Study Guide
for the DET
DIAGNOSTIC ENTRANCE TEST

Penelope Arnett RN, EdD
Felicia Remle BBA

For additional information about this products or others, contact
Arnett CE, P.O. Box 6280, North Augusta, S.C. 29861,
Phone 803-279-6325, Fax 803-279-8646 or email info@arnettce.com.

ISBN 978-0-9842709-0-3

by Dr. Penelope Arnett and Felicia Remle

Table of Contents

Table of Contents..

Preface..

Introduction 11

Description of DET 2

Test Taking Strategies 3

General Strategies for Taking the Entrance Exam 4

Comprehensive Review for English 9

    Parts of Speech.. 11

    Correct the Sentence... 15

    Complete the Sentence... 20

    Contextual Clues.. 21

    Complete the Sentence Test & Answers... 24

    Sound Alike, Similarly Spelled Words.. 28

    Reading Comprehension... 40

    Reading Comprehension Passages 42

Comprehensive Review for Critical Thinking.. 55

    Critical Thinking... 57

    Critical Thinking Practice Test... 59

    Critical Thinking Answers and Explanations 62

Comprehensive Review for Charts and Graphs.. 72

Comprehensive Review for Mathematics 81

    Integers 83

    Prime Numbers.. 84

    Prime Numbers Test and Answers 85

    Rounding... 86

    Rounding Test and Answers 87

    Adding Integers... 88

Adding Integers Tests and Answers 88

Subtracting Integers 90

Subtracting Integers Test and Answers 90

Multiplying Integers 92

Multiplying Integers Test and Answers 93

Dividing Integers 94

Dividing Integers Test and Answers 96

Fractions 97

Addition of Fractions 98

Addition of Fractions Test and Answers 98

Addition of Mixed Numbers 101

Addition of Mixed Numbers Test and Answers 101

Subtraction of Fractions 102

Subtraction of Mixed Numbers 103

Subtraction of Mixed Numbers Tests and Answers 103

Multiplication of Fractions 104

Multiplication of Fractions Test and Answers 104

Division of Fractions 105

Division of Fractions Tests and Answers 105

Comparing or Ordering Fractions 106

Decimals 108

Changing a Decimal to a Fraction 109

Decimal/Fraction Converting Test and Answers 109

Adding Decimals 110

Adding Decimals Test and Answers 111

Subtracting Decimals 111

Subtracting Decimals Test and Answers 111

Multiplying Decimals 112

Multiplying Decimals Test and Answers 112

Dividing Decimals 114

Dividing two decimals..115

Dividing Decimals Tests and Answers 115

Percents 117

Decimal to Percents Test and Answers 117

Percents to Decimals Test and Answers 118

Percents to Fractions Test and Answers 119

Fractions to Percents Test and Answers 120

Percent Problems 121

Percent Tests and Answers 122

Ratio and Proportion 123

Conversions or Equivalents Formula Use 124

Conversions Test and Answers 125

Roman Numerals 127

Word Problems 128

Word Problems Test 132

Word Problem Answers 136

Optional Test Science..145

Comprehensive Review for General Science...147

Scientific Method 148

Significant Figures 150

Comprehensive Review for Biology 155

Cells..157

Animal Cell Structure and Components...157

Cell Functions and Processes 159

Movement of Substances In or Out of the Cell 160

Plants 165

Plant Cell Structure and Components...167

Plant's Structure and Components 169

Plant Cell Functions and Processes 173

Plant Cells and Animal Cells Differences 179

The Implications and Importance of Plants to Humans 179

Protists 181

Microorganisms 183

Phylum Mastigophora 185

Phylum Protozoa 186

Sporozoa (Sporozoans) 186

Animals 187

Lower Intervertebrates 189

Higher Invertebrates 190

The Human Being 191

Practice Test for Biology 197

Practice Test for Biology Answers 204

Comprehensive Review Section for Chemistry 205

Introduction 207

Chemistry Fundamentals 208

Laws of Matter and / or Energy 210

States of Matter 211

Atomic Quantum Numbers 217

Periodic Table 218

Molecular Geometry 220

Nomenclature 221

Acids & Bases 223

Gases 225

Chemical Reactions & Chemical Equations 226

Balancing Chemical equations 228

Nuclear Decay 229

Calculations in Chemistry 231

Practice Test for Chemistry 233

Practice Test for Chemistry Answers 241

Comprehensive Review for Physical Science **243**

Introduction 245

General Terms and Relationships...245

Laws in Physics...246

Kinematics 249

Force 251

Work / Energy 253

Waves...255

Sound 258

Light...259

Relativity..261

Thermodynamics...263

Electricity...264

Magnetism 266

Heat..268

The Earth's Atmosphere..269

Practice Test for Physical Science 273

Practice Test for Physical Science Answers..278

Optional Test: Learning Styles..279

Learning Styles...281

How to Understand Learning Styles and its Relationships 283

Optional Test: Cyberspace Aptitude Analysis..287

Cyberspace Aptitude Analysis 289

User Types Explanation 290

Categories of Knowledge and Use Content...292

Blank

Preface

Thank you for selecting the **Study Guide for the DET Diagnostic Entrance Test** published by Arnett CE. This guide was developed by faculty that are directly involved in preparing students to excel in English, Mathematics, Science and have an extensive background in Nursing/Allied Health to assist you in preparation for your career.

To be successful, you will need to develop a study plan and stick to it during your preparation. This will lead to success on your first attempt at the Diagnostic Entrance Test. The key to success is preparation. You will find all the information that you need in this study guide for Nursing and Allied Health entrance exam and numerous practice questions with detailed explanations of the correct answer. This will assist you in your preparation for this exam.

This study guide has been developed by the same person that created the Diagnostic Entrance Test (DET) which has been in use since 1996 with thousands of prospective Nursing/Allied Health students having taken it every year.

Many thanks to our editors, Melissa Collins and Stella Leonard, for their hard work and dedication. This book would not be a reality without their assistance. More thanks to my husband, Jerry, for his patience, encouragement and input.

Penelope Arnett

Blank

Introduction

Overview

This section will describe an approach for studying for the school's admission test. Once you have this information, you can start to develop your study plan for the entrance exam. The better informed you are the better you will be able to prepare for this all important exam. This is your first step towards a successful career in Nursing/Allied Health.

Why do many health occupations and nursing require an entrance exam?

The main purpose of an entrance exam is to determine your current knowledge level in a variety of areas that have proven to have an impact on being successful in a Nursing/Allied health program. This also gives the admissions office an opportunity to evaluate you and other applicants on one standardized test to determine knowledge levels across a variety of non health care content areas that were developed while attending high school.

How do I get started?

One of the first things that you will want to do is determine "what do I need to study and how prepared am I?" to take a test in all of the areas for the entrance exam. You will need to review the information in this chapter about the specific types of material on which you will be tested on. Some schools include information about Biology, Physical Science or Chemistry. The next step will be to contact the school of your choice and determine what the admission requirements are and when the entrance test will be offered. You will need to sign up early to ensure you will have a space at one of the testing dates. Plan ahead and plan early to ensure you will be able to complete your application and take the entrance exam. When the test is offered will have a great impact on your study plan.

Description of DET

Diagnostic Entrance Test (DET) developed by Arnett Development Corporation is an entrance exam for registered nursing, practical/vocational nursing and allied health programs. This test consists of 148 items. The time allotted to take this test is two hours and 30 minutes. The test is divided into two major parts, i.e., English and Mathematics. There are three optional tests that can be added to the basic test, i.e., Science, Learning Styles Inventory and Cyberspace Aptitude Analysis. The decision about the optional areas is a school by school decision. Your school of choice will be able to tell you what tests you will take.

English: Basic English (20 questions), Reading Comprehension (28 questions), Grammar, Charts and Graphs (20 questions), Word Usage and Critical Thinking (10 questions).
Math: Conversion, Integers, Fractions, Word Problems, Proportions, Decimals, Percentages, Formula Use, and Basic Algebra. (60 questions)
Optional areas:
Science: Biology, Chemistry and Physical Science. (60 questions)
Learning Styles Inventory: This section has 60 questions. A sample report is provided.
Cyberspace Aptitude Analysis: This section has 60 questions. A sample report is provided.

Test Taking Strategies

There is nothing more important than developing outstanding test taking strategies to insure your success on any test that you undertake. You should approach this entrance exam the same way that you approached a test during high school or any other school or program that required you to show your knowledge in certain subject areas. The first step in this process is to identify the subject matter required to study and the kind of information that will be presented to you on the examination. Once you have determined what is to be covered on the test, the next step is to develop a plan to address your needs. This will require you to assess where you are in respect to the information that will be presented on the entrance exam.

Tips for the day prior to the entrance exam

This should be a day of rest. You should not try to study that day or during the evening. You should have a normal meal and get the normal amount of rest that you generally get. This is not a time to see how much sleep that you can get. This could make you more tired than if you had only had a few hours of sleep.

Preparation for test day

Get up at your normal time and make sure that you have eaten a balanced meal. Avoid any excessive intake of food or drink prior to the start of the test. You should plan on arriving at the test site early enough to ensure that you will not be late. Make sure you bring the required information to be able to register/enter the testing center. You should plan to wear layered and comfortable clothes the day of the test. Uncomfortable clothes will cause you to lose focus, which could impact your test. You do not know how hot or cold the test area will be. It is very important that you are as comfortable as possible; this will lower you stress level.

General Strategies for Taking the Entrance Exam

Follow the directions as given

You should make sure that you hear and understand the directions as they are being given. If you are not sure what you are to do, you should request clarification. If you misunderstand the directions and take the test the wrong way, you could fail the examination. Remember when you are not sure, you should ask for clarification.

Read each question very carefully

Always read every question and the choices very carefully. You could miss important information if you are not careful. Only read the information two or more times if you believe you do NOT have the right information about the question. Ask yourself what is the correct answer for each question presented. All of the questions are straight forward, and none of them are trick questions. Each question has ONLY one correct answer.

Set your own pace

The entrance exam is timed. However, you will need to use your time wisely and not waste time. You should wear a watch for the test. The proctor will have a time clock but, by having your own watch, you can make sure that you are setting a good pace to ensure that you do not run out of time on any section of the test. The DET is in two parts: English and Math. You may be asked to stop after the English portion. Be sure you follow the proctor's directions in regard to this.

Make sure you mark your answers correctly

There are two methods for taking the entrance exam: paper and pencil exam or a computer/online exam. Both of the exams will be scored by a computer. Whichever one you will be taking, make sure that you select the answer that you want and either darken it in with a pencil, if taking the paper and pencil test, or click on the box with the answer you want on the computer. Either type will score your answer. A problem can occur with paper and pencil answer sheets if you darken more than the area in the circle/bubble. The computer could score your answer wrong. **Fill in the circle/bubble but stay within the circle.** The correction facility CANNOT change anything on your answer sheet.

Should you guess if you don't know the answer?

Yes, you should try to choose the answer for each question that most closely matches what you think is the correct response. There are no points removed from your score for guessing, but a blank answer is an automatic wrong answer. You should always try to rule out as many answers as possible prior to making your final decision on the correct response.

Check test answer sheet for accuracy

Prior to the completion of the exam, you should always check to make sure that you did not make any mistakes. If you have some time left over prior to the completion of the test period, you may want to check any question(s) that you had to guess on and see if you can now select the correct answer. You will be able to do this on the paper and pencil test and the computer test.

What is the pass/fail or cut score for the DET?

The school will tell you what the cut score or pass score is for the test. If you ask, they will inform you what that is to meet their minimum score for consideration for entrance into their program. The testing company CANNOT give you any information.

What happens if my performance on the Entrance Exam is low?

Most schools will allow you to retest, but you must check with them as to their policy on retesting and the time you have to wait before retaking the test again. Most schools require some time to elapse between testing, and this is done to allow you time to study and better prepare for the next test. Most schools have an alternate test that will be presented to you on a retest. Also remember there are thousands of students trying to get into these schools, so the results of the entrance exam are important and will inform the school what kind of student you will be if accepted into their program.

Develop a Study Plan for Success

The first step in the study plan is to determine what you need to remember or learn. You can do this by quickly paging through this study guide. Look at the different areas that will be tested.
You should take each area, one at a time, and review the information in that area and learn how to answer questions that are specific for that section of the test. If you feel you are still weak in some areas, seek some other sources for those specific areas. This study guide will refer you to some websites you can visit to find more information. This process should continue until you feel comfortable.

Adult Learners

Adult learners are motivated with good experience that will help them in the classroom. If you have a life or career centered focus to learning and are genuinely motivated to learn, you can be successful in the education process. Learning will be successful if you take an active role in the process. Become a person who enjoys planning and evaluating their progress. It may help to write out goals and time commitments. Put down class, work, homework and time with friends and family. This will assist in planning your learning process. It is a good idea for learners to understand their learning styles. It will help to go to the counseling and/or testing center of an educational institution for this evaluation. Instruments are available through educational institutions that will evaluate learning styles and give pointers on the best ways to learn. Understanding learning styles will assist adult learners in identifying areas where they may be weak. It will also show the learning styles that best suit you, the learner.

Self Discipline / Routine

Learn how to schedule your priorities. Set small tasks at different times of the day. Do these tasks at the scheduled times. This will allow you to stay focused on your priorities. Keep a list of what you need to do and then, as you accomplish a small task, mark it off. Refer to your list often, and it will keep up on track and also show you where you are making progress one step at a time. This will help you from becoming discouraged and you will see what you have accomplished. You need to develop a routine and stay with the routine. Consistently do the task at the scheduled time of day. A routine once developed and followed, things start to become a habit. Break down tasks into smaller tasks, so you can see what you have accomplished each day. Schedule your day, your week and your month, have a "to-do" list for priority items. Decide what areas you are the weakest and work on them first. Once you start on a task, keep at it until the task becomes a habit. Don't get discouraged if you at first do not succeed with everything. Give yourself a chance and give yourself positive feedback even if you don't get something accomplished.

Procrastination

It is important to understand if procrastinating is to avoid the subject at hand or if it is a habit. Break your studying down into small segments and accomplish them one step at a time. As you accomplish one section, you motivate yourself to move forward because of your success. The most important step is the first one. Go ahead and do something regarding the task at hand. It will be easier after the first step is made. Avoid distractions. Don't let yourself get too comfortable when studying. Try to get everything you need together so you don't have to get up and down. Minimize noise. It is a good idea to turn off your telephone when studying. Television and music is also distracting. Don't lay down; you may go to sleep. Tell yourself that you can do the assignment. Self-motivation is important. Reward yourself with positive thoughts when you complete a job. Think about your goal; it will motivate you. Believe that you can succeed, and you will.

Motivation

Motivating yourself is in a student's success. You take control of your learning when you begin motivational techniques. You need to study some every day. Don't get behind and then you have to cram or read a entire book before a test. A little studying every day will make a huge difference. The most important motivational force is going ahead and doing the task at hand and not putting it off. Just accomplishing a small goal is an achievement and will make you feel good. When you finish one task, go ahead and put down your next task so you will focus to the next task at hand.

Goal Setting

Goal setting is important for academic success. To successfully set and plan a goal, you must state the goal as an outcome and specify actions. The clearer and more specific your goal the more likely your chances are of achieving it. Setting goals gives you a road map as to where you want to be. It is important to remain flexible with long range goals in case your circumstances change. Always congratulate yourself when you achieve a goal, and mark it off your list. You can look back to that achievement while starting to work on the next goal.

Concentration and Memorization

Concentration is an important attribute when studying. If you concentrate, you can focus on what you need to do and eliminate outside distractions. In order to concentrate better, it helps to have a set place to study. Keep a study routine; know what time of day is best for what kind of studying. When you study, go ahead and focus your mind on the subject at hand. Look over notes and decide what you need to accomplish. It may help to know that you will reward yourself if you concentrate. Think about a special treat at the end of a study session. Don't study one topic for hours. Vary the routine and the subject matter. By studying a bit and allowing the information to digest, you may understand it better. You need to schedule breaks for study time. Give yourself a chance to move around. Many people worry about studying, so it may be a good idea for you to schedule worry time for half an hour a day. Think about your problems then. It is amazing how scheduling time for worry decreases worry during the day.

Stress Management

Stress can be a terrible block to student success. Symptoms may show up as physical, mental or social. Your behavior may change for no reason. An increased use of alcohol or drugs may signal stress. Feelings of hopelessness and discouragement may also surface when under stress. One way to manage stress is to be organized. Organize your time. Get everything together that you need to accomplish a task. Make sure that the important things are prioritized. If smaller things have to be let go, do it. See if you can get control of your environment. See who or what is controlling you; and if you can change it, do so. Get out of the situation for a day or two, if necessary. Give yourself positive feedback. Make sure that your inner dialog is positive and uplifting. Do not be too hard on yourself. Let yourself know how well you are coping with the situation. Take care of yourself. Get enough sleep, usually seven to eight hours a night. Take breaks while you study. Get up and walk around. Get some exercise. Make sure that you eat correctly. Watch your caffeine; it can aggravate stress. Be careful about how much sugar and fat you eat, and monitor your alcohol consumption. Avoid escaping stress by drinking or taking medication. Learn how to relax. You do not have to be busy every minute, even if you have things to do. Learn how to recharge yourself. Sometimes it helps to relieve stress if you do something for others. Do something you enjoy to get your mind off the stressor.

Avoiding Test Anxiety

When you are ready to take a test, approach it with confidence. Tell yourself you will do well. Prepare yourself by studying. Pick a good place to take the test. Make sure that distractions will not affect you. Give yourself time for the tests. Stay relaxed. Don't talk with students who are not prepared. Eat something before you go into the test. As you are taking the test, make sure you read the directions and answer the questions asked. Watch your time. Skip over difficult areas and go back to them. Move around in your chair, but don't fidget. Don't worry about other students finishing first. If you go blank, start writing something on another sheet of paper. It may trigger your mind. While taking the test, stay relaxed. Don't tense up. Take deep breaths. Expect to be a little anxious, but don't let it control you. Think positive thoughts and tell yourself that you can take the test. When you have finished the test, think back over what you did and what did or did not work on the test. Congratulate yourself on a job well done.

Blank

Comprehensive Review for English

Parts of Speech

Correct the Sentence

Complete the Sentence

Vocabulary

Reading Comprehension

Blank

Parts of Speech

This portion of the test evaluates your ability to construct correct sentences. Words or groups of words are underlined. You are to determine if the words are used correctly. They can be any part of speech. Like vocabulary, this entire area cannot be learned in a day or two. The material here is to refresh your memory and present some of the more common problems found in grammar.

Nouns

A noun is a word which names a person, place or thing.
Here are some examples of nouns:

>Person: girl, boy, John F. Kennedy, uncle, teacher
>Place: stream, river, Canada, United States, school, college, classroom
>Thing: circle, day, lie, idea, story, vacation, ear, vision, flag

Nouns can be divided into 2 groups.

>Proper nouns begin with a capital letter because it is a name of a <u>specific</u> person, place or thing.
>>Some examples of proper nouns are: Canada, John F. Kennedy, Pacific Ocean, September, Sunday, Los Angeles, Connie, Front Street.
>
>Names of classes of persons, places or things are NOT capitalized (a street, the country, a college).

Words beginning with a capital letter, and not the first word of a sentence, are probably proper nouns. Common nouns are most of the nouns and are not capitalized unless they are the first word of a sentence. Nouns can be used as different parts of a sentence. A noun can be a subject or object of the sentence, or an object of a preposition.

There are some special rules for making the plural (more than one) form of a noun.
Plurals are usually formed by adding an "s" (friends) or "es" (bushes). The "es" is added if it makes a new syllable (bush-es). There are exceptions. Some plurals are formed in different ways:

ends in	then	
"y" preceded by a consonant	change "y" to "i"	sky skies
"f"	change to "ve" and add "s"	wife wives
Compound words	add "s" to main word	mothers-in-law

Pronouns

	Subjective	Possessive	Objective
Singular	I	my, mine	me
	You	your, yours	you
	He	his	him
	She	her, hers	her
	It	its	it
Plural	We	our, ours	us
	You	your, yours	you
	They	their, theirs	them
Interrogative & Relative			
People	Who	whose	whom
	whoever		whomever
Things	Which		which
	What		what
	That		that

Interrogative pronouns are used when a question requires more than a "yes" or "no" answer.
"Whose house is this?"

Relative pronouns introduce an adjective clause.
"Sally, whose bike was stolen, walked home."

Indefinite Pronouns
        everybody   everybody's   everybody

Problems
A pronoun combined with someone or something or two pronouns together,
use the pronoun as if it were alone.
            "She gave it to me."
            Then add the other person:
            "She gave it to Sam and me."
            "She gave it to him and me."

A pronoun following *except, but, than* or *as*
If it acts as if it is following a conjunction, use it as a subject.
"No one could dance as well as I."

For more information on pronouns go to:
www.towson.edu/ows/pronouns.htm

Verbs

Verbs show an action (run) or a state of being (were). Verbs may be followed by an object and sometimes they are not.
Verbs must agree in tense with their subject. Plural subjects must have plural verbs.
Most nouns ending in "s" are plural.
Verbs ending in "s" are usually singular and a form of the third person.

Regular Verbs

A regular verb has the conjugation or alteration of the word that follows a standard pattern.

first person	third person	past tense	present participle	past participle
play	plays	played	playing	have played
sit	sits	sat	sitting	have sat

Below is a list of websites that list a large number of regular verbs:
http://www.eslgold.com/grammar/verb_list.html
http://www.englishclub.com/vocabulary/regular-verbs-list.htm
There are a few rules for verbs with different endings.
Ending in:
"e", "o", or "i" or "y" as a consonant, add "s" for third person and "ed" for past tense.
"y" as a vowel (i.e., preceded by a consonant), change "y" to "i" and add "es".
single consonant (besides "y") preceded by single stressed vowel, add "s" for third person but double the consonant for past tense and past participle (zap, zaps, zapped, zapping).

Irregular Verbs

Irregular verbs have a different form

Present	Past	Past participle
break	Broke	broken
grow	Grew	grown

These sites have lists of irregular verbs:
http://www2.gsu.edu/~wwwesl/egw/verbs.htm
http://owl.english.purdue.edu/owl/resource/605/01/

More about verbs:
http://eslus.com/LESSONS/GRAMMAR/POS/pos3.htm
http://www.ccc.commnet.edu/sensen/part1/two/index.html

Linking verbs complete statements and are followed by adjectives.
Examples of linking verbs include smell, sound and taste.

The verb has six tenses:
- Present
  - The present tense indicates an action is currently taking place. "The boy is running home."
- Past
  - The past tense indicates the action is completed. "The boy ran home."
- Future
  - The future tense indicates the action has not yet occurred. "The boy will run home."
- Present perfect
  - The present perfect tense indicates an action that occurred in the past and is still occurring. "The boy has run home every night."
- Past perfect
  - The past perfect tense indicates a previous action that was completed before another action was completed. Both actions are in the past. "The boy had run home every night before he fell."
- Future perfect
  - The future perfect tense indicates a future action that takes place before another action that is even farther in the future. "The boy will have run home before his mother calls him."

Adjectives and Adverbs

Adjectives modify nouns and pronouns. Adjectives describe or provide information about the noun/pronoun.
"She picked the pretty flower." "Pretty" is the adjective that describes the flower.

Adverbs modify verbs. Adverbs answer the question "how, when, where, why".
"He crawled quickly across the floor." "Quickly" is the adverb, showing how he crawled.

First you must identify the noun/ pronoun or verb. Once this is done, it is fairly easy to identify the word modifying it as an adverb or adjective.

An exception to the rule is when you have used a linking verb. An adjective follows the linking verb. Previously a few verbs were identified as linking verbs (smell, taste, etc.). "The food tastes wonderful." "Wonderful" is an adjective. Wonderfully would be an adverb.

Prepositions

Prepositions are words that begin a phrase. These phrases are called prepositional phrases. These phrases contain a preposition and an object of that preposition. It can also contain adjectives.

Common prepositions are: in, to, by, at, with, for, of.

"She ran to the store." "to the store" is the prepositional phrase.

"For ten cents, I would go home." "For ten cents" is the prepositional phrase. The phrase needs a comma after it, if it can be moved in the sentence. "I would go home, for ten cents." Both sentences say the same thing.

Conjunctions

Conjunctions are words that join words or clauses together.

Some common ones are: and, or, for, but.

Some conjunctions are pairs of words: either/or, neither/nor, both/and.

"Suzie and her dog."

"I would run for Chief, but my time is so limited."

Correct the Sentence

For the next 15 questions: Please read the following sentences carefully. Select the underlined word(s) that is incorrect and choose it from the choices.

1. If I have seen the accident, I would have stopped.
   - A. I
   - B. have seen
   - C. I
   - D. have
   - E. No error

Answer: B

"Have seen" should be "had seen", past perfect tense.

"I" is the subject and used correctly.

"Would have" is called the "third conditional". It is for an imaginary past action, where the action DID NOT take place. It is formed by a past perfect tense in the "if" section of the sentence and a past participle in the "would have" section of the sentence.

2. All the young people who the company interviews must undergo drug testing.
   - A. All
   - B. who
   - C. interviews
   - D. undergo
   - E. No error

Answer: B

"Who" should be "whom". "The company interviews whom." Whom is an object. Try substituting the personal pronoun "he/him" or "she/her" for "who/whom." The company interviews "he"- no. The company interviews "him"- yes. This is the objective case so whom is correct.

"All" is an indefinite pronoun and can be singular or plural depending on what it refers to. If people refer to a group, it is singular. If people refer to each individual person, it is plural.

"Interviews" is a verb here and is the third person singular verb.

"Undergo" is a verb and it is active tense.

3. One in every four persons in the United States owns a dog.
   - A. One
   - B. persons
   - C. United States
   - D. owns
   - E. No error.

Answer: E

"One" is singular.

"Persons" is plural and is the proper English form.

"United States" is a proper noun and capitalized.

"Owns" is a verb and in the third person so the "s" is correct. (One owns)

4. He could only <u>guess</u> at the <u>number</u> of guests who <u>attended</u> the party.
      A. He
      B. guess
      C. number
      D. attended
      E. No error

Answer: E
"He" is a pronoun and is singular.
"Guess" is a singular verb and agrees intense with "he".
"Number" is an object of the preposition "at".
"Attended" is a past tense verb.

5. <u>That</u> is the <u>problem</u> when <u>peoples</u> have a disagreement; <u>they</u> attack each other personally.
      A. That
      B. problem
      C. peoples
      D. they
      E. No error.

Answer C:
"That" is a pronoun which represents an object not a person.
"Problem" is the object.
"Peoples" refers to nations. "People" refers to individuals. "People" should be used here.
"People" is plural so "they" is correct as it is plural and a subject. It would be "them" if it were an object.

6. By 7:30, <u>it</u> was <u>too</u> late, the show <u>had</u> already <u>began</u>.
      A. it
      B. too
      C. had
      D. began
      E. No error

Answer: D
"It" is a pronoun and refers to a thing not a person.
"Too" is the correct form. It means also and is an adverb. "To" is a preposition.
"Had" is used with the past participle of the verb.
The word should be "begun"." Began" is the past tense and occurs alone. "Begun" is the past participle and occurs after the verb 'have.'

7. The <u>person,</u> who has very little education and whose entire desire <u>is</u> to acquire a vast fortune, is not the <u>types</u> of people I want <u>to be</u> associated with.
      A. person
      B. is
      C. types
      D. to be
      E. No error

Answer: C

"Person" is a singular noun.

"Is" is a singular verb with the subject "person".

"Types" is the object and must agree with the singular subject "person". "Type" would be the correct word.

"To be" is the infinitive form of the verb.

8. Neither Connie nor Mandy, students of Ms. Miller, presented their paper before the published deadline.
    A. Neither
    B. students
    C. their
    D. published
    E. No error

Answer: C

"Neither" is a singular adjective and both nouns are singular so the verb is singular.

"Students" is a noun representing both Connie and Mandy.

Since "neither" is a singular adjective, "their" is inappropriate.

"Her" would be the appropriate word- singular.

"Published" is an adjective.

9. Each of the students is responsible for the homework.
    A. Each
    B. students
    C. is
    D. for
    E. No error.

Answer: E

"Each" is a singular pronoun and requires a singular verb.

"Students" is an object of a preposition and not the subject of the verb.

"Is" is a singular verb with "each" as its subject.

"For" is a preposition.

10. Two thirds of the contestants was chosen from the tickets before the show started.
    A. Two thirds
    B. was
    C. from
    D. started
    E. No error

Answer: B

A fraction equivalent "two thirds" is determined to be singular or plural by the noun it measures "contestant". Since contestants are plural, the verb must be plural.

"Was" is singular; and since the noun "measured" is plural, the verb must be plural.

"From" is a preposition.

"Started" is the verb of the prepositional phrase. Since the "show" is being talked about in the past tense, the verb must be in the past tense.

11. The car, <u>as well as</u> the <u>girl's</u> purse, <u>were</u> stolen by the <u>thief</u>.
>   A. as well as
>   B. girl's
>   C. were
>   D. thief
>   E. No error

Answer: C

"As well as" is not a conjunction but a preposition here.

"Girl's" is possessive as it is her purse.

"Were" is a plural verb and the subject "car" is singular. "Was" would be the singular verb.

"Thief" is the object of a preposition.

12. Children <u>seem</u> more adult <u>than</u> <u>they're</u> parents did at the <u>same</u> age.
>   A. seem
>   B. than
>   C. they're
>   D. same
>   E. No error

Answer: C

"Seem" agrees with children.

"Than" is a conjunction connecting children and parents.

"They're" is a contraction meaning "they are". "Their" would be the possessive word that should be here.

"Same" is an adjective modifying age.

13. It was <u>difficult</u> to not throw up as <u>we</u> passed the waste <u>purifying</u> station, because it <u>stunk</u> so much.
>   A. difficult
>   B. we
>   C. purifying
>   D. stunk
>   E. No error

Answer: E

"Difficult" is called an adjective complement and follows the verb "was".

"We" is a plural pronoun.

"Purifying" is an adjective here describing the noun "station".

"Stank" or "stunk" are both considered the past tense of "stink". Either is correct.

14. The captain of the volleyball team was a <u>senior</u>, last year's junior <u>co-captain</u>, when <u>she</u> fell from the bleacher and broke <u>her</u> leg.
>   A. senior
>   B. co-captain
>   C. she
>   D. her
>   E. No error

Answer: E

"Senior" is the object of the verb was.

"Co-captain" is a noun referring to the noun "captain".

"She" is a singular pronoun referring to the noun "captain".

"Her" is an adjective modifying leg.

15. The <u>girl</u> has <u>past</u> the course, since <u>she</u> is <u>in</u> the advanced course.
     A. girl
     B. past
     C. she
     D. in
     E. No error

Answer: B

"Girl" is the subject of the sentence.

"Past" is the incorrect word. The correct word is "passed".

"She" is a pronoun and the subject of that clause.

"In" is a preposition.

Complete the Sentence

Sentence completion is part of the measurement of reading comprehension. Sentence completion is a test of your vocabulary and your ability to appropriately use a word in a sentence. Understanding the structure of the sentence will also help you determine which word is appropriate.

When looking at the possible choices, you may find that, some or all of them can "fit" or "make sense" in the sentence. Only one is correct. You must initially read the sentence with the word missing. What is the meaning of the sentence? What is the idea behind the sentence? Look for "clue" words or phrases.

Don't look at the choices until you have an idea about the meaning of the sentence. Once you decide this, you can then look at each word and see if one "fits" with the meaning. Always look at every answer before choosing one. If the one you wanted is not there see if there is a synonym. A synonym is a word that can mean the same thing or be used interchangeably.

Be sure to think of all the "meanings" of a word. In the English language many words have several meanings. Don't just think of the most common meaning. Also look at the use of the word in terms of sentence structure and parts of speech. Is it a noun, a verb, etc.? Many words can be more than one part of speech. When used as a different part of speech the word can have a different meaning.

Words can have a literal and or a figurative meaning. This becomes especially problematic for applicants not living in the United States. Literal meaning is the dictionary definition, the concrete meaning. Figurative words do not mean exactly what they say.
"That is cool!" The way cool is used here does not mean cold but that the person finds that "alright, very good". Figurative words/language is context based. You must read the surrounding words to understand the context in which this is being used. See the Reading Comprehension section for more information on this.

Have you heard the word before? What type of a sentence was it used in? You may not remember the definition but have an idea of its meaning. Does the word or sentence have a "positive" or "negative" meaning? If it is positive look for words that have some form of positive meaning and vice versa.

Many times two or more choices may relate to the content of the question but are not the answer. These are chosen to draw you to them because they relate to the content. They are not necessarily the answer.

Contextual Clues

When reading the sentence, look for context clues. These give clues to help determine the meaning of the word. They can be: definition, description or example, explanation, contrast or compare synonym or antonym.

Definition

The actual definition of the word is given in the sentence.
The child appeared _____ in class because she had never answered incorrectly.

Any of the following words would be correct based on the meaning in the sentence: infallible, unerring, unfailing, errorless, faultless, flawless, impeccable, certain, foolproof, perfect.

Description or Example

In this sentence a description of the item or event is given or an example is offered.
Ralph is an accomplished piano player. But Molly is more _____; she sings, acts, paints and writes poetry, and also plays the piano.
Here several items are listed that describe the missing word "versatile".

Explanation

Here the word or phrase is actually explained.
We could tell by the _____ smell, that something putrid was in our trash can.
Using the explanation clue, "something putrid was in our trash can" in this sentence explains the missing word, "rotten".

Comparison and Contrast

In comparison clues, the sentence has words or a phrase that have the same or similar meaning as the missing word. The following words link the missing word to the rest of the sentence that gives the comparison.

similarly	likewise	also	both
are similar in that	the same as	as	

We stopped at the _____, which is as large as the department store, for bath supplies and powder.

Compared to "which is as large as the department store"; emporium, retail outlet, outlet center.

In contrast clues, the sentence has words or a phrase that mean the opposite of the missing word.
The following words link the missing word to the rest of the sentence that gives the contrast.

also differ in	even though	not only...but also
although	however	on the other hand
but	in contrast	still
conversely	in spite of	unlike
despite	instead of	whereas
different from, different in	more than	yet

In the pirate story, there were the good guys against the _____.

Contrasted with "good guys": marauder, pillager, plunderer, raider, privateer, hijacker.

Other words that are similar but do not relate to the idea of what a "pirate" does are: looter, robber, burglar, housebreaker, stealer, thief, and rustler.

Synonyms

A synonym is a word that means the same thing or something very similar. In this type, the word means the same as the other word.

The hurricane caused _____, disastrous damages in the state.

Disastrous: catastrophic, cataclysmal, cataclysmic, destructive.

The saturated, _____ dog ran in the house after falling in the swimming pool.

Saturated: drenched, dripping, soaked, sodden, soggy, waterlogged.

Antonyms

An antonym is a word that means the opposite of that word.

Sentences or phrases connected by the following words are looking for an antonym.

but	instead of	though
however	on the other hand	unlike
in contrast	opposite of	

I thought the church trip would be awkward, but it ended up _____ .

Opposite words for awkward: comfortable, easy, agreeable, pleasant.

Cause and Effect

The unknown word depends on the cause/effect relationship with other words.

As a result of	For this reason	Therefore
Accordingly	Hence	Thus
Because	If...then	
Consequently	so...that	

He is in better _____ shape now because he spends more time exercising.

The missing word is "physical". This is a direct result of exercising.

There are so many words in our language that trying to learn enough to take a test in a few days is impossible. Many words are made up of two or three parts: prefixes, suffixes and root words. It is better to spend some time learning some of each of these and working to put them together to define words. Remember that at least 50 percent of the words we use have a Latin origin. If you know a foreign language, it can help you figure out the meaning of words also.

Prefixes

Prefixes are letters placed together at the beginning of a word to add a meaning to that root or word. Listed here are some common prefixes and their meaning(s):

a- without, to, completely
ab- away from, take from
ad- move towards, add to
ante- before
anti- against
aqua- water
audio- related to hearing
auto- self, on own
be- completely; affect
bi- two

bio- life
circum- go around
com- jointly
contra- against
counter- opposite direction; go against
de- down
di- two
dia- across
en- bring in, put in
ex- out, former
frater- brother
geo- earth
heni- half
hetero- mixed

homo- same
hyper- more than
hypo- less, under
im- not
in- in, towards
infra- below
inter- between
micro- small
mono- one
nomen- name
ob-hide, conceal
out- better than, more than
over- above
peri- around

phage- eat
post- after
poly- many
pre-before
pro-favor, for
semi- half
sub- loser than
syn-together, with
tele- distance
trans-across
ultra- beyond
un- reverse
under- below, lower than

Suffixes

These are letters added to the end of a word to change the meaning. Listed here are some common suffixes and their meaning(s):

able, ible- capable
age- result of
algia- pain
ceed, cede- yield, give up
cide - kill
cise, cision - cut
clude- close
clusive- close
cy- function

cycle- circle
duce, duct- lead, drain, pull
er, or - one who
esis, osis - process
fy- make
ion, sion, tion -act, result
ject- throw
ist- person
ive- making

ment- result
ous- having
scrib, script- write
sect- cut, separate
spect- look, see
vert- turn
y- tend to do

Root Words

Root words are words that either a prefix or suffix can be added to. There are so many root words that it is impractical to try to list them all here for you. There are some web sites that have long lists of root words that you can go to and review these. We have listed them here for you.
www.virtualsalt.com/roots.htm
www.msu.edu/~defores1/gre/roots/gre_rts_afx1.htm
www.betterendings.org/homeschool/words/root%20words.htm
www.espindle.org/roots.html
Each of these websites have lists of root words many with examples.

Complete the Sentence Test & Answers

1. Due to the drought, the land has been barren for years, the farmers must now _____ most of their food.
A. develop   B. consume   C. produce   D. purchase

Answer: D
"Develop" and "produce" are synonyms. Both cannot be correct so delete them as possibilities. The clue word is "barren" which in this context means "empty" or "not able to produce". If the land is not able to produce the farmer cannot grow his own food so he must "purchase" it.

2. Summer thunderstorms may be brief, but sometimes the conditions make them ____ for some time.
A. wander   B. wane   C. persist   D. abate

Answer: C
The sentence says they may be "brief" but ... The "but" indicates an antonym. "Wane" and "abate" mean go away or stop. "Wander" would mean they do not stay in the same place. "Persist" is the opposite of brief.

3. His _____ over his parent's favoritism caused him to avoid his family as an adult.
A. rancor   B. love   C. grief   D. tolerance

Answer: A
"Avoid" is a negative word. "Love" and "tolerance" are not negative. "Grief" could be a possibility until we look at "rancor" which means bitterness or ill will. "Grief" is bereavement or sorrow. It does not fit well in this context; "rancor" fits better.

4. The three days of meeting sessions were listed in _____ order, from 1 to 50.
A. random   B. reverse   C. chronological   D. scrambled

Answer: C
This is a definition, "1 to 50". "Chronological" means in time order.
"Random" means in any order.
"Scrambled" means out of order.
"Reverse" means in the opposite direction (50 to 1).

5. The thief was sent to the _____, after the jury found him guilty.
A. penitentiary   B. school   C. house   D. dormitory

Answer: A
The jury found him guilty so he is to be punished. Sending him to his "house" would be setting him free. Sending him to "school" doesn't make any sense. A "dormitory" is a sleeping facility usually for a school. A "penitentiary" does not refer to its cell blocks as dormitories.

6. The fact that the professor's office was totally disorganized was one indication of his _____.

A. conscientiousness   B. indifference   C. diligence   D. absentmindedness

Answer: D

Other words for "disorganized" are confused, disordered, shuffled, chaotic, jumbled.

"Conscientiousness" means painstaking, thoroughness.

"Diligence" is another word for conscientiousness.

Other words for "indifference" are emotionlessness, unconcern, unemotional.

This leaves us with "absentmindedness" which means preoccupied, inattentive. A "disorganized" office would not be surprise for this type of person.

7. Samuel was _____ by the rejection of his stories; as a result, he continued to send them to other publishers.

A. encouraged   B. undaunted   C. elated   D. discouraged

Answer: B

His stories were rejected (negative word). He would not be happy. "Elated" means extremely happy. "Encouraged" is a possibility but means emboldened, heartened, and inspired. If he was "discouraged", the opposite of "encouraged", he would not have kept on. "Undaunted" means not put off or beaten. This is a better choice than "encouraged".

8. The owner was distressed that the salesman was not meeting his deadlines; the owner warned the salesman that if he continued to _____, he would be fired.

A. be dispassionate   B. procrastinate   C. be autonomous   D. dissemble

Answer: B

The clue here is "not meeting his deadlines".

"Procrastinate" means to put off, delay. This would match this definition.

To "dissemble" means to pretend, misrepresent.

"Autonomous" means independent, self-directed.

"Dispassionate" means unemotional, somber, unruffled.

9. A solemn tone was necessary for the eulogy; the minister lapsed into _____ which was distressing rather than comforting.

A. loquaciousness   B. levity   C. morbidity   D. rambling

Answer: C

The eulogy was "distressing" not "comforting." The clue word is "distressing" and a eulogy is at a funeral.

"Morbidity" means excessively gloomy. This would then complete the thought.

"Loquaciousness" is over talkative, a long speech.

"Levity" is lack of seriousness, frivolity.

"Rambling" would mean wordy, going from topic to topic. These other three words would not make the eulogy "distressing".

10. When asked, the principal responded with _____ and failed to respond with clarity and precision.
A. lucidity   B. vagueness   C. candor   D. fervor

Answer: B
The clue here is "failed to respond with clarity and precision". We are looking for an opposite.
"Lucidity" means easily understood, intelligible.
"Candor" means fair-minded, impartial.
"Fervor" means passion, excitement.
"Vagueness" means hazy, indistinct, and unclear. This would be the opposite of "clarity and precision".

11. The rows of houses for sale, the lines at the unemployment office, the lines at the soup kitchens, all _____ the idea that the economy is in the recovery stage.
A. validate   B. denigrate   C. belie   D. avouch

Answer: A
This sentence gives examples. The last part shows recovery which is the opposite of the examples.
"Validate" means to formalize, ratify.
"Denigrate" means to falsely charge, belittle.
"Avouch" means affirm, acknowledge.
"Belie" means contradict, negate. This word is the opposite of the last part of the sentence.

12. The judge ordered that the Court would _____ the acts of the defendant and fine him for his actions.
A. impeach   B. detain   C. expunge   D. denounce

Answer: D
The defendant was found guilty. What would the Court say about his acts?
"Impeach" means file a charge against, challenge the honesty of. This would be against a person.
"Detain" means confine, imprison, delay. He was fined not imprisoned.
"Expunge" means delete, cancel, excise. If he was found not guilty the judge could expunge the record.
"Denounce" means condemn, criticize. This would be the appropriate answer.

13. While reading the book for submission to the publisher, the reader found offensive material and decided to _____ it before allowing it to be entered for publishing.
A. refute   B. expurgate   C. challenge   D. dismiss

Answer: B
The sentence provides the definition of the word.
"Refute" means rebut, contradict.
"Expurgate" means to remove offensive material from a publication.
"Challenge" means justify, take exception to, dare.
"Dismiss" means reject, fire an employee, put out of one's mind.

14. I expected the truth from the administrator; I was shocked by his _____.
A. candidness   B. forthrightness   C. mendacity   D. honesty

Answer: C
This is a contrast sentence. The answer is the opposite of the "truth".
"Candidness" means impartiality, directness.
"Forthrightness" means directness, candidness, without evasion.
"Honesty" is truthfulness, displaying integrity.
"Mendacity" is untruthfulness, lying. This is the opposite.

15. The professor's lectures were so _____ that only people with his erudition could understand them.
A. elitist   B. scholarly   C. egalitarian   D. pretentious

Answer: B
This is a definition sentence. "Erudition" is the definition of the word.
"Elitist" means a sense of entitlement.
"Egalitarian" means believing in equality in all areas for all people.
"Pretentious" means unjustified claims of merit, ostentatious.
"Scholarly" means intellectual, erudite, having great knowledge.

Sound Alike, Similarly Spelled Words

Below is a list of some of the words that often get mixed up when spelling or writing. They do not have the same meaning and cannot be used interchangeably. Review them and their meanings. Try using them in a sentence. This is NOT an exhaustive list.

On the DET there will be a blank space and below will be listed two or more words. You must choose which word fits the meaning of the sentence. Read the entire sentence and, then read the sentence with each word inserted, to see if it makes sense.

A

accept:	to agree to, to receive
except:	exclude, leave out
access:	to give permission or allow to enter
assess:	evaluate, determine value of
excess:	more than needed, left over
acclamation:	loud approval by cheering or applause
acclimation:	adapt to new environment or surroundings
addict:	devotee, must follow a strong habit
edict:	a decree, official proclamation
addition:	adding to, the part added on
edition:	latest version, number of times a book/document was revised
affect:	influence, a feeling.
effect:	(Noun) result from something
	(Verb) to make the result happen, accomplish
ail:	to cause trouble, to be sick
ale:	a drink, similar to beer
aisle:	passageway, walkway
I'll:	contraction for "I will"
isle:	small land mass surrounded by water, an island
all most:	two words: all: the whole group and most: the greatest amount
almost:	very nearly, not quite completed
allude:	to refer to indirectly
elude:	to avoid or escape

B

bad: evil, unpleasant, spoiled, defective

bade: past tense of bid: issue a command, a greeting

bail: (Noun) form of security to release one from jail
(Verb) to remove or empty water from

bale: a large package of raw material that is wrapped or tied, evil, anguish

bases: plural of base- lowest part, point of attachment, chief ingredient, a cosmetic, a military center

basis: fundamental principal, schedule for preceding

basses: Plural of bass- male who sings the lowest range of notes

beat: (Noun) heart sound, musical sounds, regular route usually for police or reporters
(Verb) hit or strike several times, pound, mix quickly, defeat, shine on intensely
(Adjective) fatigued, exhausted

beet: edible root of a specific plant, red in color

berth: room to maneuver, boat's place at a dock, built in bed on a boat or train, job,

birth: when being born, origin, from the beginning

billed: past tense of bill- list of charges, menu, program (printed).

build: (Noun) physical makeup, physique
(Verb) construct, put together, create, develop a basis for

board: (Noun) flat piece of wood, an organized body of people, surface on which a game is played or scores are posted, prepaid meals

bored: past tense of bore-
(Noun) dull, repetitive, not kept one's attention
(Verb) make a hole with a tool, form a tunnel with equipment, advance steadily

brake: (Noun) device that slows or stops an object

break: (Noun) a crack or opening, beginning of something, an escape, piece of luck, brief time off work, a sudden change
(Verb) separate into pieces, smash, fracture a bone, escape from, detach, find flaw in, lessen effect of, cancel an appointment

bread: (Noun) food made from flour or rice and baked, form of making a living
(Verb) in cooking, to cover a food with a substance before frying or baking

bred: Past tense of breed- to mate, to develop, a group within a species

bridal: about a bride or a wedding

bridle: (Noun) headgear for a horse to control it
(Verb) slow or check, resent

broach: to pierce a hole in, debate, start a discussion
brooch: a large piece of jewelry usually pinned on clothing

C

cache: hiding place, a hidden store of something, area of computer memory
cash: (Noun) money, no credit
(Verb) converts or turns into smaller forms of money

canvas: fabric that ships sails are made from, woven fabric used for oil painting, background of a scene
canvass: (Noun) an examination, a survey
(Verb) scrutinize, make a survey

capital: (Noun) seat of government of a state, city that is the center of an activity, material wealth that can be used as collateral, an asset, a letter that is in the capital form (capital letter)
(Adjective) excellent, serious, relating to death, most important
Capitol: Refers to a specific building in Washington DC that houses the U. S. Congress

carton: container made from cardboard to package multiple quantities of an object
cartoon: humorous picture: satirical, political drawing, several continuous drawings with captions depicting a story

casual: by chance, irregularly, not planned, relaxed, little interest
causal: having to do with a cause, relating to an effect

cease: bring to an end, discontinue
seize: take, grab, have an overwhelming effect on, capture, come to a halt

ceiling: upper part of a room, highest limit, base of the could layer
sealing: to close, make waterproof, bind for life

cell: small room, smallest part of an organism, smallest unit of a group of people, a space on a spreadsheet
sell: exchange for money, persuade as to worth of something, gain acceptance

cellar: underground room for storage or protection
seller: vendor, person who sells

census: official counting of population done periodically
senses: (Noun) five faculties of the body that receive stimuli from the outside, a feeling or sensation, ability to think soundly, conveyance of a meaning
(Verb) grasp, understand

D

dairy: business related to milk, place processing milk
diary: personal record of events, appointment book

deceased: dead, no longer living
diseased: having a pathological condition, an illness, an abnormal condition

decree:	(Noun) a legal order
	(Verb) establish, decide, dictate
degree:	steps in a process, certification of higher level learning, social rank, a unit of math, classification of injury
detract:	take away from, divert, reduce the value of
distract:	turn attention from, pull in different directions emotionally
dew:	small drops of moisture
do:	perform, carry out, play a part, bring about, travel, meet the needs of
die:	(Noun) a metal piece used to stamp or shape material especially metal
	(Verb) expires, stop living, fade, and experience suffering
dye:	(Noun) a substance that changes something's color
	(Verb) to change the color of
divers:	(Noun) people who go underwater for sport or work
diverse:	(Adjective) different, having variety
dose:	(Noun) quantity of a drug, an amount of something unpleasant
doze:	sleep on and off

E

eight:	cardinal number after seven
ate:	past tense of eat- take into the body by the mouth, to destroy, erode
elicit:	evoke, arrive at
illicit:	unlawful, not allowed by custom
emerge:	to rise from, become apparent
immerge:	submerge, plunge
eligible:	qualified for, worthy of choice, available
illegible:	unable to make out writing, hard to read
ineligible:	unfit, disqualified
elusive:	prevent capture, difficult to describe
illusive:	deceptive, seems real but false (illusion)
enable:	make possible, make able
unable:	lacking means, incapable, incompetent
envelop:	to enclose, to attack, to cover
envelope:	container for a letter, a wrapping
erasable:	capable of being removed, not permanent
irascible:	easily angered, short tempered
erotic:	concerning sexual love or desire

erratic:	wandering, inconsistent
expand:	increase in size or volume, enlarge on, spread out
expend:	to use up, to spend, consume
expansive:	able to get larger, talkative, large scale (social)
expensive:	costly, high priced

F

facetious:	funny, humorous
factitious:	artificial, not genuine
factious:	internal dissension, internal disagreement, quarrels
fictitious:	imaginary, assumed to deceive
facility:	ease in doing, equipment needed for an activity, building for a specific function
felicity:	happiness, bliss, pleasing manner
fair:	(Noun) exhibition or market or event benefitting an organization
	(Adjective) pleasing appearance, free of clouds, promising, follows the rules, free to hunt
fare:	(Noun) fee to ride, food
	(Verb) get along, to dine, to travel
farther:	more distant, to a greater distance (physical)
further:	in additional or more (non-physical)
finale:	concluding part of play or musical presentation
finally:	at the end, ultimate, unattainable
finely:	splendid, in small parts, delicate manner
flagrant:	offensive, glaring, outrageous
fragrant:	pleasant odor, smell good
flair:	knack, elegant style
flare:	(Noun) bright light, sudden flame, burst of emotion, an opening outward,
	(Verb) flame up, become angry suddenly
flecks:	small marks or spots, small pieces
flex:	(Noun) electrical cable, pliancy
	(Verb) bend, contract, show off
flicks:	(Noun) a light touch, sound made by the contact
	(Verb) hit lightly, snap, remove by this motion
for:	(Preposition) indicates purpose of action, destination, in favor of, in place of, as a result of
	(Conjunction) since, because
fore:	(Noun) at the front,
	(Adjective and Adverb) earlier in order, forward
	(Interjection) golf term- ball coming
four:	Cardinal number one more than three

foreword:	introduction in a book, preface of a book	
forward:	(Noun) player in sports in the front line of defense	
	(Adjective) near the front, eager, progressive, exceptionally advanced	
	(Adverb) towards the front, in the future, a different time	

G

gage:	an object used to signify a challenge
gauge:	an instrument used to measure, means of evaluating, thickness or diameter of something
garnish:	embellish, decorate
garnishee:	withhold part of wages to pay a debt
gene:	hereditary unit containing DNA
jean:	work clothes or pants made of heavy material or denim
gibe:	jeer or taunt derisively
jibe:	agree with
gist:	main idea, point
jest:	prank, witty remark, joke
gild:	cover with gold, give false appearance
guild:	trade association, association of merchants
gleam:	(Noun) trace, glow
	(Verb) glow, shine
glean:	gather, collect information in small bits
grate:	(Noun) annoy, a metal covering made from iron bars
	(Verb) shred, make irritating sound
great:	(Noun) person who is extraordinary
	(Adverb) very well
	(Adjective) large in size, a long distance, important, powerful
guessed:	predicted with little information, estimate
guest:	invited person, visitor

H

hall:	passageway or lobby, building for public gatherings
haul:	(Noun) a distance, a load, the take as in a robbery
	(Verb) pull, drag or move in a truck
hear:	sound received by the ear, be told by others, listen carefully
here:	in this place, now, at this point
higher:	farther up, advanced in development, in upper range of pitched, elevated in rank
hire:	employ, use for fee

hole:	hollow place, deep cavity, squalid surroundings, a predicament	
whole:	complete, full amount of time, healed	
hour:	a measure of time equaling sixty minutes, a particular time, a unit of educational credit	
our:	belonging to us	

I

idle:	(Verb) pass time without working, run car at slow speed without moving (Adjective) not busy, lazy, not in use
idol:	adored, object used to worship
immunity:	free from legal obligation, ability to resist disease, protected
impunity:	freedom from punishment
in:	(Noun) a person with position or power
	(Preposition) within limits, into, function of, by means of, with reference to
	(Adverb) Toward the inside, within a place, under one's control, position of success
inn:	a hotel, a tavern or bar, place to sleep
incite:	provoke, prompt, set off
insight:	perception, see inner nature of
indelible:	memorable, irremovable
inedible:	unfit to eat
inhabit:	live in, fill
inhibit:	restrain, forbid
insolent:	arrogant, rude
insulate:	protect from, prevent heat or cold from reaching
intense:	to extreme, strong
intents:	aim, meaning
it's:	contraction of it is
its:	possessive of it

J

jam:	(Noun) a preserve made from whole fruit
	(Verb) put in a tight position, hit hard, cram, overfill
jamb:	sides of a door or window
jewelry:	ornaments made of metal and other materials worn by women
jury:	panel of judges, people chosen to hear evidence and make a decision in a court

K

knew:	past tense of know
new:	fresh, original, or not used before

kernel:	small part of corn or a nut, essential part
colonel:	commissioned rank in the military

knead:	massage, roll and push into lump of dough
need:	something required, obligation, poverty

know:	perceived, skilled in, experienced, fixed in the mind
no:	refusal, denial, not

L

later:	comparative form of late, afterwards
latter:	near the end second of two people or groups

lay:	produce, put against, devise plans for, give importance past tense of lie
lie:	(Noun) animal's lair, position of an object, (Verb) tell an untruth, put oneself flat, to exist, to extend (land).
lye:	caustic liquid from wood ash

lead:	Two words spelled exactly the same but pronounced differently. 1. gray metal used to write with 2. initiative, first position, dog leash, an example, part in a play, a clue
led:	past tense of lead (2)

lean:	(Noun) an incline, thin, little fat (Verb) rely on, prefer, to cause to tilt
lien:	secure an interest in, legal hold on property for a debt

lessen:	reduce, belittle
lesson:	period of instruction, class, a reprimand

lightening:	brighten, make less heavy
lighting:	equipment to illuminate, act of illuminating
lightning:	electrical discharge in the sky, flash in the sky from electrical discharge during a storm

local:	from a limited area, not widespread,
locale:	particular location, scene

M

made: produced, invented, successful
maid: female servant, unmarried girl

main: principal pipe, largest part
mane: long hair on horse, person

marital: relating to marriage, spousal
marshal: (Noun) military officer, city law enforcement officer
                   (Verb) arrange or place in order, organize, place in order
martial: relating to war, characteristic of a warrior

meat: edible part of an animal, the essence of
meet: (Noun) contest
                   (Verb) come together, introduced to, deal with

missed: not make contact with, omit, let go, feel loss of
mist: fine drops of liquid, haze before the eyes, dimness, moisturize

morality: system of right and wrong
mortality: death rate, rate of failure

N

naval: relating to the Navy or shipping
navel: middle, middle of abdomen where umbilical cord was attached (belly button)

O

one: single item, undivided
won: past tense of win- achieve victory, receive prize, reach with difficulty, gain affection of

our: possessive of we, belonging to
are: the plural form of the present tense of be

P

packed: crowded together, compressed
pact: agreement, bargain

pain: unpleasant sensation, irritation
pane: transparent material set in a window

parameter: measurable factor, boundary
perimeter: the outer limits, area around the edges

partition: a divider, a wall, storage space on a hard drive
petition: formal written document asking for something

passed: proceed, go beyond, allow in, succeed
past: (Noun) already happened
                   (Adjective)   former times
                   (Preposition) after

paunch:	protruding abdomen	
punch:	(Noun) a tool to make holes	
	(Verb) poke or hit, drive or vigor	
peak:	(Noun) a pointed top	
	(Verb) bring to its highest point	
peek:	glance, look quickly	
pique:	feeling of sharp anger or resentment	
peer:	(Noun) person on the same level	
	(Verb) look at intently	
pier:	platform extending over the water for ships to dock.	
peruse:	examine with care	
pursue:	chase, accomplish, advance, haunt	

Q

quiet:	hushed, calm
quit:	leave, give up
quite:	to a degree, completely alone or finished

R

rain:	(Noun) drops of water falling from the sky, a large amount
	(Verb) pour, give a large amount
reign:	(Noun) rule of a sovereign, large influence over
	(Verb) prevails, dominate, or act as the ruler
rein:	(Noun) leather straps used to control a horse, a restraint, form of power over people
	(Verb) hold someone back with invisible power, control
really:	truthfully, genuinely
reality:	way things are, what exists, fact
realty:	land, real estate
recluse:	person who stays alone, hermit
recue:	disqualify due to some involvement
relieve:	lessen, assist, ease pain, give aid, reduce monotony
relive:	live over, re-experience
retch:	(Verb) throw up, spasms of stomach with or without emptying contents of it
wretch:	(Noun) despicable, unfortunate, unhappy
root:	(Noun) part of plant that lives under the ground, basis for, base of, primary source, belonging to a group, mathematical number, source of
	(Verb) become settled, to establish firmly, dig, rummage, or applaud
route:	road, highway, path to follow, course of action

S

scene:	setting for play, site of a happening, public display of strong emotion
seen:	past participle of to see- saw with the eye, mental image, imagine
shear:	(Noun) tool used to cut, a force that removes or tears off a portion
	(Verb) removes by cutting, deprive, prune, trim
sheer:	(Adjective) see through, thin, absolute, unqualified, steep, vertical
	(Verb) change course, trend
soar:	rise quickly, glide, effortlessly
sore:	(Noun) wound, ulcer
	(Adjective) tender, painful, cause distress or irritation
staid:	straight-laced, sober
stayed:	past tense of stay- remain, wait, persist, delay
stair:	a step
stare:	(Noun) fixed look
	(Verb) regard, contemplate, look at fixedly
statue:	molded, carved or casted likeness of something
stature:	height , esteem, regard
statute:	decree, a law

T

tail:	(Noun) end of an animal especially the elongated portion, end of an object, bottom, last place, end of the line, formal dress for men
	(Verb) to follow, pursue
tale:	lie, story, gossip
tenant:	renter, occupant
tenet:	opinion, doctrine, creed, principle
theirs:	(Pronoun) belonging to them
there's:	contraction of there is
tracked:	followed, left dirt on, watch progress of, a course of study
tract:	a piece of land, a group of related organs in the body

U

undo:	reverse, open, take apart, ruin, confuse
undue:	excessive, not proper, unjustified

V

vale:	valley, dale
veil:	(Noun) cloth over head or face, screen
	(Verb) hide, transform, make obscure

W

waist:	middle, narrow part of the body above the abdomen
waste:	(Noun) garbage, undigested food expelled by the body
	(Verb) consume inefficiently, not take advantage of, kill
waive:	give up, not insist on
wave:	(Noun) a sudden sensation, an upward movement of the water which follows a pattern, trend, mass movement
	(Verb) move freely back and forth
weather	(Noun) day to day atmospheric changes
	(Verb) exposes to the elements, survive, endure
whether	conjunction introducing an indirect question

Y

ewe:	female sheep
yew:	a form of an evergreen tree
you:	the one being spoken to
yoke:	close fitting garment, a bar connecting two animals, bond,
yolk:	yellow portion of an egg used by a developing embryo
you're:	contraction meaning you are
your:	possessive pronoun belonging to you

Reading Comprehension

What is the purpose of testing for reading comprehension? While you are a student, you will spend a huge amount of time reading material that you are expected to understand, remember and use in different ways. If you cannot take the material you read, summarize it, reorganize it and retain it, you will not be successful in any Nursing or Allied Health program. These reading passages are followed by questions. These questions help determine if you were able to extract the important ideas and information from the passage. These passages are not about how fast you can read, but about your ability to understand what you read.

On this test you are required to answer a series of questions about the reading passage. These questions vary in what they are asking. Some of the major points asked are "What is the main idea?" "What is the author inferring in this passage?" "What is the meaning of this word as it is used here?" "What fact supports the author's idea that...?" Some questions are about the meaning of words, others are about specific facts in the passages, and some are about the idea or ideas the writer is trying to impart.

The first thing you should do before reading the passage is to read the question stems following the passage. Don't read the answer choices just the questions. This then helps you focus on what you need to determine from the reading. The main goal on the test is to answer the questions. To do this you must have some idea of what you are looking for. Answer any of the questions that can be answered after this reading.

The next step is to look over the passage. If it has a title, what is it? How many paragraphs are there? Then read the first and last sentence of each paragraph. What is the passage about? Now quickly read the entire passage. Don't dwell on it. Read it for the main points keeping in mind the questions you have to answer. Main ideas are usually in the first and last sentence of a paragraph. Don't read word for word. Read groups of words. This is called skimming. Don't move your lips when reading; this causes you to take longer to read the passage.

Next, discover the facts. Try to answer some basic questions. Follow the five W's: who, what, where, when and why. These give you the facts. Facts are things that we know happened, are true or exist. The author always provides some facts. Then observe for opinions. Opinions are things we believe to have happened or are true. There are clues to help determine it is an opinion, but no facts. With an opinion, one person could get one meaning while another person got a completely different meaning. You can disagree with an opinion, but not with a fact. Opinions often include words like: think, should, ought, could, good, important, and interesting. Opinions are usually supported by facts.

Separate main ideas from supporting ideas. The main idea is the overall idea of the passage. The rest of the passage should be encompassed under the main idea. In other words, the other sentences or paragraphs should support or define the main idea. If you decide on the main idea and then find a sentence or paragraph that cannot fit under that idea, then it is not the main idea. Supporting ideas are often explanations or examples.

When reading a passage, especially about a controversial idea, keep an open mind. Do not let your personal feelings or beliefs prevent you from seeing what the author is saying. The questions will ask what the author said, not what you believe. You do not have to agree with what the author is saying; just see what the author is saying.

Answer easy questions first. Questions asking for a fact or a definition are usually easier. While answering the question, eliminate answers that you know are not correct first. This leaves you with a few possible answers. Refer back to the passage and try to find the answer in the paragraphs. If you have scrap paper, jot down the idea of each paragraph in a few words (supplies to bake cake, good recipes). This will quickly help you to find the correct area of the passage to find your information.

What point of view did the author take to present the material? There are three points of view: first, second and third. First person is personal. The author is speaking about him or herself or his or her feelings and experiences. The first person attempts to create a bond between the author and the reader. The second person, you, makes the reader a part of the passage. It involves the reader in the action. The third person creates a distance between the author and the reader. This is more impersonal and more objective. You must understand that the author still may present an opinion in the third person, but the author hopes it seems more reasonable.

Continued Practice of these skills, when reading, will increase your ability to read more critically and thoroughly. Read the sample passages and answer the questions. After answering the questions, read the explanation of the paragraph and each answer. Go back to the passage, if necessary, and find where the explained parts of sentences or paragraphs are and how they fit. By reviewing the explanations, you can learn to read better for understanding.

Reading Comprehension Passages

As a young person growing up near the Atlantic Ocean, one of my main desires was to become a shark fisherman. For years, I watched as a shark fisherman would float the bloody shark bait out away from the beach using only balloons attached to the fishing line to carry the bait on the waves out into the ocean. When the bait was at the fisherman's desired location, the fisherman would jerk and tug hard on
5   the fishing line until the balloons would pop and the bait would sink to lie on the floor of the ocean. The fisherman would sit and wait for hours to have a chance for a shark to pick up the bait and take off with it. As the shark moved away with the bait, the fisherman's reel would start clicking, the sound would get louder and louder, the shark would be moving faster and faster, and then all of a sudden the clicking would stop. The fishing line would go slack, and nothing would happen. The fisherman would grab the rod and
10   give a huge tug, two or three times on the line. Then suddenly the reel would sing, the shark swallowed the bait and ran with the line. The fight was on. The fisherman would reel in some line, the shark would pull some more line out, the fisherman would reel in more line, and on and on. The shark could pull out several hundred yards of fishing line from this huge fishing reel, designed to catch very large fish in the ocean. Depending on the size of the shark, this fight between man and shark could go on for several hours, tiring
15   both the man and the shark.

      What process does the fisherman go through to prepare to battle large sharks? Let's follow the process. The first step is to determine what size shark the fisherman plans to try to catch. If the fisherman desires to catch a very small shark, one to three feet in length, then he chooses a lighter fishing rod and fishing tackle (fishing line, hook(s), leader wire or heavy duty monofilament line, swivels, etc.). If the
20   fisherman does not choose the correct size fishing equipment, the shark will break the line; and the fisherman will lose the shark and all the line and its attachments. The bigger the shark the fisherman plans on hooking, the larger and heavier the fishing equipment will have to be if the fisherman plans on landing this shark. Of course, the larger and heavier the equipment, the more expensive the supplies are. One thing the fisherman will tell you is that you may plan on a small shark; however, this does not mean that a large
25   shark will not take your bait. The chance of landing a large shark, on light fishing equipment though, is very rare.

      The next step is to make the best selection of available fishing bait. Sharks love bait that has a very strong smell and are also attracted to bloody fish parts. These parts are available around docks where fisherman have just cleaned and skinned the fish they brought in from a catch. They will usually allow
30   someone to just take the bloody head and discarded, non edible parts of the fish. This is great bait.

      Once the bait is selected, the fisherman is now ready to locate the best area that attracts sharks. Sharks are known to stay around piers, fishing docks and any man made reefs or natural reefs that will keep fish in that area. The fish use these areas to try to hide from their predators, and this is where they find their food. If the fisherman sees a large school of fish on the surface of the ocean, he can be assured
35   that sharks are close behind. Sharks follow this school of fish and attack it as a ready supply of food. Sharks are known as scavengers of the ocean, and they are always looking for food. If all these preparations are successful, the fisherman may go home with a trophy that he can talk about for a long time. Sometimes the fisherman wins and sometimes the shark wins. That is the thrill.

1. What is the main idea of this passage?
    A. The success of shark fishing depends on the bait chosen.
    B. The battle between man and shark is exciting.
    C. If a fisherman prepares properly he will catch a shark.

2. The author implies that shark fishing is:
    A. exciting
    B. time consuming
    C. expensive
    D. all the above

3. One may infer from the passage that:
    A. man is smarter than sharks.
    B. sharks are smarter than man.
    C. luck plays a large part in the catch.

4. Which statement is *true* based on the passage?
    A. The young man became a shark fisherman.
    B. The proper equipment guarantees once a shark is on the line the fisherman will catch it.
    C. Sometimes the fish wins and sometimes man wins.

5. What does the word "ran" in the story mean?
    A. roamed
    B. melted
    C. escaped
    D. dissolved

6. In this passage the word "sing" means:
    A. croon
    B. whistle
    C. reveal

Let's analyze this passage. The first paragraph describes the "hooking" and beginning battle of catching a shark. The next three paragraphs describe the preparation necessary for this battle between man and shark to begin. The last two sentences of the passage tell us that if the fisherman wins he can brag about this win; and the last sentence tells us that even if he doesn't win he gets the thrill out of trying.

Answers:
1. B
2. D
3. C
4. C
5. C
6. B

1. The main theme of this passage is that "the battle between man and shark is exciting." This is what the first paragraph leads up to. The main idea does not necessarily have to be in the first sentence of a passage. It doesn't even have to be in the first paragraph. All other information in the passage should be able to be included under the main idea. The rest of this passage describes how the fisherman would get ready; and then if he was lucky, he might go home with a shark.

2. Two statements indicate that shark fishing is "exciting": "The fight was on," and "That is the thrill". "The fisherman would sit and wait for hours" tells us that it is "time consuming". "he chooses a lighter fishing rod and fishing tackle (fishing line, hook(s), leader wire or heavy duty monofilament line, swivels, etc.). If

the fisherman does not choose the correct size fishing equipment, the shark will break the line and the fisherman will lose the shark and all the line and its attachments" implies that this is expensive. Obviously the fisherman does not want to lose all of this equipment. Since all three are in the passage, then the answer is "all the above".

3. Answer A and answer B are opposite of each other. There are no supporting statements to indicate that either man or shark is smarter. There are statements though that supports the idea that catching the fish is, for a large part, luck. These statements are: "The chance of landing a large shark, on light fishing equipment though, is very rare." and "Sometimes the fisherman wins, and sometimes the shark wins". If man were smarter than the fish then he would catch the fish most often and vice versa.

4. There is no evidence in the passage that the young man ever became a shark fisherman. The young man "watched" the fisherman, but nothing is said that he became one. A lot is said about the proper equipment, but the passage indicates the fisherman does not always win with the statement "the fisherman may go home with a trophy". The last paragraph states "Sometimes the fisherman wins, and sometimes the shark wins." This is a statement of fact.

5. To determine the meaning of "ran", the reader should look at the part of the sentence before, "the shark swallowed the bait" and the sentence after the word, "The fisherman would reel in some line, and the shark would pull some more line out". Now look at the part of the sentence with the word "and ran with the line". Ran means all of the words listed, but "escaped" fits what the author is saying. The fish took the bait, had the line in his mouth and tried to run away with it.

6. Again look at the parts of the sentence and the sentences around the word. "The reel would start clicking, the sound would get louder and louder," and "and ran with the line." The clicking was when the fish was going slowly. Now that he was going fast, the reel would make a much different sound. Crooning is a soft sound. Reveal is also another meaning for sing but certainly out of context here. Whistle is the only choice left. As the fishing line spins the reel changes from a clicking sound to a more consistent sound, like a whistle.

Reading Passage 2

At the age of 60, I am nearing retirement. I am very worried about the current debt in the U.S. and the proposed changes in healthcare. Our elected representatives in Congress, the Senate and even the President are trying to change our current healthcare system. Are they trying to match either the Canadian
5 *or European system or create a unique system? We need to provide quality healthcare for every citizen in the United States. Some will tell you that we need to make changes to the system and refine the process. However, 92% of Americans are very happy or mostly satisfied with their current health insurance. Do we need to completely change the system or modify it to accommodate the other 8% of the uninsured people in the United States?*
10 *One of the biggest arguments for change in the system is the cost of healthcare. If something is not done to reduce the costs, it is going to bankrupt the country. The country does need to look at ways of cutting costs but, at the same time, not diminish the quality of care. The Congressional Budget Office has recently published a report stating that healthcare, to include Medicare, is 12% of the Gross National Product (GNP). At the rate of increase in healthcare costs in the next 10 years, these costs could be 20% of*
15 *the GNP.*
Many in Congress and the President are pointing the finger at a few areas that are responsible for the high cost of healthcare. Every year we are being told about the billions of dollars that are being wasted by abuse of the government's Medicare system. However, it doesn't seem as if the government can correct

this problem. Another area is the doctors that make the clinical diagnosis of the medical problem(s) and perform the procedures that fix the problem(s). Some feel they are doing unnecessary tests and procedures to increase their profit. Are they or are they covering the chance of expensive litigation? Are they paying the high price of malpractice insurance, staff to file the Medicare/Medicaid and insurance forms, etc.? The other culprit is insurance companies who are charging more and more each year for coverage and limiting the amount they will cover. Insurance companies have raised the costs of healthcare coverage based on the amount of money they have to put out for the various procedures and surgeries. Are insurance companies loosing that much money or wasting it on excessive compensation for the executives and perks for special employees?

Many in the Congress and the President feel that the answer to this issue is to have a "public option", a government run healthcare plan. We already have a government run health care program, Medicare; and it is in the billions of dollars in the red. There is a lot of debate on this issue, and citizens of all ages are speaking out about this issue. Only time will tell how this will turn out.

1. What is the main idea in this passage?
   A. The insurance companies and doctors are ruining healthcare.
   B. A "public option" healthcare plan is needed.
   C. Healthcare needs changing, but how is yet undetermined.

2. The author's attitude toward the healthcare in the U. S. is:
   A. Healthcare needs reform.
   B. The Government needs to take over healthcare.
   C. There is no need to change healthcare.

3. What percent of the people in the U. S. are uninsured?
   A. 92%
   B. 12%
   C. 20%
   D. 8%

4. "Many in the Congress and the President feel that the answer to this issue is to have a "public option", a government run healthcare plan" is intended to express:
   A. the government's interest in increasing everyone's healthcare.
   B. the creation of the first government run healthcare plan.
   C. an alternative to expensive insurance.

5. In the next 10 years, what would be the increase in the Gross National Product from the increase in healthcare costs?
   A. 8%
   B. 10%
   C. 12%
   D. 20%

6. Which statement is true based on the passage?
   A. Insurance costs have reached their peak.
   B. Every citizen deserves quality healthcare.
   C. Doctors are doing unnecessary tests and surgeries to increase their profits.

7. What does the word "culprit" mean as used here?
    A. person being wronged
    B. wrongdoer
    C. receiver of evil

Let's analyze this passage. The first paragraph describes the issue of healthcare and raises a few questions about what is actually being suggested. The second paragraph discusses the cost of healthcare and its effect on the country. The third paragraph describes the perceived causes of the high cost of healthcare, and the author provides some alternative ideas. The last paragraph provides a solution that has been offered to solve the problem. It also indicates that there is no agreement as to the solution of this problem.

Answers:
1. C
2. A
3. D
4. C
5. A
6. B
7. B

1. "The insurance companies and doctors are ruining healthcare." is offered as one of the causes of the high costs of healthcare. The paragraph includes three of these, so it cannot be the overall idea. "A 'public option' healthcare plan is needed." is offered as one possible solution to the problem. The author presented at least one other possible solution, "to make changes to the system and refine the process." "Healthcare needs changing, but how is yet undetermined" is the best choice for the overall idea of the passage. It includes all the other points as reasons for the cause and possible solution to the problem.

2. The author indicates in several places that "healthcare needs reform". "There is no need to change healthcare" is the opposite of this position. The "Government needs to take over healthcare" is one possible solution, but the author indicates "There is a lot of debate on this issue, and citizens of all ages are speaking out about this issue."

3. The first paragraph states" the other 8% of the uninsured people in the United States". This answers the question. "92% of Americans are very happy or mostly satisfied with their current health insurance" is also stated in the first paragraph, but this is the opposite of what is asked. 12% refers to the "Gross National Product (GNP)" in the second paragraph. 20% is what percent the "healthcare costs in the next 10 years" could be.

4. There is no mention of "the government's interest in increasing everyone's healthcare." The government is interested in providing everyone some form of healthcare coverage. This passage does not specify. The government already runs a healthcare system, as indicated by "of the government's Medicare system". The "'public option'", a government run healthcare plan" would not be the first. This leaves "an alternative to expensive insurance" as the only correct option. The author does discuss the "insurance companies who are charging more and more each year for coverage and limiting the amount they will cover." This statement indicates that insurance is expensive and getting more so every year.

5. The question asks what the increase would be. The passage states "is 12% of the Gross National Product (GNP). At the rate of increase in healthcare costs in the next 10 years, this cost could be 20% of GNP." 12 from 20 is 8. The answer is that the INCREASE would be 8%.

6. There is no indication from the passage that insurance costs have peaked. The passage actually states "who are charging more and more each year." "We need to provide quality healthcare for every citizen in the United States" is stated in the first paragraph. The statement, "Some feel they are doing unnecessary tests and procedures to increase their profit", is not a proven statement just what some people feel.

7. The word culprit means "wrongdoer". The other two choices are the receiver of the culprit's actions, the opposite.

Reading Passage 3

5   *In the last decade there have been a huge number of midlife missteps by our elected officials. It has been rampant throughout the political arena, starting with a former President of the United States, congressmen, senators, governors and other state officials. There seems to be a feeling in the political arena that these politicians can do whatever they desire and the public, who elected these people, should say nothing about these indiscretions nor make any comment about these issues. Most of these men are pronounced church-going Christians who have run their political careers on a platform as strong Christians with a great love of family and country. These individuals have made a commitment to be faithful to their elected community and their family. When their clandestine activities are exposed, the individual states, that he is very sorry for the hurt to his family and his failure to the voters and desires forgiveness from all of*
0   *us for his actions. If we cannot believe what they say during their political campaigns and during the time they are serving us in the office that this individual has been elected to, how can they now expect us to believe that they are going to represent our needs in the community or country? One Governor was forced to resign from office after his affair became public. Another Governor's wife left him, and he was not reelected.*

5   *The latest to fall into the trap of midlife missteps is the Governor of South Carolina. He is a pronounced Christian who railed against our former President for his sexual escapades while in the White House. In the summer of 2009, it came to light that he was having an affair with a divorced Argentinean woman. The Governor attempted to conceal the affair and stated that he met her on the internet.   The Governor's wife recently was quoted as saying, "Mark has issues that he needs to work on, about*
0   *happiness and what happiness means". The Governor states that family is very important to him. He goes on by stating that he wants reconciliation with his wife and family. At this point, this is questionable. He and his wife are not living together, and his wife states that she is not sure that this is fixable. Many people in politics and his constituents have asked for his resignation. To date, he has refused to resign.*
        Recently Stephen Arterburn, the author of Every Man's Battle, states that one piece of good news
5   *amid the seemingly unending parade of political men and others getting tripped up by sexual temptations is that Christian men increasingly have been joining small men's groups to discuss these issues. Some of the relationship experts are reporting that those temptations are still out there and often hit home during the midlife years. The experts state that the top level potholes for men are problems with sexuality, past business failures or money problems and the inability to talk to their partner about the problems that they*
0   *are having or have encountered*

1. What is the main idea of this passage?
   A. Midlife sexual encounters can be avoided.
   B. Many elected officials in the political arena feel they can have extramarital encounters without repercussions.
   C. Officials caught having extramarital affairs should resign.

2. The author's attitude toward the commitment to the public by these officials is?
   A. apathy
   B. objection
   C. ambivalence

3. The passage suggests that clandestine extramarital affairs are:
   A. expected of elected officials
   B. unrelated to politics
   C. unacceptable for elected officials

4. What is meant by "missteps"?
   A. blunder
   B. incident
   C. accident

5. The author uses the word "potholes" to mean:
   A. hazards
   B. pits
   C. hollows

Let's analyze this passage. The first paragraph describes the issue of extramarital affairs by elected officials. It describes their beliefs and how they seem to feel about being "caught". The second paragraph describes a specific example and the results of his indiscretions. The last paragraph indicates that there are an increasing number of middle aged men seeking help before they make this error.

Answers:
1. B
2. B
3. C
4. A
5. A

1. "Many elected officials in the political arena feel they can have extramarital encounters without repercussions" is supported in this passage by "There seems to be a feeling in the political arena that these politicians can do whatever they desire and the public, who elected these people, should say nothing about these indiscretions nor make any comment about these issues". In the last paragraph, the author cites another author who talks about men trying to discuss these issues. He does not state whether these men are trying to avoid this problem or have already committed this indiscretion. There are no comments in this passage to support the idea that the author thinks these officials should resign. There is a statement that "One Governor was forced to resign from office after his affair became public".
   2. The author's attitude of objection is supported in the first paragraph by "If we cannot believe what they say during their political campaigns and during the time they are serving us in the office that this individual has been elected to, how can they now expect us to believe that they are going to represent our

needs in the community or country?" Apathy is indifference, and there is no support in this passage for this conclusion. Ambivalence is uncertainty or indecisiveness. The author seems to have a very definite point of view, disapproval.

3. Because these indiscretions have "been rampant throughout the political arena" does not mean they are expected. The author does not deny that others have these affairs ("seemingly unending parade of political men and others"), but the words "rampant throughout the political arena" focuses the reader on these particular men and the seemingly large number that are politicians. The tone of the passage certainly gives the impression that these are not acceptable behaviors for people who make public statements about their beliefs.

4. A "misstep" can be a stumble or misplaced step. This passage does not mean the act of walking. There is no indication from the passage that the author is talking about an "accidental happening". This word here means "inappropriate conduct" or "blunder". An "incident" is an occurrence or happening but does not mean an error.

5. A "pothole' is a "pit" or "hollow" in the ground. Here it is used figuratively and not literally. Here it means a source of danger or "hazard". Problems of this nature of those listed can undermine a person's self confidence and cause them to look for sources of admiration or fulfillment in the wrong places.

Reading Passage 4

The gift of motherhood is one of the most spectacular events in a woman's life. The birth of a child is a very special moment; and the responsibilities for the feeding, changing and caring for the infant is huge during the child's early years. Parenting skills are not necessarily inherent. Children do not come with instruction manuals, and very little training is provided or required for parents before a child is placed in their care. The state has very strict guidelines for the protection of a child. If these are not followed, the local officials could bring charges against the parent(s); and if the neglect or abuse is significant, the child could be removed from their care.

Recently, a mother, with a five-year old child and a new baby only six weeks old, was charged for the extraordinary neglectful act of leaving a child in a hot vehicle. This act by the mother resulted in the six-week old child dying in the car due to the extreme heat. The mother discovered that the child was not in the house and went to the car, only to find the child still in the car seat. The mother called 911 for assistance. The temperature inside the car was found to be 129 degrees. The mother told the police that she and her cousin had taken the child to a doctor's appointment; and when arriving home, the mother thought that the cousin had taken the child out of the car. The mother did not realize that the child was missing for more than an hour. As a result of the extraordinary neglect, the mother was taken into custody and charged with felony murder.

This is an incident that is too common and needs rectifying. According to a study published in the Pediatrics Journal, 2009, 29 deaths of infants left inside hot vehicles have occurred so far in 2009 in the United States. This study by the Department of Geosciences of San Francisco State University found that since 1998 a total of 441 children have died after being left in hot vehicles. According to the University of Michigan Health System, "Studies show that regardless of the color of the car, its seats, or if the windows are cracked, interior temperatures can rise from 96 degrees to 150 degrees in a matter of 20 minutes, with a sharp rise in the first 10 minutes."

To prevent incidents like these and others, one recommendation is for parents to receive mandatory parenting classes on this and other safety issues for their newborns. Ignorance is no excuse when a helpless child is injured or dies due to relegating the parental responsibility to another or being so preoccupied with other things that the child is endangered.

1. What is the main idea of this passage?
    A. People forget and make mistakes and should be excused.
    B. Parenting classes should be mandatory before having a child.
    C. A parent must take the responsibility for the protection of their child.

2. The purpose of stating the facts on the quick temperature rise in the vehicle is to:
    A. demonstrate neglect
    B. educate
    C. place blame

3. The author's attitude towards parents leaving children in cars is:
    A. critical
    B. disbelief
    C. admiration
    D. condescension

4. The primary purpose of paragraph 2 is to:
    A. explore outcomes
    B. give an example
    C. show the need for change

5. What is the death toll for 2009?
    A. 29
    B. 96
    C. 129
    D. 441

6. Which statement is true based on the passage?
    A. Law enforcement and the state are trying to take children away from their parents.
    B. Parenting skills are inherent.
    C. Children are more resilient than adults.
    D. The state has strict guidelines to protect children.

Let's analyze this passage. The first paragraph describes parenting and the responsibilities that go with it. It tells us that these skills are not inborn. The second paragraph provides an example of the lack of these skills. The third paragraph reports the frequency of this particular act. The last paragraph provides a possible solution to reduce the number of this particular incident.

Answers:
1. C
2. B
3. A
4. B
5. A
6. D

1. The fact that people forget and make mistakes is not the issue here. Nowhere does the author excuse this behavior, as it resulted in the death of a helpless six- week old infant. This is not a broad enough idea to take in the rest of the information provided. "One recommendation is for parents to receive mandatory parenting classes on this and other safety issues for their newborns" is just that one recommendation. The entire passage is broader than this. That "parents must take the responsibility for the protection of their child" is the overall idea. The first paragraph talks about the protection of a child, and the last paragraph talks about "parental responsibility".

2. Inserting the facts about how quickly the temperature rises in a vehicle in the heat is inserted to "educate" and demonstrate that the timeframe for removing a person from a hot car is so brief before damage can occur. There is no purpose to "placing blame" on the parent. The court determines who is to blame. The purpose of facts has nothing to do with demonstrating neglect. The example "demonstrates neglect".

3. The author's disapproval of this action is evident throughout the passage. The example, the statistics, and even the recommendation demonstrate this. There is no evidence in the passage that the author feels "disbelief" that this has occurred and keeps occurring. To "condescend" is to act superior. There is no indication that the author feels superior or looks down on these people.

4. Paragraph two gives an example of lack of protection of a helpless child and the result of this action. Paragraph three demonstrates a need for change. The statistics of this happening support the need. An outcome is the result or consequences. The consequences the parent(s) of this child are not even mentioned. The point of the passage was not what happens to the parent as a result of the neglect, but that such incidences need to be prevented.

5. The death toll for 2009 is stated as "29". "96" degrees is the beginning temperature in the car. "129" degrees is what was measured in the car when the child was found. "441" is the total number of deaths by this route since 1998.

6. The statement that "if the neglect or abuse is significant the child could be removed from their care" is a last resort. There is no information that this is the goal of the state. The passage states that "Parenting skills are not necessarily inherent." This passage focused on children. There is no indication from any information that "children are more resilient than adults". Actually children dehydrate much more quickly that adults, but there is no reference to any of this as to why they die so quickly. "The state has very strict guidelines for the protection of a child" is in the first paragraph is a fact.

Reading Passage 5

     The financial and housing market meltdown of 2007 was caused by too many banks and financial institutions making questionable loans to people that were not able to make the payments at the level required. The result of the financial meltdown not only impacted the housing market, but it had a major impact on the automobile industry and the whole U. S. economy. This caused millions of people to lose their jobs, and the recession progressed into 2009. As a result of the failure of these large banks, President Bush and his staff starting looking at ways to spark the economy and assist people to get back to work.

     During the same time, the automobile industry had been struggling due to high gas prices; and the problem with the economy made their businesses get into even more trouble. In the fall of 2008, Ford, Chrysler, and Chevrolet were looking for government assistance or some type of Federal bailout to keep their companies from going bankrupt. The government had come up with the term "too large to fail" for many of the financial companies. The auto industry felt that they were in the same category also. The

*Congress met with representatives of the big three automakers, Ford, Chrysler and Chevrolet, to discuss
ways to assist them to prevent bankruptcy. The Congress and the President felt if the U. S. auto industry*
15   *were allowed to go bankrupt, there would be a long reaching negative impact on the U. S. economy. They
were not ready to have this happen. So the government agreed to aide these companies with major loans
but required them to restructure.*

*During the analysis process of the auto industry and reviewing the type of cars being built, the
decision was made to do something about the "gas guzzling autos". Someone came up with the idea of*
20   *doing a program called "Cash-for-Clunkers". This program was designed to assist the automakers to sell
millions of cars that were on their car lots all over the United States. It was believed that if you assist
people to trade in the gas guzzling vehicles for autos that had better fuel efficiency, this would reduce the
dependency on foreign oil and boost the economy by having the public spend money in the U. S. and keep
the money in the U. S. The President and the Congress approved a total of three billion dollars for the*
25   *implementation of the "Cash-for-Clunkers". This program would give anyone, trading in a vehicle that met
the program requirements, up to $4,500.00 for the traded-in vehicle. The program was stopped in August
of 2009 because they ran out of money. This was one of the only government programs that had been
successful in boosting spending. The automakers are now hiring people back and have restarted
manufacturing more vehicles. The report of the "Cash-for-Clunkers" states that over 690,000 gas guzzling*
30   *vehicles were taken off the road. Now the process of paying the car dealers the $4,500.00 per car and
turning these gas guzzlers into scrap metal is under way.*

1. What is the main idea in this passage?
   A. The auto industry is the main stay of the economy.
   B. "Gas guzzling vehicles" caused the crash of the U.S. economy.
   C. To end a recession, the public must spend money.

2. One may infer from the passage that:
   A. The auto industry was too large to fail.
   B. Any spending program will stop the recession.
   C. The cost of oil caused the recession.

3. Which statement is true based on the passage?
   A. The "Cash-for Clunkers" program ran out of money.
   B. The auto industry is a small part of the U.S. economy.
   C. The loans from the government kept the auto industry from going bankrupt.

4. What is the total number of vehicles taken off the road from the program?
   A. 2008
   B. 4,500
   C. 690,000

5. What does the word "clunkers" mean?
   A. junk cars
   B. cars making noise
   C. cars using gas inefficiently

Let's analyze this passage. The first paragraph describes the original cause of the recession and the need to spark spending to recover. The second paragraph describes a particular industry and its difficulties. The third paragraph describes a strategy that was adopted to increase spending and help turn the tide towards recovery.

Answers:
1. C
2. A
3. A
4. C
5. C

1. The crisis was caused by "The financial and housing market meltdown of 2007". The auto industry is a smaller part of the economy. The banks caused the recession not the oil (gas) issue. The spending of money is what has turned the recession around. This is supported by "The automakers are now hiring people back and have restarted manufacturing more vehicles."

2. The government found a way to save the auto industry. This implies it was too large to fail. "This was one of the only government programs that had been successful in boosting spending" tells us that not all spending programs work. The crisis was caused by "The financial and housing market meltdown of 2007".

3. "'Cash-for-Clunkers' program ran out of money" is a stated fact. The auto industry was large enough for the government to find a way to prevent them from bankruptcy. The "Cash-for-Clunkers" program rescued the auto industry not loans.

4. The statement "The report of the 'Cash-for-Clunkers' states that over 690,000 gas guzzling vehicles were taken off the road" is the actual number of cars removed from service. "2008" is the year the auto industry asked for a bailout. "$4,500.00" is the rebate on turning in the gas guzzler.

5. The word "clunkers" here does not mean a "noisy car" or a "junk car". It was used here to signify a car that got less miles per gallon.

Blank

Critical Thinking

Critical Thinking Practice Test

Critical Thinking Answers and Explanations

Blank

Critical Thinking

Critical Thinking can be defined in many ways. One way is to say it is thinking clearly and having rational thought. It requires the ability to analyze information, determine what is fact and opinion, and either develop conclusions or validate the conclusions someone else has developed.

Critical thinking requires a set of skills and attitudes. The knowledge base must already be present. Critical thinking cannot occur if the person has no knowledge of the subject that they are to think about. The content in the critical thinking section is general information that everyone should have knowledge of. The situations are everyday type situations.

The critical thinking attitudes include such items as inquisitiveness, open mindedness, flexibility in thought, honest about personal beliefs, openness to change (to reconsider conclusions), systematic in solving problems, and persistence. Personal experiences must be put aside, and the problem must be approached from the information given and the idea that ANYONE could solve this problem. If you interject personal experience or local environmental issues, you add information that anyone would not have access to.

Some situations present an argument. This is different than a dispute or controversy. An argument is a set of sentences that present a premise or claim to some information. Usually the argument claims it is fact and correct. The real question is "are the conclusions presented valid based on the information given?" The test taker must ask his/her self if the argument presented is valid? Is the information presented complete or were parts left out? Is the argument a person's personal opinion or are there facts presented?

To uncover the meaning of all of these questions requires the person to use the set of skills that comprise Critical Thinking Skills. These skills include: Interpretation, Analysis, Evaluation, Inference, and Explanation.

Interpretation

Interpretation includes recognizing a problem and being able to describe it and its parts. This may include seeking others input and more data to understand the issue. It also requires the individual to correctly understand what was presented. If the language used (technical, medical, slang) is not understood, then the correct definitions of those terms must be found. Any symbols, numbers, drawings must be understood.

Analysis

Analysis requires the person to determine the relationships between statements. The person must determine each statement's purpose in the group of statements. What effect is the statement meant to have on the reader of the statement? Is it to bring a feeling of sympathy, anger, etc.? Can the reader rephrase these statements to present the meaning in a more understandable way? Are these statements presented to support or disagree with the main idea? What point of view did the author of these statements take? Are there any statements that could be left out and not change the idea (extraneous material)?

Evaluation

Evaluation includes determining the validity or believability of the statements made. The reader must determine the strength of the relationship between the statements. Is the author presenting facts or opinions? Are these statements true, probably true or not sure about them?

Inference

Inference requires the reader to determine if further information is needed to determine conclusions. If inadequate information is given, there is no ability to draw conclusions. The reader then must review the conclusions drawn and determine their reasonableness. Are there alternative conclusions that can be drawn from the information given? Are the conclusions logical? Can the reader supply reasons to select one conclusion over another?

Explanation

Explanation is a statement of the results of one's own thinking process about the problem presented and the methods the reader used to come to his/her conclusion. To record or explain the entire process that resulted in his/her conclusions. To present one's own argument(s) or reasons for accepting or refuting the conclusions presented.

These competencies or skills are possessed by at different levels for different individuals. All of these skills are not necessary at the same level for one to think critically. The development of these skills begins early in life and develops at different speeds in each of us. The purpose of these questions is to determine the level of critical thinking one possesses at this point. All health education programs aim to further develop these skills throughout the educational process.

Several critical thinking questions are presented to assist you to practice answering these types of questions.

Critical Thinking Practice Test

1. You need a babysitter, and you have four options. You can call your sister who lives 32 miles away; it will cost you $20.00; and it will take her 45 minutes to get to your house. You can call your neighbor, who lives one mile away; it will cost you $35.00; and it will take her 25 minutes to get to your house. You can call your mother, who lives 63 miles away; it will not cost you; and it will take her 72 minutes to get to your house. You can call the babysitter, who lives 35 miles away; it will cost you $25.00; and it will take her 40 minutes to get to your house. Which one of the four can get to your house faster?

    A. babysitter
    B. neighbor
    C. mother
    D. sister

2. Five children (Lauren, Olivia, Daniel, Matthew and Ali) were playing hide and go seek; but Mr. Smith, the finder, chased them back to base. Daniel made it to base third, and Ali was fourth. Matthew made it to base after Ali. Olivia did not make it back second. Which child made it back to base first, and which was last?

    A. Lauren, Matthew
    B. Olivia, Ali
    C. Olivia, Matthew
    D. Daniel, Matthew

3. Anthony, Joseph, Andrew, and Sarah are waiting in line to get school pictures taken. Joseph is not first, Andrew is between Anthony and Joseph. Sarah is before Anthony. Anthony is not first. What is the order in which the students are standing in line?

    A. Sarah, Anthony, Andrew, Joseph
    B. Joseph, Anthony, Sarah, Andrew
    C. Andrew, Sarah, Anthony, Joseph
    D. Anthony, Joseph, Andrew, Sarah

4. Rebecca is planning her wedding. She has three bridesmaids (Michelle, Kelly, and Christina) and five groomsmen (Brian, Josh, Adam, Mike, and Kevin). After going over her budget, she can only afford for one bridesmaid and two groomsmen to be in her wedding. She must now pick whom she wants to be in her wedding. Michelle and Christina are competing against each other as the "best bridesmaid." Michelle and Kevin previously dated. Josh and Mike do not like one another. Brian and Adam are mean to each other. Who will be in Rebecca's wedding?

    A. Michelle with Kevin and Adam
    B. Kelly with Josh and Mike
    C. Christina with Brian and Mike
    D. Kelly with Brian and Adam

5. The kids in Mrs. Smith's class (Frank, Charles, Suzzie and Betty) are coloring a Halloween page. Each child picked a different color crayon to color with. The colors were Orange, Purple, White, and Black. Frank did not pick Orange or Purple. Charles did not like the colors Purple or White. Suzzie chose White. Betty chose a color that both Charles and Frank did not pick. What child picked what color?

    A. Frank - Black, Charles - Purple, Suzzie - White, Betty - Orange
    B. Frank - White, Charles - Orange, Suzzie - Purple, Betty - Black
    C. Frank - Black, Charles - Orange, Suzzie - White, Betty - Purple
    D. Frank- Purple, Charles - Black, Suzzie - White, Betty - Orange

6. If Nathan has more than Alyssa, Alyssa has more than Noah, and Christopher has more than Nathan. What is the order from most to least?
	A. Noah, Nathan, Alyssa, Christopher
	B. Nathan, Noah, Alyssa, Christopher
	C. Christopher, Nathan, Alyssa, Noah
	D. Alyssa, Nathan, Noah, Christopher

7. Emily, Ava, Mia, and Ann went to the farm. They saw four pigs. Pinky and Squeaky were pink with short tails. Oinky and Porky were white with long curly tails. Pinky and Oinky were eating. Squeaky and Porky were running. Emily didn't want a pink pig. Ava didn't want a pig with a long tail. Mia didn't pick a pig that was eating. Ann picked a pig that Mia and Emily didn't want. Who picked which pig?
	A. Ann - Oinky, Ava - Pinky, Mia - Porky, Emily - Squeaky
	B. Ann - Pinky, Ava -Squeaky, Mia - Porky, Emily - Oinky
	C. Ann - Squeaky, Ava - Pinky, Mia - Oinky, Emily - Porky
	D. Ann - Porky, Ava- Oinky, Mia - Pinky, Emily - Squeaky

8. For the past three nights, Betty has washed her hair in the sink. Tonight, Betty will:
	A. wash her hair in the sink.
	B. wash her hair in the shower.
	C. wash her hair in the tub.
	D. maybe not wash her hair.

9. Barbara went to the mall to go shopping. The mall has both food and clothing. What did Barbara go to the mall for?
	A. food
	B. clothing
	C. both
	D. cannot tell

10. Jason was in the class with the nerds; he must be a nerd. This conclusion is valid only if which of these statements was true?
	A. Nerds are often in his class.
	B. Only nerds are in the class.
	C. Nerds must be in the class.
	D. Nerds are never in the class.

11. Bob bought a car. Bob doesn't like the color of his car. The dealership has a satisfaction guarantee on every car that is sold there. Bob took his car back to the dealership. What did Bob do?
	A. got a new car
	B. got his money back
	C. either one: got the car or got the money back
	D. kept the old car

12. Some Santa's wear glasses. All Santa's have beards. All Santa's that have beards are chubby. Based on the information given, which one of the following is a true statement?
	A. Some Santa's that wear glasses are chubby.
	B. Santa's that are chubby wear glasses.
	C. Santa's are chubby.
	D. Small Santa's wear glasses and have beards.

13. Brenda, a clothing designer, opened up a clothing store about six months ago. One day, a lady walked into Brenda's store and stated, "I didn't know that you had a variety of clothes in this store. I thought that you had to have a special order to purchase anything." Brenda knew that she needed to do some advertising so people knew that she was a clothing store and not just a "special order" store. Which of the following methods would Brenda use to increase her business?
    A. Advertise in the local paper the variety of clothing that is in the store.
    B. Move her store to a well populated area.
    C. Attend the next clothing expo and advertise her specially made clothes.
    D. Making coupons available for 50% off entire purchase.

14. Marsha owns five pigs. She has always wondered which one of the five eats the most. When the pigs were eating, Marsha noticed that Snorti eats more than Babe. Pungey eats more than Wilbur but less than Porky. Wilbur eats more than Babe. Porky eats less than Snorti. List the pigs in the order of who eats the most to who eats the less.
    A. Snorti, Porky, Pungey, Wilbur, Babe
    B. Snorti, Pungey, Porky, Babe, Wilbur
    C. Pungy, Porky, Wilbur, Snorti, Babe
    D. Babe, Wilbur, Pungey, Snorti, Porky

15. Richard is a truck driver who took the written driving test. Which statement can be logically deduced from which of the following statements?
    A. Most truck drivers have taken the written driving test.
    B. Every truck driver either took the written driving test or was grand fathered in.
    C. Some truck drivers have to take the written driving test.
    D. Every truck driver has to pass the written driving test.

16. Elizabeth must be a cheerleader; she is wearing a cheerleading outfit. This conclusion above is valid only if it is true that:
    A. only cheerleaders wear cheerleading outfits.
    B. all cheerleaders wear cheerleading outfits.
    C. cheerleaders never wear any kind of outfit other than their cheerleading outfits.
    D. cheerleaders often wear cheerleading outfits.

17. Paula went to the store. The store has both groceries and gifts. What will Paula get?
    A. groceries
    B. gifts
    C. both
    D. cannot tell

Critical Thinking Answers and Explanations

1. Correct answer: B

        A. What are you being asked? Who can get to your house the fastest?

        B. Ignore the miles and cost. This is just distracting information.

        C. Look at the times:

Person	time/minutes
Sister	45
Neighbor	25
Mother	72
Babysitter	40

Looking at all each of the choices you will see that it only takes the neighbor 25 minutes to get to your house, and all other choices are longer.

2. Correct answer: C

        A. What are you being asked? Which child made it back to base first, and which was last? This is a two-part question.

        B. Number your chart 1-5 as there are five children.

        C. Use the clues that the question gives you. It tells in what order some children made it back. List what you know in the chart.

Person	order to base
	1
	2
Daniel	3
Ali	4

Matthew after Ali, if Ali was 4th, and there are five children, Matthew had to be 5th.

We now know that 3rd, 4th, and 5th slots are filled. That leaves us with who came in first and second.
We do not know anything about Lauren, except she cannot be 3rd, 4th or 5th.
We also now know that Olivia is not second, but we also know she is not 3rd, 4th or 5th, so she has to be first.
Now your chart looks like this:

Person	order to base
Olivia	1
Lauren	2
Daniel	3
Ali	4
Matthew	5

Look at the question "Which child made it back to base first, and which was last?"
Olivia was first, and Matthew was last.

3. Correct answer: A

A. What are you being asked? What is the order in which the students are standing in line?

B. Number your chart 1-4 as there are four children.

Person	order in line
	1
	2
	3
	4

C. Use the clues that the question gives you. It tells in what order some are in. List what you know.

1. We know that Andrew is between Anthony and Joseph.

So far you can have:

Anthony   or   Joseph
Andrew   Andrew
Joseph   Anthony

This immediately eliminates answers:

    A. Sarah, Andrew, Anthony, Joseph,

    B. Joseph, Anthony, Sarah, Andrew and

    D. Anthony, Joseph, Andrew, Sarah

You actually do not need to go further, as C is the only answer left.

For sake of discussion let's go on.

2. We also know that Joseph is not first. That means someone is before Joseph.

This immediately again eliminates answer

    B: Joseph, Anthony, Sarah, Andrew.

3. We also know that Sarah is before Anthony.

This immediately again eliminates answer

    B: Joseph, Anthony, Sarah, Andrew and

    D: Anthony, Joseph, Andrew, Sarah

So we now have three correct orders:

Sarah   or   Sarah or   Andrew
Anthony   Joseph   Sarah
Andrew   Andrew   Anthony
Joseph   Anthony   Joseph

You would need to look to see which of the three possible correct orders is present as a choice.

Of course for this question, it is C: Andrew, Sarah, Anthony, Joseph.

4. Correct answer: C

A. What are you being asked? Who will be in Rebecca's wedding?

B. What do we know? From the three bridesmaids, she has to pick one; and from the five groomsmen, she has to pick two.

1. Ignore "Michelle and Christina are competing against each other as the 'best bridesmaid'." This is just distracting information, since she is only going to have one bridesmaid.

2. Michelle and Kevin previously dated. This eliminates answer A: Michelle with Kevin and Adam

3. Josh and Mike do not like one another. This eliminates answer B: Kelly with Josh and Mike

4. Brian and Adam are mean to each other. This eliminates answer D: Kelly with Brian and Adam

Therefore, the answer is C: Christina with Brian and Mike

Another way to do this is to create a two-way table for each group.

	Michelle	Kelly	Christina
Brian			
Josh			
Adam			
Mike			
Kevin	x		

Now we know that all the girls could pair with Brian, Josh, Adam and Mike, and that Kelly and Christina could also pair with Kevin.

This eliminates answer A: Michelle with Kevin and Adam

The groomsmen's table would look like this:

	Brian	Josh	Adam	Mike	Kevin
Brian	X		X		
Josh		X		X	
Adam	X		X		
Mike		X		X	
Kevin					X

Josh pair with	Brian pair with	Adam pair with	Mike pair with	Kevin pair with
Brian	Josh	Josh	Brian	Josh
Adam	Mike	Mike	Adam	Brian
Kevin	Kevin	Kevin	Kevin	Adam
				Mike

This table then eliminates answer B: Kelly with Josh and Mike and answer D: Kelly with Brian and Adam

5. Correct answer: C.

    A. What are you being asked? What child picked what color?

    B. Create a chart of each child and every color.

       When the question states "did not like" or "did not pick", place an X in that space.

       When the question states "chose", place an O in that space.

    C. Use the clues that the question gives you.

       1. Frank did not pick Orange or Purple. Place an X under Orange and Purple.

       2. Charles did not like the colors Purple or White. Place an X under Purple and White.

       3. Suzzie chose White. Place an O under White.

       4. Betty chose a color that both Charles and Frank did not pick. Purple has an X for both Charles and Frank. Place an O under Purple.

	Orange	Purple	White	Black
Frank	X	X		
Charles		X	X	
Suzzie			O	
Betty		O		

Answer D has Frank with Purple. Therefore, eliminate answer D.

Answer A has Charles with Purple. Therefore, eliminate answer A.

Answer B has Suzzie with Purple. Therefore, eliminate answer B.

You are left with answer C.

6. Correct answer: C.

    A. What are you being asked? What is the order from most to least?

    B. Create a chart. Number your chart 1-4, as there are four people.

Person	most to least
	1
	2
	3
	4

    C. What do we know?

       1. Nathan has more than Alyssa. Nathan is 1st, and Alyssa is 2nd.

       This eliminates answer D: Alyssa, Nathan, Noah, Christopher

       2. Alyssa has more than Noah. This makes Noah 3rd.

       This eliminates answer A: Noah, Nathan, Alyssa, Christopher and

       Answer B: Nathan, Noah, Alyssa, Christopher

       Answer C is the only one left.

       3. Christopher has more than Nathan. This makes Christopher 1st, and everyone else moves down one. This would also make all the other answers wrong, as Christopher is last in answer A, B, and D.

Person	most to least
Christopher	1
Nathan	2
Alyssa	3
Noah	4

7. Correct answer: B

A. What are you being asked? Who picked which pig?

B. Create a chart of the pigs and their characteristics.

C. Use the clues that the question gives you. When the question states "were" about the pig, place an O in that space.

On the chart with the children's names and the pigs, when the question states "did not want or like" or "did not pick", place an X in that space. When the question states "picked", place a O in that space. List what you know in the charts.

1. Pinky and Squeaky were pink with short tails.
2. Oinky and Porky were white with long curly tails.
3. Pinky and Oinky were eating.
4. Squeaky and Porky were running.

Characteristic Pig	Pink	White	Short tail	Long, curly tail	Eating	Running
Oinky		X		X	X	
Porky		X		X		X
Pinky	X		X		X	
Squeaky	X		X			X

1. Emily didn't want a pink pig. (Pinky & Squeaky)

This eliminates answer A: Ann - Oinky, Ava - Pinky, Mia - Porky, Emily - Squeaky and Answer D: Ann - Porky, Ava- Oinky, Mia - Pinky, Emily - Squeaky

2. Ava didn't want a pig with a long tail. (Oinky & Porky)

This eliminates answer D: Ann - Porky, Ava- Oinky, Mia - Pinky, Emily - Squeaky

3. Mia didn't pick a pig that was eating. (Oinky & Pinky)

This eliminates answer C: Ann - Squeaky, Ava - Pinky, Mia - Oinky, Emily - Porky

4. Ann picked a pig that Mia and Emily didn't want. (Pinky)

This was only in answer B.

Pig Child	Oinky	Porky	Pinky	Squeaky
Emily			X	X
Ann			O	
Ava	X	X		
Mia	X		X	

Since Ann picked Pinky, Ava could only pick Squeaky.

With Pinky and Squeaky gone, Mia could only pick Porky; and then Emily could only pick Oinky.

The chart could be completed in this manner:

(Little "o" - ended picking)

(Little "x" - couldn't pick as already chosen)

Pig Child	Oinky	Porky	Pinky	Squeaky
Emily	o	x	x	x
Ann	x	x	o	x
Ava	x	x	x	o
Mia	x	o	x	x

8. Correct answer: D
    A. What are you being asked? What will Betty do?
    B. What do we know?
        1. For the past three nights, Betty has washed her hair in the sink.
    C. What choices are we given? Tub, shower, sink, won't wash it.
    D. Questions to ask?   Does she have a shower? Do not know
                       Does she have a tub? Do not know.
                       Does she wash her hair EVERY day? Do not know.
    E. What can we say for SURE from what we know? We don't know what she will do, answer D.
Conclusions can only be drawn from FACTS given. We do not have enough information to support
answers A, B, or C. What we know is what she did for the past three days only.
Do NOT jump to conclusions.

9. Correct answer: D
    A. What are you being asked? What did Barbara go to the mall for?
    B. What do we know?
        1. Barbara went to the mall to go shopping.
        2. The mall has both food and clothing.
    C. What choices are we given?   Food, clothing, both, cannot tell.
    D. Questions to ask?   Could she buy food? Yes.
                       Could she buy clothes? Yes.
                       Could she buy both? Yes.
                       Could she buy nothing? Yes.
    E. What can we say for SURE from what we know? We don't know what she will buy, if anything.
Conclusions can only be drawn from FACTS given. We do not have enough information to support
answers A, B, or C. What we know is she went to the mall. Do NOT jump to conclusions.

10. Correct answer: B
    A. What are you being asked? This conclusion is valid only if which of these statements were true?
    B. Evaluate each statement.
        1. Answer A: Nerds are often in his class. This statement does NOT say all students in the class
        are nerds. Jason may not be a nerd. False statement.
        2. Answer B: Only nerds are in the class. If all students in the class were nerds, then Jason would
        be a nerd. True statement.
        3. Answer C: Nerds must be in the class. This statement does NOT say all students in the class
        are nerds. Jason may not be a nerd. False statement.
        4. Answer D: Nerds are never in the class. If there are NEVER nerds in the class, then Jason
        CANNOT be a nerd. False statement.
    Since answer B is a true statement, then is the answer.

11. Correct answer: C

    A. What are you being asked? What did Bob do?

    B. What do you know?

        1. Bob bought a car.

        2. Bob doesn't like the color of his car.

        3. The dealership has a satisfaction guarantee on every car that is sold there.

        4. Bob took his car back to the dealership.

    C. Evaluate each statement.

        1. Answer A: got a new car

    It just said Bob took his car back. False statement.

        2. Answer B: got his money back

    It just said Bob took his car back. False statement

        3.Answer C: either one: got a new car or got the money back

    This would be the two options open to him. True statement.

        4. Answer D: kept the old car.

    It said Bob took his car back. False statement.

12. Correct answer: C

    A. What are you being asked? Based on the information given, which one of the following is a true statement?

    B. What do you know?

        1. Some Santa's wear glasses.

        2. All Santa's have beards.

        3. All Santa's that have beards are chubby.

So we know that ALL Santa's have beards and are chubby. Not all Santa's wear glasses.

    C. Evaluate each statement.

        1. Answer A: Some Santa's that wear glasses are chubby.

    Since ALL Santa's are chubby this is a FALSE statement, because ALL Santa's who wear glasses are chubby.

        2. Answer B: Santa's that are chubby wear glasses.

    Not all Santa's wear glasses so this statement is FALSE.

        3. Answer C: Santa's are chubby.

    Since all Santa's have beards and are chubby, this is a TRUE statement.

        4. Answer D: Small Santa's wear glasses and have beards.

    There is no evidence that Santa's are tall or small, so this is a FALSE statement.

13. Correct answer: A

    A. What are you being asked? Which of the following methods would Brenda use to increase her business?

    B. What do you know?

        1. Brenda, a clothing designer, opened up a clothing store about six months ago.

        2. One day, a lady walked into Brenda's store and stated, "I didn't know that you had a variety of clothes in this store; I thought that you had to have a special order to purchase anything."

        3. Brenda knew that she needed to do some advertising so people knew that she was a clothing store and not just a "special order" store.

    C. The problem is that people need to know Brenda is a clothing store and not just a "special order" store.

    D. Evaluate each statement.

        1. Answer A: Advertise in the local paper the variety of clothing that is in the store.
        This would let people know what is in the store. Correct answer.

        2. Answer B: Move her store to a well populated area.
        This would not help to let people know what is in the store. Incorrect answer.

        3. Answer C: Attend the next clothing expo and advertise her specially made clothes.
        She doesn't want to highlight the "special made." Incorrect answer.

        4. Answer D: Making coupons available for 50% off entire purchase.
        This wouldn't let anyone know what is in the store. Incorrect answer.

14. Correct answer: A

    A. What are you being asked? List the pigs in the order or who eats the most to who eats the less.

    B. Who do we have: Snorti, Babe, Pungey, Wilbur, Porky

    C. What do we know?

        1. Snorti eats more than Babe.

        2. Pungey eats more than Wilbur but less than Porky.
        This means Pungey eat more than Wilber, and Porky eats more than Pungey. (reverse the statement)

        3. Wilbur eats more than Babe.

        4. Porky eats less than Snorti or Snorti eats more than Porky. (reverse the statement)
        By making them all go in the same direction, "eats more than," it is easier to order them.

        Now we have; Snorti - Babe   ("-" means more than)

            Pungey -Wilber

            Porky- Pungey

            Wilbur-Babe

            Snorti - Porky

    We can rearrange these statements:

            Snorti - Porky

            Porky- Pungey

            Pungey -Wilber

            Wilbur-Babe

The statement "Snorti - Babe" isn't even necessary.

So Snorti is before Porky, who is before Pungey, who is before Wilber, who is before Babe.

Only answer A is in this order.

15. Correct answer: D

  A. What are you being asked? The statement can be logically deduced from which of the following statements? In other words, which statement would insure that a person could NOT drive a truck without passing the driving test?

  B. Evaluate each statement.

    1. Answer A: Most truck drivers have taken the written driving test.
    This is weak, in that it leaves open the chance that there might be truck driver who did not pass the driving test. Statement is FALSE.

    2. Answer B: Every truck driver either took the written driving test or was grand fathered in.
    There is no connection between being grand fathered in and taking the driving test. Therefore, this statement is FALSE.

    3. Answer C: Some truck drivers have to take the written driving test.
    This is weak, in that it leaves open the chance that there might be truck driver who did not pass the driving test. Statement is FALSE.

    4. Answer D: Every truck driver has to pass the written driving test.
    This statement rules out the chance that a person could be driving a truck without having passed the driving test.

16. Correct answer: A

  A. What are you being asked? This conclusion above is valid only if it is true that the question is: "Is Elizabeth a cheerleader?"

  B. What do we know?

    1. She is wearing a cheerleading outfit.

  C. Evaluate each statement.

    1. Answer A: Only cheerleaders wear cheerleading outfits.
    If this is true, then Elizabeth has to be a cheerleader, as ONLY cheerleaders wear the outfit. Statement is TRUE.

    2. Answer B: All cheerleaders wear cheerleading outfits.
    This statement leaves the possibility that someone else COULD wear a cheerleading outfit. Statement is FALSE.

    3. Answer C: Cheerleaders never wear any kind of outfit other than their cheerleading outfits.
    This statement does not address the issue of who is a cheerleader based on their dress. Statement is FALSE.

    4. Answer D: Cheerleaders often wear cheerleading outfits.
    This statement leaves the possibility that someone else COULD wear a cheerleading outfit and other outfits. Statement is FALSE.

17. Correct answer: D

A. What are you being asked? What will Paula get?

B. What do you know?
1. Paula went to the store.
2. The store has both groceries and gifts.

C. What choices are we given? Groceries, gifts, both or cannot tell.

D. Questions to ask?
1. Could she buy groceries? Yes.
2. Could she buy gifts? Yes.
3. Could she buy both? Yes.
4. Could she buy nothing? Yes.

E. What can we say for SURE from what we know? We don't know what she will buy, if anything. Conclusions can only be drawn from FACTS given. We do not have enough information to support answers A, B or C. What we know is she went to the store. Do NOT jump to conclusions. There is not enough information to tell what she did.

Comprehensive Review for Charts and Graphs

Graphs are used in newspapers, magazines, history books, and science texts. Graphs are a great way to show a lot of information. Reading and interpreting graphs can be confusing. Answering questions about graphs can be harder still.

To understand statistics and data (facts and figures), you have to understand how to read a chart, table, bar graph, line graph or pie graph. With this information you can make informed choices.
First check the title so you know what the whole chart or graph is about. Then see what is being compared. The labels on the rows or columns of a table and the labels of the up and down (vertical) or flat (horizontal) axis of a graph show the variables.

The most common mistake made seems to be trying to interpret the graph before really understanding the graph. Graphs can be read just like you read the words in a story. Look at the title, the words describing the X and Y axis (the bottom and side of the graph), and the information that is presented. As you read the graph, think about whether the information makes sense. Does the information seem to make sense with what you know? If it does, it is likely that you are reading the graph correctly. If it doesn't make sense, try to figure out why it is not making sense before you try to answer the questions!
The second mistake people make when reading and interpreting graphs is they do not understanding the questions. Break down each question to make sure you understand it.

There are three types of graphs you will see most often. Each type of graph is used for different reasons. No matter which type of graph you are reading, it will be important to read and understand the graph before you answer any questions about the graph.

Bar Graph

Bar graphs are used to compare information or look at information over time such as years.
Bar Graphs are used to compare the value of related things.

Charts or Tables

One way to organize a collection of facts is to make a table. Then this data can be used to make a decision or answer a question.

Pie Chart

Pie charts show percentages. If you add up all the percentages in a pie chart, the total would be 100%. Pie charts are very good for looking at the parts of a whole.
Pie charts are often in the shape of a circle, but they do not have to be a circle. Circle or Pie Graphs are circle charts used to show percentage or fractions of the whole.

Line Graphs

Line graphs present information visually with data connected by a rising or falling line. The line shows changes or trends usually over time.

School Attendance and Math Grades

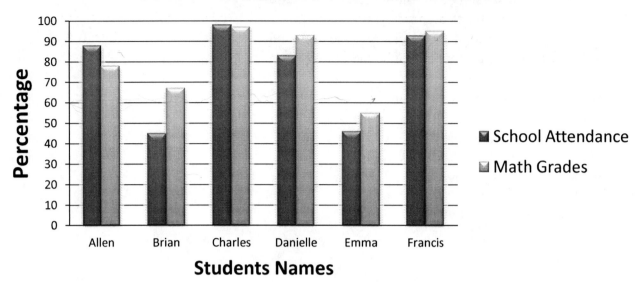

1. If a math grade below 60% is failing, how many students failed math?
    A. 1
    B. 0
    C. 2
    D. 4

2. The bar chart shows the correlation of school attendance and the student's math grade. Study the bar chart to see which statement is TRUE.
    A. The difference between Brian's and Emma's attendance versus grades is equal
    B. Three students had higher grade percentages than the percentage of school attendance
    C. If Brian and Emma had worked together; they could have gotten 100% in math
    D. The higher percentage of grades, the higher the percentage of attendance

3. The student with the best grade and attendance was
    A. Allen
    B. Charles
    C. Danielle
    D. Francis

4. The student with the MOST equal school attendance and grade percentage was
    A. Allen
    B. Danielle
    C. Charles
    D. Brian

5. Brian was what number in order from the student with the top grade to the lowest grade of the six listed?
    A. 2
    B. 3
    C. 6
    D. 5

6. Which statement of the following is true?
    A. Brian and Emma will not be promoted to the next grade
    B. School attendance affects the math grade
    C. Danielle and Allen attended school about the same number of days
    D. Charles would get a better grade if he did not attend school so regularly

7. Which student had the lowest math grade?
    A. Brian
    B. Charles
    C. Danielle
    D. Emma

8. Whose attendance was under 50%?
    A. Allen
    B. Brian
    C. Danielle
    D. Francis

9. Which of the following students had a grade of less than 80%?
    A. Allen
    B. Charles
    C. Danielle
    D. Francis

10. This bar chart shows that students with good school attendance have high math grades.
    A. True
    B. False
    C. Not enough information to say

Answers
1. A
2. D
3. B
4. C
5. D
6. B
7. D
8. B
9. A
10. A

Solutions

Let's analyze the chart. The dark bars to the left are "School Attendance". The light bars to the right are "Math Grades". Each set of bars (dark, light) represent 1 student. There are a total of 6 students. The student's names are listed across the bottom of the chart. The percentages of possible grade are listed on the side of the chart.

1. A. What are you being asked? How many students had grades lower than 60%?
   B. What do we know from the chart?
      Find 60 on the left side of the chart. How many light bars are (grades) are below 60?
      Only 1- Emma. Answer: A

2. A. What are you being asked? Each statement must be evaluated using the chart.
   a. Is the difference between Brian's and Emma's attendance and grades equal? Find the difference between each child's attendance versus grades then see if they are equal. Brian 68-44=28 Emma 54-45=9 No Not true.
   b. Three students had higher grade percentages than the percentage of school attendance? Is this true? You are looking for how many students had higher dark (attendance) bars higher than light (grades) bars. 4- Brian, Daniele, Emma, and Francis –NOT true.
   c. Brian and Emma together could equal 100%. Add Brian's and Emma's light (grade) bars together. Brian 68 + Emma 54 = 122% not 100% - Not true
   d. Higher attendance equals higher grades. Make a chart with the person with the highest attendance first. Use this when you can.

Child	Grade	Attendance
Charles	98	97
Francis	94	92
Allen	78	89
Danielle	92	84
Brian	68	44
Emma	54	45

   This chart shows that this statement is true. Answer

3. A. What are you being asked? Who has the best grades and attendance? (See chart in 2d.) - Charles Answer B

4. A. What are you being asked? Whose attendance and grades are MOST equal? Look at the difference in each child's grade versus attendance. (See chart in 2d.) Charles has only 1 point difference. All the others are larger. Answer C

5. What number is Brian ranked regarding grade from highest to lowest? There are six children. The chart you made in 2d. is from the highest to the lowest. Count down Brian is 5th. Answer D

6. A. What are you being asked? Each statement must be evaluated using the chart.

a. Brian and Emma will not be promoted to the next grade. We do not know what passing is. Cannot evaluate this statement so it is not correct.

b. School attendance affects the math grade. Review the chart in 2d. The higher the grade the higher the attendance was. Answer B

c. Danielle and Allen's attendance were equal. (See chart in 2d.) Danielle 84% and Allen 89%   Not equal.

d. Did children with lower attendance have higher grade? (See chart in 2d.) Children with lower attendance had the lowest grades. Not true.

7. A. What are you being asked? Who had the lowest attendance and lowest grade? (See chart in 2d.) Emma had the lowest grade. Answer D

8. A. What are you being asked? Whose attendance was under 50%? (See chart in 2d.) Brian and Emma both had attendance below 50%. Whose name was listed as a possible answer? Brian Answer B

9. A. What are you being asked? Whose grade is less than 80%? (See chart in 2d.) Allen, Brian, and Emma. Whose name was listed as a possible answer? Allen Answer A

10. A. What are you being asked? Does this bar chart show that good attendance equals high grades? (See chart in 2d.) For three of the six students the lower attendance showed lower grades. Two had the highest attendance and the highest grades. True Answer A

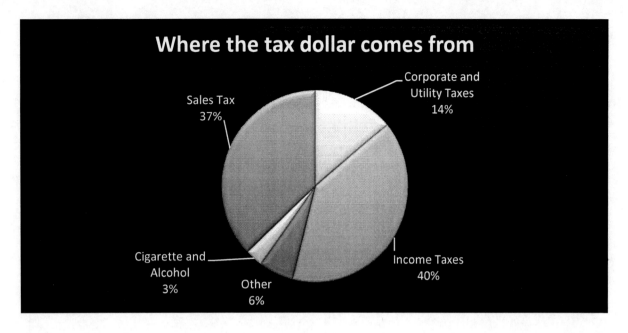

Where the tax dollar comes from

Sales Tax 37%

Corporate and Utility Taxes 14%

Cigarette and Alcohol 3%

Other 6%

Income Taxes 40%

1. What is the largest source of revenue?
   - A. Corporate tax
   - B. Income tax
   - C. Sales tax
   - D. Utility tax

2. Corporate and utility taxes make up ___ cents of every tax dollar.
   - A. 3
   - B. 6
   - C. 14
   - D. 37

3. Income tax and sales tax make up ___ cents of every tax dollar.
   - A. 20
   - B. 51
   - C. 54
   - D. 77

Answers
1. B   2. C   3. D

Solutions

Let's analyze the chart. Each "slice" has been assigned a "tag+ and a "%". A Pie chart adds up to 100%. You can look at the "size" of each slice or look at the % assigned to each slice. Each "slice" equals % of total number of dollars.

1. A. What are you being asked? Which slice is the largest? Look for the largest "slice". Now look at the "tag". Is it the largest number? 40% is the largest "tag". Answer B
2. A. What are you being asked? Corporate and utility taxes equal how many cents? Percent is ?/100. A dollar is 100 pennies. So % equals amount of dollar. 14 % = 14 cents. Answer C
3. Income tax and sales tax equal how many cents? Add Income tax and sales tax 40 +37+77%=77 cents Answer D

The pie charts below are from the 1995 1040 Forms and Instructions published by the Internal Revenue Service.

Major Categories of Federal Income and Outlays for Fiscal Year 1994

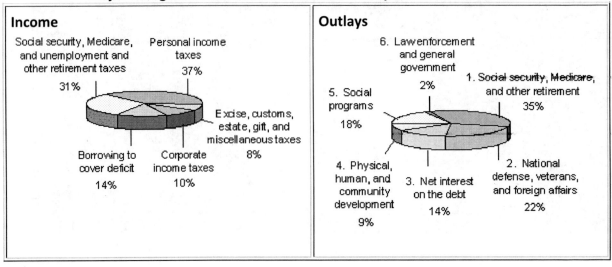

1. What is the largest source of income for the U.S. Government?
   A. Corporate taxes
   B. Excise, customs, estate gift and other miscellaneous taxes
   C. Personal income taxes
   D. Social security, Medicare, unemployment and other retirement taxes

2. Borrowing to cover the deficit is what percent of the federal income?
   A. 3
   B. 6
   C. 14
   D. 37

3. Personal income taxes and social security, Medicare unemployment and other retirement taxes make what percentage of the federal income?
   A. 45
   B. 51
   C. 57
   D. 68

4. Law Enforcement, general government, armed forces and veterans receive what percentage of the federal income?
   A. 2
   B. 14
   C. 22
   D. 24

5. The area which receives least amount of federal money the is:
   A. #1
   B. #3
   C. #4
   D. #6

6. Social security, Medicare, and other retirement programs plus social programs receive what percentage of the outlays?
   A. 32
   B. 40
   C. 53
   D. 57

Answers
1. C
2. C
3. D
4. D
5. D
6. C

Solutions

Let's analyze the chart. Each "slice" has been assigned a "tag+ and a "%". A Pie chart adds up to 100%. You can look at the "size" of each slice or look at the % assigned to each slice. Each "slice" equals % of total number of dollars. Each chart is labeled. The left chart is INCOME and the right chart is Outlays (paid out).

1. A. What are you being asked? What is the largest source of income? Use the left chart. Which slice is the largest? Look for the largest "slice". Now look at the "tag". Is it the largest number? 37 personal income taxes   Answer C

2. A. What are you being asked? Borrowing to cover the deficit is what percent of the federal income? Use the left chart. What % is borrowing to cover the deficit? 14 % Answer C

3. A. What are you being asked? "Personal income taxes" + "social security, Medicare unemployment and other retirement taxes" make what percentage of the federal income? Use the left chart. Add "Personal income taxes" + "social security, Medicare unemployment and other retirement taxes" together 31 = 37 = 68 Answer D

4. A. What are you being asked? "Law Enforcement, general government" +" armed forces and veterans" receive what percentage of the federal income? Use the right chart. "Armed forces" is not listed but "national defense" starts this list. Armed forces= national defense. Add the two parts together. 2 + 22 = 24 Answer D

5. A. What are you being asked? Which AREA receives least amount of federal money? There are 6 areas. Which choices are we given: 1, 3, 4, 6.   1= 35, 3=14, 4=9, 6=2 Area 6 has the least. Answer D

6. A. What are you being asked? Which AREA receives least amount of federal money? There are 6 areas.

Blank

Comprehensive Review for Mathematics

Integers

Prime Numbers

Roman Numerals

Fractions

Decimals

Percentages

Conversions

Word Problems

Blank

Integers

INTEGERS are all the whole numbers on the number line, both positive and negative. A positive number has an OPPOSITE, its negative number. A negative number has an OPPOSITE, its positive number.

If a number is greater than 0 it is a positive integer (number).

If a number is less than 0 it is a negative integer (number). A negative number is a number that you add to that number to get 0.

0 is neither positive nor negative. It is called neutral.

The **ABSOLUTE** number is the number regardless of its sign (− or +). It is written as $|3|$. -3 or +3 are equal to the absolute number $|3|$. This is used in different mathematical operations.

PRIME numbers are integers that can only be divided by the number 1 and itself. The first four prime numbers are: 2,3,5,7.

Prime numbers in the first 100 numbers are:

2 3 5 7 11 13 17 19 23 29 31 37 41 43 47 53 59 61 67 71 73 79 83 89 97

The number 1 is not a prime number because it has only itself, one number, to be divided by.

Prime numbers are also important to know as they are also used in different mathematical operations.

A **COMPOSITE** number is a "NON-PRIME" number that is positive (+) and can be divided by 1 or more prime or composite numbers other than the number one and itself. These numbers that can be divided into another number are called **FACTORS**. **Prime factors** are the prime numbers that can only be divided into another non-prime number.

REMEMBER: The number 1 is NOT a "prime" factor it is just a factor.

The factors of 4 are: 1, 2, 4.

The prime factor of 4 is: 2.

10 is a Composite number with factors: 1, 2, 5, 10 and the Prime factors of 2, 5.

Prime Numbers

Prime numbers are numbers that cannot be divided by any other number but 1 and itself. It has NO factors.
A Composite number can be divided evenly by numbers other than 1 or itself.

Prime numbers in first 100 numbers
2 3 5 7 11 13 17 19 23 29 31 37 41 43 47 53 59 61 67 71 73 79 83 89 97

Number 12
  Made up of 1, 2, 3, 4, 6, 12; composite
        2*6 = 12
        3*4 = 12

Examples: (factors then the number)
I.   1, 2, 7, 14; composite (14 is the number)
II.   1, 2, 4, 7, 14, 28; composite
III.   1, 19; prime
IV.   1, 5, 7, 35; composite
V.   1, 23; prime
VI.   1, 2, 11, 22; composite
VII.   1, 2, 3, 5, 6, 9, 10, 15, 18, 30, 45, 90; composite
VIII. 1, 2, 3, 4, 6, 8, 9, 12, 18, 24, 36, 72; composite
IX.   1, 71; prime
X.   1, 2, 4, 6, 7, 12, 14, 21, 42, 84; composite
XI.   1, 7, 13, 91; composite
XII.   1, 3, 9, 27, 81; composite
XIII. 1, 13; prime
XIV.   1, 2, 4, 5, 10, 20, 25, 50, 100; composite
XV.   1, 101; prime
XVI.   1, 2, 3, 4, 6, 8, 12, 18, 24, 36, 48, 72, 144; composite
XVII. 1, 2, 3, 4, 5, 6, 10, 12, 15, 20, 25, 30, 50, 60, 75, 100, 150, 300; composite
XVIII. 1, 2, 4, 6, 8, 9, 12, 16, 18, 24, 32, 36, 48, 72, 144, 288; composite

Prime Numbers Test and Answers

Tell if the Number is Prime or Composite, then List its Factors, then List its Prime Factors

	Prime (P) or Composite (C)	Factors	Prime factors
e.g. 91 C		1, 7, 13, 91	7, 13
1. 27	_____	_____	_____
2. 12	_____	_____	_____
3. 35	_____	_____	_____
4. 72	_____	_____	_____
5. 17	_____	_____	_____
6. 79	_____	_____	_____
7. 23	_____	_____	_____
8. 30	_____	_____	_____
9. 44	_____	_____	_____
10. 59	_____	_____	_____

Answers

1.	27 C	1, 3, 9, 27	3
2.	12 C	1, 2, 3, 4, 6, 12	2, 3
3.	35 C	1, 5, 7, 35	5, 7
4.	72 C	1, 2, 3, 4, 6, 8, 9, 72	2, 3
5.	17 P	1, 17	17
6.	79 P	1, 79	79
7.	23 P	1, 23	23
8.	30 C	1, 2, 3, 5, 6, 10, 15, 30	2, 3, 5
9.	44 C	1, 2, 4, 11, 22, 44	2, 11
10.	59 P	1, 59	59

Rounding

Rounding is reducing a number by 1 or more digits. **Digits** are the number of numbers or places in a number. 10 has 2 digits/places (ones and tens). 125 has three digits/places (ones, tens, hundreds). 0.10 has 2 digits/places (tenths and hundredths). 0.125 has three digits/places (tenths, hundredths, thousandths).

A 2 digit number (tens) has 2 places: numbers 10-99.
The rules of rounding are:

1. If the number to the right of the number you are rounding to is between 0-4, leave the number to the left the same and the number to the right is changed to a 0.
   53 is rounded to 50.   The 3 is less than 5, so the 5 is left as is and the 3 is changed to a 0.   0.53 is rounded to 0.5 The last digit is 0 so it is dropped.
   If the number to the right of the number you are rounding to is between 5-9, change the number to the left by adding 1 and the number to the right is changed to a 0.
   56 is rounded to 60. The 6 is more than 5, so the 5 is changed to a 6 and the 6 is changed to a 0.
   0.56 is rounded to 0.6 The last digit is 0 so it is dropped.

A 3 digit number (hundreds) has 3 places: numbers 100-999.
   Using the rounding rules:
   1.   If the digit is 0-4: 133 is rounded to 130. 0.133 is rounded to 0.13 The last digit is 0 so it is dropped. If told to round to the hundredths place the answer is 0.13. (Instead of changing the 3 to a 0 you drop the 3 or that digit. The number becomes a 2 digit number.)
   2.   Digit is 5-9: 125 is rounded to 130. If told to round 0.125 to the hundredths place the answer is 0.13. (Instead of changing the 5 to a 0 you drop the 5 or that digit. The number becomes a 2 digit number.)

A four digit number (thousands) has 4 places: numbers 1000-1999.
Using the rounding rules:
   1.   Digit is 0-4: 1631 is rounded to 1630. If told to round 0.1631 to the thousandths place the answer is 0.163 (Instead of changing the 1 to a 0 you drop the 1 or that digit. The number becomes a 3 digit number.) If told to round to the hundredths place the answer is 0.16 (Instead of changing the 3 and the 1 to 0, you drop the 3 and the 1. The number becomes a 2 digit number.)
   2.   Digit is 5-9: 1257 is rounded to 1260. If told to round 0.1257 to the thousandths place the answer is 0.126. (Instead of changing the 7 to a 0 you drop the 7 or that digit. The number becomes a 3 digit number.) If told to round to the hundredths place the answer is 0.13. (Instead of changing the 5 and the 7 to 0, you drop the 5 and the 7. The number becomes a 2 digit number.) If told to round 0.1257 to the tenths place the answer is 0.1 (You do not chain rounding. You only round the number closest to the number you are rounding to.)

Rounding Test and Answers

Round to the

	Thousandths	hundredths	tenths
1. 0.33	_____	_____	_____
2. 0.88	_____	_____	_____
3. 0.647	_____	_____	_____
4. 0.906	_____	_____	_____
5. 0.833	_____	_____	_____
6. 0.7869	_____	_____	_____
7. 0.4885	_____	_____	_____
8. 0.5433	_____	_____	_____
9. 0. 824	_____	_____	_____
10. 0.6741	_____	_____	_____

Answers

1.			0.3
2.			0.9
3.		0.65	0.6
4.		0.91	0.9
5.		0.83	0.8
6.	0.787	0.79	0.8
7.	0.489	0.49	0.5
8.	0.543	0.54	0.5
9.		0.82	0.8
10.	0.674	0.67	0.7

Adding Integers

The rules for adding integers are:

1. When adding two positive (+) integers: add the absolutes and give the answer the same sign. 3 or +3 added to 5 or +5= +8 or just 8. (The number is considered a positive number unless there is a − sign in front of it).
2. When adding two negative (-) integers: add the two absolutes and give it the same number sign. -7 added to -5= $|7| + |5| = |12|$ given the − sign = -12.
3. When adding integers with different signs (one + and one -): find the absolute of each number. Subtract the smaller number from the larger number. Give the answer the sign of the largest absolute number. 6 or +6 added to -8. This is $|6|$ and $|8|$. 6 from 8 is 2 and give it the sign of the largest number (− sign). The answer is -2.

Addition Words: add ... and, plus, sum ...and

Add 54 and 21 is   54   21 plus 33 is   21   Sum 45 and 87 is   45

                +21   +33   +87

Adding Integers Tests and Answers

1. 5 plus 5=   _____
2. -3 plus -6=   _____
3. add -5 and -9 =   _____
4. sum 3 and -6 =   _____
5. 8 plus 8 =   _____
6. add -9 and +3 =   _____
7. sum 2 and 10 =   _____
8. add -10 and -4 =   _____
9. -22 plus -25 =   _____
10.   -62
     +45   _____

Answers

1. 10 or +10
2. -9   like signs get the same sign
3. -14   like signs get the same sign
4. -3   = $|3| + |6| = |3|$ the larger number was -6 so the answer is -3
5. 16 or +16
6. -6   = $|9| + |3| = |6|$ the larger number was -9 so the answer is -6
7. 12 or +12
8. -14   like signs get the same sign
9. -47   like signs get the same sign
10. -17 = $|62| + |45| = |17|$ the larger number was -62 so the answer is -17

Adding numbers that have a sum greater than 9 in a digits place.

57 plus 43=   57

$\qquad$ +43   7+3=10 Place the 0 under the 3, **carry** the 10 to the tens place

Remember the problem looks like 50 + 7

$\qquad\qquad\qquad\qquad$ 40 + 3

and now you add ten   +10

$\qquad\qquad\qquad\qquad$ ‾‾‾‾‾‾

The problem looks like this now   ?0 + 0   so 5 + 4 + 1 =10 the answer is 10 + 0 (three places) = 100 and 100 + 0 =100

Two or Three Numbers

1. 22	2. 35	3. 40	4. 51	5. 53
+44	+18	+37	+12	+24

6. 263	7. 387	8. 26	9. 596	10. 49
+361	+534	+37	+975	+54

Four or Five Numbers

11. 1246	12. 1395	13. 54794	14. 81143	15. 7369
+2551	+5623	+71623	+21776	+6413

16. 4564	17. 7178	18. 6008	19. 5136	20. 64921
+4857	+4857	+2993	+8976	+35431

Answers

1. 66	6. 624	11. 3797	16. 9421
2. 53	7. 921	12. 7018	17. 12035
3. 77	8. 63	13. 126417	18. 9001
4. 63	9. 1571	14. 102919	19. 14112
5. 77	10. 103	15. 13782	20. 100352

Subtracting Integers

The rules for subtracting integers are:
1. Add the smaller number's opposite to the number.   Subtract 3 from 7.   The opposite of 3 is -3. Add -3 to +7 = +4.

```
  6                                    +6
 -4   the opposite of 4 is -4. The problem becomes + (-4)    Change to absolute values and
The answer is:                         +2       give the answer the sign of the largest number.
```

Subtracting 2 or more digits when one digit is smaller than the digit it is being subtracted from.
```
   52   Write this as 50 + 2
  -18   Write this as 10 + 8
```

Since 2 is smaller than 8 you must "borrow" 10 from 50.
This makes the numbers   40 +12
The bottom numbers stay   10 + 8

You subtract 8 from 12 = 4 and 10 from 40 = 30 the answer is 30 + 4 or 34

```
40 +12
10 + 8
30 + 4 or 34
```

Subtracting 2 or more digits when one or more digits are smaller than the digit(s) it is being subtracted from. When 2 digits are smaller than those it is being subtracted from you use the borrowing principle in both digit places as below:

```
 326   300 + 20 + 6        200 +119 + 16
-147   100 + 40 + 7        100 + 40 +   7
                           100   79     9 or 179
```

Subtraction Words: Reduce... By, Subtract ... From, Minus

```
Reduce 295 by 90 is 295      Subtract 62 from 99 is 99      32 minus12 is 32
                -  90                        -62                      -12
```

Subtracting Integers Test and Answers

Question		Answers	
1. 32 minus 21 =	_____	1. 11	32-21
2. 319 minus 138 =	_____	2. 181	319-128
3. subtract 129 from 605 =	_____	3. 476	605-129
4. reduce 646 by 312 =	_____	4. 334	646-312
5. 77 minus 13 =	_____	5. 64	77-13
6. 88 reduced by 59 =	_____	6. 29	88-59
7. 92 minus 56 =	_____	7. 36	92-56
8. 871 minus 430 =	_____	8. 441	871-430
9. 640 reduced by 410 =	_____	9. 230	640-410
10. 543	_____	10. 265	543-278
-278			

Two or three numbers

1.   63
   -52
	2. 25
	   -13
		3. 98
		   -87
			4. 86
			   -54
				5. 59
				   -38

6.   972
  - 641
	7. 871
	  -430
		8. 748
		  -526
			9. 640
			  -410
				10. 512
				  -311

Answers

1. 11   2. 12   3. 11   4. 32   5. 21
6. 331   7. 441   8. 222   9. 230   10. 201

Four or Five Numbers

1.   2563
  -1522
	2. 3285
	  -1749
		3. 9748
		  -8637
			4. 7288
			  -5422
				5. 5563
				  -4038

6.   96724
  - 63417
	7. 28781
	  -14303
		8. 57498
		  -52631
			9. 6409
			  -3421
				10. 6392
				  -4815

Answers

1. 1041	3. 1111	5. 1525	7. 14478	9. 2988
2. 1536	4. 1866	6. 33307	8. 4867	10. 1577

Multiplying Integers

Multiplying is adding the same number together X number of times. 3 times 4 is 3 added together 4 times.
 3 + 3 + 3 + 3 = 12

The answer received is called the PRODUCT. The number that you are multiplying by is the MULTIPLIER. The number being multiplied is the MULTIPLICAND.

```
        MULTIPLICAND
X          MULTIPLIER
           PRODUCT
```

There are 2 laws or properties that can be used in multiplication: Commutative Property and the Associative Property.

Commutative Property: When a and b are whole numbers, $a \times b = b \times a$. In other words order doesn't change the answer. You can multiply b by a or a by b.
6 times 4 is the same as 4 times 6.

Associative Property: When a and b and c are whole numbers, $(a \times b) \times c = a \times (b \times c)$.
 $(2 \times 4) \times 3$ is the same as $2 \times (4 \times 3)$. In other words, the order doesn't change the answer.

7 times 10=
This is 7 tens   (10 + 10 + 10 + 10 + 10 + 10 + 10) or 10 sevens (7 + 7 + 7 + 7 + 7 + 7 + 7 + 7 + 7 + 7)

Remember: 1 times any number is that number.   0 times any number is 0.
              Any number times 1 is that number. Any number times 0 is 0.

Single digit multiplication:
4 times 7= 28 (7 + 7 + 7+ 7)

Double digit multiplication.
```
   12
 x14
```

Here you multiply 4 times 12 first, and place the 8 under the 4 (ones place) and the 4 under the 1 (tens place).
```
   12
 x14
   48
```

Then you multiply the 1 times the 12.
```
   12
 x14
   48
 120
 ___
 168
```
120   Since you are multiplying with the "tens" place you move over one place or place a 0
         in the ones place.

The problem can also be looked at as multiplying 12 by 4 and 12 by 10 and adding the two results.

```
12      12
x4    + x10
48     120 = 168
```

A few tips to remember about multiplication!
  1. 4 times a number
         2 times the number and times two again.
         4 times 8 =   is 2 times 8 = 16 times 2 = 32
  2. 5 times a number
         always ends in 5 or 0
  3. 11 times a number
         10 times the number and then add the number to it.
         11 times 5= 10 times 5 is 50 plus 5=55
  4. 10 times a number
         always ends in 0
Multiplication words: the product of .. and ..,   multiply ... by ..., ... times ... Or (a) (b)

The product of 45 and 12 is   45   Multiply 10 by 5 is   10   7 times 33 is   33   (6) (7) is 6
                                x 12   x 5   x 7   x7

Multiplying Integers Test and Answers

Problems

1. 93	2. 52	3. 73	4. 519	5. 928
x 3	x 2	x 3	x 47	x 62

6. 6724	7. 117	8. 749	9. 845	10. 92
x 17	x 303	x 631	x421	x48

Answers

1. 279   2. 104   3. 219   4. 24393   5. 57536

```
  93              52              73              519              928
 x 3             x 2             x 3             x 47            x 62
 279             104             219             3633            1856
                                                 2076            5568
                                                 24393           57536
```

6. 114308   7. 35451   8. 472619   9. 355745   10. 4416

```
  6724            117             749             845              92
 x   17          x303           x 631           x421             x48
 47068            351             749             845             736
 6724            3510            2247            1690             368
114308           35451           4494            3380            4416
                                 472619          355745
```

Dividing Integers

Division is the opposite of multiplication. It is also defined as separating a number into two or more parts. The DIVIDEND is the number being divided. The DIVISOR is the number that you are dividing with. The QUOTIENT is the answer received.

        <u>QUOTIENT</u>
  DIVISOR | DIVIDEND

If a x b = c then a=c/b

Division is written as a/b (a divided by b) or $\underline{a}$.
                                                b

Division rules can be used to help determine what numbers can be divided into a number.
A number can be divided by:

2	if	the "ones" digit is even (2, 4, 6, 8, 10) 3244/2=1622
	3	if the sum of all the digits is divisible by 3. If a big number results still keep doing it until it is a small enough number to tell it is divisible by three.
		456 4 + 5 + 6= 15/3 = 5
4	if	the number created by the last 2 digits is divisible by 4. 712 12/4=3
5	if	the last digit ends in 0 or 5. 5250
6	if	the number can be divided by both 2 and 3 4326 4326/2= 2163
		4326/3=1442
	7	if double the last (ones) digit and subtract that from the remaining number. If big number results still keep doing this until it is a small enough number to tell it is divisible by 7. 371
		double the 1=2 37 -2=35/7=5
		Another way: 3X+L X= digits before last one L= last digit 245 (3x24)+5=77/7= 11
8	if	the last three digits are divisible by 8 2592 592/8=74
9	if	the sum of all the digits is divisible by 9 4266 4+2+6+6=18/9=2
10	if	the last number is 0 89990
11	if	add the ones digit to every other digit (ones, hundreds, ten thousands). Add the tens digit and every digit left (tens, thousands, hundred thousands). Subtract the "ones" answer from the "tens" answer. If answer is 0 or 11 it is divisible by 11. 276353
		2+6+5=13 7+3+3=13 13-13=0
12	if	the number can be divided by both 3 and 4 37224 3+7+2+2+4=18/3=6
		24/4=6
	13	if Drop the last number (ones). Multiply the dropped digit by 9. Take the remaining number and the answer just obtained. Subtract the smaller of the two from the larger. If it is divisible by 13.
		299 9x9=81 81-29=52/13=4

Remainders: The remainder is the number left over that is not divisible by the divisor. Use the rules above and

2	if	the "ones" digit is uneven (3, 5, 7, 9) 5/2=2 r1
3	if	the sum of all the digits is not divisible by 3. 7/3=2 r1
4	if	the number created by the last 2 digits is not divisible by 4. 13 13/4=3 r1
5	if	the last digit does not end in 0 or 5. 27 27/5=5 r2
6	if	the number can not be divided by both 2 and 3 26 26/2= 13 26/3=5 r1
7	if	double the last (ones) digit and subtract that from the remaining number. If it is not divisible by 7. 373 double the 3=6 37 - 6=31/7=4 r3
8	if	the last three digits are not divisible by 8 2593 593/8=74 r1
9	if	the sum of all the digits is not divisible by 9 4267 4+2+6+7=19/9=2 r1

| 10 | if | the last number is not 0 | 89992 | 89992/10=8999 r2 |

11 if add the ones digit to every other digit (ones, hundreds, ten thousands).
Add the tens digit and every digit left (tens, thousands, hundred thousands). Subtract the "ones" answer from the "tens" answer. If answer is not 0 or 11 it is not divisible by 11.
276354   2+6+5=13   7+3+4=14   14-13=1   r1

12 if the number can be divided by both 3 and 4   37225   3+7+2+2+5=19/3=6 r1
25/4=6 r1

13 if Drop the last number (ones). Multiply the dropped digit by 9. Take the remaining number and the answer just obtained. Subtract the smaller of the two from the larger. If it is divisible by 13.
298   9x8=72   72-29=43/13=3 r4

How to divide:

$\overline{37|333}$ The first step is to determine how many places of the dividend the divisor (37) will go into at least once. That place is the hundreds. Now under the hundreds and the tens places you place a 0 and carry that number down, as below.

```
     00
37|333
   0
   30
   333
```

Now you have to determine how many times 37 might go into 333. 33 goes into 100 3 times so try 9.
9 x 7=63

```
    009
37|333
   0
   30
   333
```

3 carry the 6. 3x9=27 +6 = 33   Place this under the hundreds and tens places.

```
    009
37|333
   0
   30
   333
   333
     0
```

If the number does not end evenly, it can be carried out to decimals places. To do this you add a decimal point and 0s. Carry the decimal point to the quotient also. The number of decimals can be specified or you carry it out a few places.

```
     009.
37|337.00    add the decimal point and start adding 0s. Carry the 0 down next to the 4.
   0
   30
   337
   333
    40    37 goes into 40 1 time
```

```
        009.1088
37|337.000
    0
   30
   337
   333
      40
      37
       300
       296
        40
        37    Write the 37 here, subtract and leaves a remainder of 3
              3
```

This answer can now be written as 9.1088 or rounded to 9.109.

Division words … divided by …, … over …., divide … by …,

32 divided by 4 is   4|32̄   12 over 3 is 3|1̄2̄   divide 45 by 9 is   9|4̄5̄

Dividing Integers Test and Answers

Problems

```
         ‾‾‾‾              ‾‾‾‾              ‾‾‾‾‾          ‾‾‾‾‾        ‾‾‾‾
  1.   45|1215    2. 37|962    3.  87 |8613    4. 61 |3294  5. 21 |567

         ‾‾‾‾              ‾‾‾‾              ‾‾‾‾          ‾‾‾‾‾        ‾‾‾‾
  6. 52|2548       7. 39 |858    8. 73|1241       9. 132|4489   10. 82|7793
```

Answers

1. 27   2. 26   3. 99   4. 54   5. 27

```
     __27_        _26_          _99_           _ 54_          _27__
45|1215        37|962        87 |8613        61 |3294        21 |567
    90           74            783            305             42
   315          222            783            244            147
   315          222            783            244            147
```

6. 49   7. 22   8. 17   9. 34.007 or 34.01 (rounded)   10. 95.036 or 95.04 (rounded).

```
     49         22          17           34.007                    95.036
52|2548      39 |858     73|1241     132|4489.000               82|7793.000
   208         78          73            396                       738
   468         78         511            529                       413
   468         78         511            528                       410
                                        1000                       300
                                         924                       246
                                          76                       540
                                                                   492
                                                                    48
```

Fractions

A **fraction** is a part of the whole.
It is made up of two parts- the **numerator** and the **denominator**.
The numerator is the number above the line and is the "part" of the number below.
The denominator is the number below the line and is the whole number.

A point to remember when working with fractions: As the denominator gets larger, the value of the fraction gets smaller. In other words, 1/8 of a pizza is less than ¼ of it. ¼ of the pizza is smaller than ½ of it.

A **MIXED NUMBER** is a whole number and a fraction. 1 1/3.
Remember: a whole number can be expressed as a fraction. These forms are both the same number: 10, 10/1.

If the numerator ends up bigger than the denominator (IMPROPER FRACTION) you must convert that number to a whole number and the remainder fraction. This is called a MIXED NUMBER.
Improper fraction: $^6/_4$ makes the mixed number: $1^1/_2$

Addition or Subtraction of a Fraction

Step one (1) in either adding or subtracting a fraction, is to make the denominator either the same number or a number that is divisible by both.
1.Denominators NOT divisible.
$\frac{1}{3}$ and $\frac{1}{4}$
You can multiply both denominators together 3 x 4 = 12
You then divide 12 by the denominator and the answer becomes the numerator.
$\frac{12}{3} = 4$ and $\frac{12}{4} = 3$

$\frac{1}{3}$ becomes $\frac{4}{12}$ and $\frac{1}{4}$ becomes $\frac{3}{12}$

2. Denominators divisible.
Way   a.
$\frac{1}{8}$ and $\frac{1}{2}$
You can divide 8 by 2 so make the denominator of ½= 8.
You then divide 8 by the denominator 2 and the answer becomes the numerator
$\frac{1}{2}$ becomes $\frac{4}{8}$.

Way   b.
Another way of doing this is to multiply both the numerator and the denominator by the number received by dividing the denominator.
$\frac{1}{3}$ and $\frac{1}{4}$ becomes

$\frac{12}{3} = 4$ $\frac{12}{4} = 3$

$\frac{1}{3} \times \frac{4}{4} = \frac{4}{12}$ $\frac{1\times4=4}{3\times4=12}$ $\frac{1}{4} \times \frac{3}{3} = \frac{3}{12}$ $\frac{1\times3=3}{4\times3=12}$
Once you have converted the fractions to like denominators you can then perform the requested operation.

Addition of Fractions

When adding fractions you add the two numerators together. The denominator stays the single or common number. If the answer can be reduced you then need to do that.

$$\frac{1}{3} + \frac{1}{3} = \frac{2}{3}$$

If the answer can be reduced you then need to do that.
1/8 plus 1/2 is   1/8 plus 4/8   equals 5/8. 5/8 cannot be reduced.
3/8 plus 1/8=   4/8 which can be reduced to 1/2.
Always reduce the answer if possible.

If the numerator ends up bigger than the denominator (improper fraction), that number must be converted to a whole number and the remainder fraction. This is called a MIXED NUMBER.

$\frac{5}{6}$ stays $\frac{5}{6}$

$+\frac{2}{3}$ becomes $\frac{4}{6}$ $\frac{5}{6} + \frac{4}{6} = \frac{9}{6}$

$\frac{9}{6} = 1\frac{3}{6} = 1\frac{1}{2}$ Divide the 6 into 9. This equals 1 with 3 left over. Place the 3 over the 6 to become

$\frac{3}{6}$ which reduces to ½.

Addition of Fractions Test and Answers

Problems

Once the denominators are alike, add the numerators.

1. $\frac{1}{2}$ 2. $\frac{3}{8}$ 3. $\frac{1}{2}$ 4. $\frac{1}{2}$ 5. $\frac{2}{3}$ 6. $\frac{7}{9}$

$+\frac{1}{4}$ $+\frac{1}{4}$ $+\frac{2}{10}$ $+\frac{1}{3}$ $+\frac{2}{3}$ $+\frac{3}{4}$

7. $\frac{11}{16}$ 8. $\frac{2}{3}$ 9. $\frac{4}{5}$ 10. $\frac{6}{7}$ 11. $\frac{3}{8}$ 12. $\frac{1}{3}$

$+\frac{5}{8}$ $+\frac{7}{10}$ $+\frac{1}{3}$ $+\frac{3}{7}$ $+\frac{5}{6}$ $+\frac{1}{2}$

13. $\frac{3}{10}$ 14. $\frac{2}{5}$ 15. $\frac{2}{9}$

$+\frac{3}{5}$ $+\frac{1}{2}$ $+\frac{3}{4}$

Answers

1. $\frac{3}{4}$

$$\frac{1}{2} = \frac{?}{4} \quad \times 2 = \frac{2}{4}$$

$$+\frac{1}{4}$$

$$\frac{1}{4}$$

$$\frac{3}{4}$$

2. $\frac{5}{8}$

$$\frac{3}{8} \qquad\qquad \frac{3}{8}$$

$$+\frac{1}{4} = \frac{?}{8} \times \frac{2}{1} = \frac{2}{8}$$

$$\frac{5}{8}$$

---

3. $\frac{7}{10}$

$$\frac{1}{2} = \frac{?}{10} \times \frac{5}{1} = \frac{5}{10}$$

$$+\frac{2}{10} \qquad\qquad \frac{2}{10}$$

$$\frac{7}{10}$$

4. $\frac{5}{6}$

$$\frac{1}{2} = \frac{?}{6} \times \frac{3}{1} = \frac{3}{6}$$

$$+\frac{1}{3} \quad \frac{?}{6} \times \frac{2}{1} = +\frac{2}{6}$$

$$\frac{5}{6}$$

---

5. $1\frac{1}{3}$

$$\frac{2}{3}$$

$$+\frac{2}{3}$$

$$\frac{4}{3} = 1\frac{1}{3}$$

6. $1\frac{19}{36}$

$$\frac{7}{9} = \frac{?}{36} \times \frac{4}{1} = \frac{4}{36} \times \frac{7}{1} = \frac{28}{36} \quad \text{(multiply the numerator)}$$

$$+\frac{3}{4} = \frac{?}{36} \times \frac{9}{1} = \frac{9}{36} \times \frac{3}{1} = +\frac{27}{36} \quad \text{(multiply the numerator)}$$

$$\frac{55}{36} = 1\frac{19}{36}$$

---

7. $1\frac{5}{16}$

$$\frac{11}{16} \qquad\qquad \frac{11}{16}$$

$$+\frac{5}{8} \quad \frac{?}{16} \times \frac{2}{1} = \frac{2}{16} \times \frac{5}{1} = +\frac{10}{16} \quad \text{(multiply the numerator)}$$

$$\frac{21}{16} = 1\frac{5}{16}$$

8. $1\frac{11}{30}$

$$\frac{2}{3} \quad \frac{?}{30} \times \frac{10}{1} = \frac{10}{30} \times \frac{2}{1} = \frac{20}{30}$$

$$+\frac{7}{10} \quad \frac{?}{30} \times \frac{3}{1} = \frac{3}{30} \times \frac{7}{1} = +\frac{21}{30}$$

$$\frac{41}{30} = 1\frac{11}{30}$$

9. $1\frac{2}{15}$

$\frac{4}{5}$ $\frac{?}{15}$ x $\frac{3}{1}$ = $\frac{3}{15}$ x $\frac{4}{1}$ = $\frac{12}{15}$

$+\frac{1}{3}$ $\frac{?}{15}$ x $\frac{5}{1}$ = $\frac{5}{15}$ x $\frac{1}{1}$ = $+\frac{5}{15}$

$$\frac{17}{15} = 1\frac{2}{15}$$

10. $1\frac{2}{7}$

$\frac{6}{7}$

$+\frac{3}{7}$

$$\frac{9}{7} = 1\frac{2}{7}$$

---

11. $1\frac{5}{24}$

$\frac{3}{8}$ $\frac{?}{48}$ x $\frac{6}{1}$ = $\frac{6}{48}$ x $\frac{3}{1}$ = $\frac{18}{48}$

$+\frac{5}{6}$ $\frac{?}{48}$ x $\frac{8}{1}$ = $\frac{8}{48}$ x $\frac{5}{1}$ = $+\frac{40}{48}$

$$\frac{58}{48} = 1\frac{10}{48} = 1\frac{5}{24}$$

12. $\frac{5}{6}$

$\frac{1}{3}$ $\frac{?}{6}$ x $\frac{2}{1}$ = $\frac{2}{6}$

$+\frac{1}{2}$ $\frac{?}{6}$ x $\frac{3}{1}$ = $+\frac{3}{6}$

$$\frac{5}{6}$$

---

13. $\frac{9}{10}$

$\frac{3}{10}$ $\frac{7}{10}$ x $\frac{1}{1}$ = $\frac{1}{10}$ x $\frac{3}{1}$ = $\frac{3}{10}$

$+\frac{3}{5}$ $\frac{?}{10}$ x $\frac{2}{1}$ = $\frac{2}{10}$ x $\frac{3}{1}$ = $+\frac{6}{10}$

$$\frac{9}{10}$$

14. $\frac{9}{10}$

$\frac{2}{5}$ $\frac{?}{10}$ x $\frac{2}{1}$ = $\frac{2}{10}$ x $\frac{2}{1}$ = $\frac{4}{10}$

$+\frac{1}{2}$ $\frac{?}{10}$ x $\frac{5}{1}$ = $\frac{5}{1}$ x $\frac{1}{1}$ = $+\frac{5}{10}$

$$\frac{9}{10}$$

---

15. $\frac{35}{36}$

$\frac{2}{9}$ $\frac{?}{36}$ x $\frac{4}{1}$ = $\frac{4}{36}$ x $\frac{2}{1}$ = $\frac{8}{36}$

$+\frac{3}{4}$ $\frac{?}{36}$ x $\frac{9}{1}$ = $\frac{9}{36}$ x $\frac{3}{1}$ = $+\frac{27}{36}$

$$\frac{35}{36}$$

Addition of Mixed Numbers

Mixed numbers can be added in two ways. The whole numbers can be added and the fractions can be added separately.

$$1\frac{1}{3}$$
$$+\,2\frac{1}{2}$$
$$\overline{\,3\frac{5}{6}}$$

You can add the whole numbers 2 + 1 = 3
You then add the fractions:

$\frac{1}{3} = \frac{2}{6}$ and $\frac{1}{2} = \frac{3}{6}$

$\frac{2}{6} + \frac{3}{6} = \frac{5}{6}$

The answer becomes $3\frac{5}{6}$

If the numerator of the fraction is larger than the denominator (improper fraction), the fraction must be converted to a mixed number and the whole number added to the whole number in the problem.

Instead of the answer being 3 5/6 say it was 3 7/6. The 7/6 becomes 1 1/6. The one is added to the 3 and the answer is 4 1/6.

The second way is to convert the whole number to a fraction and just work with fractions.

$$1\frac{1}{3}$$
$$+\,2\frac{1}{2}$$
$$\overline{\,4\frac{5}{6}}$$

$1 = \frac{3}{3}$ $\qquad \frac{3}{3} + \frac{1}{3} = \frac{4}{3}$ then $\frac{4}{3}$ is equal to $\frac{8}{6}$

$2 = \frac{4}{2}$ $\qquad \frac{4}{2} + \frac{1}{2} = \frac{5}{2}$ then $\frac{5}{2}$ is equal to $\frac{15}{6}$

$\frac{8}{6} = \frac{15}{6} = \frac{23}{6}$ which is equal to $3\frac{5}{6}$

Addition of Mixed Numbers Test and Answers

Problems

1. $3\frac{3}{4}$
   $+3\,\frac{1}{4}$

2. $5\frac{3}{8}$
   $+2\frac{1}{5}$

3. $6\frac{4}{9}$
   $+3\frac{1}{3}$

4. $7\frac{1}{10}$
   $+8\frac{3}{5}$

5. $4\frac{2}{7}$
   $+6\frac{1}{14}$

6. $4\frac{7}{12}$
   $+3\,\frac{3}{4}$

7. $2\frac{8}{16}$
   $+4\,\frac{1}{4}$

8. $9\frac{3}{15}$
   $+7\frac{11}{30}$

9. $6\frac{7}{18}$
   $+5\frac{1}{3}$

10. $5\frac{8}{24}$
    $+3\frac{3}{24}$

Answers

1. 7

$$3\tfrac{3}{4}$$
$$+3\tfrac{1}{4}$$
$$6\tfrac{4}{4} = 7$$

2. 7 23/40

$$5\tfrac{3}{8} \quad \tfrac{?}{40} \times \tfrac{5}{1} = \tfrac{15}{40}$$
$$+2\tfrac{1}{5} \quad \tfrac{?}{40} \times \tfrac{8}{1} = + \tfrac{8}{40}$$
$$7 \qquad\qquad\qquad\quad \tfrac{23}{40}$$

3. 9 7/9

$$6\tfrac{4}{9} \qquad\qquad \tfrac{4}{9}$$
$$+3\tfrac{1}{3} \quad \tfrac{?}{9} \times \tfrac{3}{1} = + \tfrac{3}{9}$$
$$9 \qquad\qquad\qquad \tfrac{7}{9}$$

4. 15 7/10

$$7\tfrac{1}{10} \qquad\qquad \tfrac{1}{10}$$
$$+8\tfrac{3}{5} \quad \tfrac{?}{10} \times \tfrac{2}{1} = + \tfrac{6}{10}$$
$$15 \qquad\qquad\qquad \tfrac{7}{10}$$

5. 10 5/14

$$4\tfrac{2}{7} \quad \tfrac{?}{14} \times \tfrac{2}{1} = \tfrac{4}{14}$$
$$+6\tfrac{1}{14} \qquad\qquad\quad + \tfrac{1}{14}$$
$$10 \qquad\qquad\qquad\quad \tfrac{5}{14}$$

6. 8 1/3

$$4\tfrac{7}{12} \qquad\qquad \tfrac{7}{12}$$
$$+3\tfrac{3}{4} \quad \tfrac{?}{12} \times \tfrac{3}{1} = + \tfrac{9}{12}$$
$$7 \qquad\qquad \tfrac{16}{12} = 1\tfrac{4}{12} = 1\tfrac{1}{3}$$
$$7 + 1 = 8 \qquad\qquad\qquad\qquad \tfrac{1}{3}$$

7. 6 3/4

$$2\tfrac{8}{16} \qquad\qquad \tfrac{8}{16}$$
$$4\tfrac{1}{4} \quad \tfrac{?}{16} \times \tfrac{4}{1} = + \tfrac{4}{16}$$
$$6 \qquad\qquad\quad \tfrac{12}{16} = \tfrac{3}{4}$$

8. 16 17/30

$$9\tfrac{3}{15} \quad \tfrac{?}{30} \times \tfrac{2}{1} = \tfrac{6}{30}$$
$$+7\tfrac{11}{30} \quad \tfrac{?}{30} \times \tfrac{1}{1} = + \tfrac{11}{30}$$
$$16 \qquad\qquad\qquad\qquad \tfrac{17}{30}$$

9. 11 13/18

$$6\tfrac{7}{18} \qquad\qquad \tfrac{7}{18}$$
$$+5\tfrac{1}{3} \quad \tfrac{?}{18} \times \tfrac{6}{1} = + \tfrac{6}{18}$$
$$11 \qquad\qquad\qquad\qquad \tfrac{13}{18}$$

10. 8 11/24

$$5\tfrac{8}{24}$$
$$+3\tfrac{3}{24}$$
$$8\tfrac{11}{24}$$

Subtraction of Fractions

When subtracting fractions you subtract the two numerators. The denominator stays the single or common number. If the answer can be reduced you then need to do that.

5/8 – 3/8 = 2/8=1/4

Subtraction of Mixed Numbers

The whole numbers can be subtracted and the fractions can be subtracted separately or convert the whole number to a fraction and just work with fractions.

$6\ 4/10 - 1\ 3/10 = 64/10 - 13/10 = 51/10 = 5\ 1/10$

Subtraction of Mixed Numbers Tests and Answers

Problems

1. $9\frac{3}{4}$
   $-6\frac{2}{10}$

2. $7\frac{5}{8}$
   $-5\frac{1}{8}$

3. $10\frac{4}{6}$
   $-4\frac{3}{9}$

4. $\frac{1}{2}$
   $-\frac{1}{4}$

5. $42\frac{5}{12}$
   $-32\frac{1}{36}$

6. $\frac{7}{9}$
   $-\frac{3}{4}$

7. $5\frac{8}{6}$
   $-3\frac{2}{6}$

8. $\frac{5}{8}$
   $-\frac{1}{8}$

9. $13\frac{20}{60}$
   $-4\frac{3}{10}$

10. $\frac{7}{6}$
    $-\frac{1}{4}$

Answers

1. $3\frac{11}{20}$

$$9\frac{3}{4} \qquad \frac{?}{40} \times \frac{10}{1} = \frac{30}{40}$$
$$-6\frac{2}{10} \qquad \frac{?}{40} \times \frac{4}{1} = -\frac{8}{40}$$
$$3 \qquad\qquad \frac{22}{40} = 3\frac{11}{20}$$

2. $2\frac{1}{2}$

$$7\frac{5}{8}$$
$$-5\frac{1}{8}$$
$$2\frac{4}{8} = 2\frac{1}{2}$$

3. $6\frac{1}{3}$

$$10\frac{4}{6} \qquad \frac{?}{36} \times \frac{6}{1} = \frac{24}{36}$$
$$-4\frac{3}{9} \qquad \frac{?}{36} \times \frac{4}{1} = -\frac{12}{36}$$
$$6 \qquad\qquad \frac{12}{36} = 6\frac{1}{3}$$

4. $\frac{1}{4}$

$$\frac{1}{2} \qquad \frac{?}{4} \times \frac{2}{1} = \frac{2}{4}$$
$$-\frac{1}{4} \qquad\qquad\qquad -\frac{1}{4}$$
$$\qquad\qquad\qquad\qquad \frac{1}{4}$$

5. $10\frac{7}{18}$

$$42\frac{5}{12} \qquad \frac{?}{36} \times \frac{3}{1} = \frac{15}{36}$$
$$-32\frac{1}{36} \qquad\qquad\qquad -\frac{1}{36}$$
$$10 \qquad\qquad\qquad \frac{14}{36} = 10\frac{7}{18}$$

6. $1/36$

$$\frac{7}{9} \qquad \frac{?}{36} \times \frac{4}{1} = \frac{28}{36}$$
$$-\frac{3}{4} \qquad \frac{?}{36} \times \frac{9}{1} = -\frac{27}{36}$$
$$\qquad\qquad\qquad\qquad\qquad \frac{1}{36}$$

7. 3

$$5\frac{8}{6}$$
$$-3\frac{2}{6}$$
$$2\frac{6}{6} = 3$$

8. $\frac{1}{2}$

$$\frac{5}{8}$$
$$-\frac{1}{8}$$
$$\frac{4}{8} = \frac{1}{2}$$

9. $9\ 1/30$

$$13\frac{20}{60} \qquad\qquad \frac{20}{60}$$
$$-4\frac{3}{10} \qquad \frac{?}{60} \times \frac{6}{1} = -\frac{18}{60}$$
$$9 \qquad\qquad\qquad \frac{2}{60} = 9\frac{1}{30}$$

10. $11/12$

$$\frac{7}{6} \qquad \frac{?}{24} \times \frac{4}{1} = \frac{28}{24}$$
$$-\frac{1}{4} \qquad \frac{?}{24} \times \frac{6}{1} = -\frac{6}{24}$$
$$\qquad\qquad\qquad\qquad\qquad \frac{22}{24} = \frac{11}{12}$$

Multiplication of Fractions

When multiplying fractions the numerators are multiplied by each other and the same in the denominator.

The rule is

$$\frac{a}{c} \times \frac{b}{d} = ab \qquad \frac{Numerator \times numerator}{Denominator \times denominator}$$

$$\frac{3}{4} \times \frac{2}{3} = \frac{3 \times 2}{4 \times 3} = \frac{6}{12} = \frac{1}{2}$$

Here we introduce the idea of cancelling. Cancelling means finding a number in the numerator that will evenly go into a number in the denominator or vice versa.

$$\frac{3}{4} \times \frac{2}{3} =$$ 3 in the denominator goes into 3 in the numerator evenly making the 3 a 1.

2 in the numerator goes into 4 in the denominator 2 times making the 4 a 2.
The answer is still ½

What you are actually doing is finding the factors of each number and then cancelling them out.
$$\frac{3}{4} \times \frac{2}{3} = \frac{3}{2 \times 2} \times \frac{2}{3}$$ this becomes $$\frac{1}{2} \times \frac{1}{1} = \frac{1}{2}$$

If the fraction is a mixed number, convert the number to a fraction and add it to the fraction.
$$1\frac{3}{4} = \frac{7}{4}$$

Multiplication of Fractions Test and Answers

Problems

1. $\frac{2}{3} \times \frac{3}{4}$ 2. $\frac{1}{7} \times \frac{2}{5}$ 3. $\frac{3}{8} \times \frac{5}{2}$ 4. $\frac{1}{2} \times 7$ 5. $\frac{18}{35} \times \frac{5}{2}$

6. $\frac{24}{55} \times \frac{8}{9}$ 7. $\frac{9}{3} \times \frac{3}{9}$ 8. $\frac{35}{12} \times \frac{9}{14}$ 9. $1\frac{1}{2} \times 1\frac{9}{4}$ 10. $6\frac{7}{8} \times 5\frac{1}{3}$

Answers

1. 1/2

$$\frac{2}{3} \times \frac{3}{4} = \frac{2 \times 3}{3 \times 2 \times 2} = \frac{1}{2}$$

2. 2/35

$$\frac{1}{7} \times \frac{2}{5} = \frac{1 \times 2}{7 \times 5} = \frac{2}{35}$$

3. $\frac{15}{16}$

$$\frac{3}{8} \times \frac{5}{2} = \frac{3 \times 5}{8 \times 2} = \frac{15}{16}$$

4. $3\frac{1}{2}$

$$\frac{1}{2} \times 7 = \frac{1}{2} \times \frac{7}{1} = \frac{1 \times 7}{2 \times 1} = \frac{7}{2} = 3\frac{1}{2}$$

5. $1\frac{2}{7}$

$$\frac{18}{35} \times \frac{5}{2} = \frac{2 \times 9}{5 \times 7} \times \frac{5}{2} = \frac{9}{7} = 1\frac{2}{7}$$

6. $\frac{64}{165}$

$$\frac{24}{55} \times \frac{8}{9} = \frac{3 \times 8}{55} \times \frac{8}{3 \times 3} = \frac{8 \times 8}{55 \times 3} = \frac{64}{165}$$

7. 1

$$\frac{9}{3} \times \frac{3}{9} = \frac{1}{1} \times \frac{1}{1} = 1$$

8. $1\frac{7}{8}$

$$\frac{35}{12} \times \frac{9}{14} = \frac{5 \times 7}{3 \times 4} \times \frac{3 \times 3}{2 \times 7} = \frac{5}{4} \times \frac{3}{2} = \frac{15}{8} = 1\frac{7}{8}$$

9. $4\frac{7}{8}$

$$1\frac{1}{2} \times 1\frac{9}{4} = \frac{3}{2} \times \frac{13}{4} = \frac{39}{8} = 4\frac{7}{8}$$

10. $36\frac{2}{3}$

$$6\frac{7}{8} \times 5\frac{1}{3} = \frac{55}{8} \times \frac{16}{3} = \frac{55}{8} \times \frac{4 \times 4}{2 \times 4} \times \frac{4 \times 4}{3} = \frac{55 \times 2}{3} = \frac{110}{3} = 36\frac{2}{3}$$

Division of Fractions

In division a RECIPROCAL is used. A reciprocal is the fraction "flipped" upside down. 3/4 becomes 4/3.

Only one fraction is "flipped" in division. Once this is done you multiply numerator times numerator and denominator times denominator.

A little memory idea: flip the second fraction and multiply.
$$\frac{3}{4} \times \frac{2}{3} = \frac{3}{4} \times \frac{3}{2} = \frac{3 \times 3}{4 \times 2} = \frac{9}{8} = 1\frac{1}{8}$$

Division of Fractions Tests and Answers

Problems

1. $\frac{2}{3} \div \frac{3}{4}$ 2. $\frac{4}{7} \div \frac{8}{6}$ 3. $\frac{5}{6} \div \frac{7}{8}$ 4. $\frac{9}{12} \div \frac{3}{4}$ 5. $\frac{6}{15} \div \frac{9}{30}$

6. $\frac{14}{11} \div 2$ 7. $\frac{16}{9} \div \frac{1}{6}$ 8. $\frac{3}{8} \div \frac{2}{7}$ 9. $4\frac{2}{5} \div 1\frac{1}{10}$ 10. $\frac{35}{8} \div 5$

Answers

1. $\frac{8}{9}$

$$\frac{2}{3} \div \frac{3}{4} = \frac{2}{3} \times \frac{4}{3} = \frac{2 \times 4}{3 \times 3} = \frac{8}{9}$$

2. $\frac{3}{7}$

$$\frac{4}{7} \div \frac{8}{6} = \frac{4}{7} \times \frac{6}{8} = \frac{2 \times 3}{7 \times 2} = \frac{3}{7}$$

3. $\frac{20}{21}$

$$\frac{5}{6} \div \frac{7}{8} = \frac{5}{6} \times \frac{8}{7} = \frac{5 \times 2 \times 4}{2 \times 3 \times 7} = \frac{5 \times 4}{3 \times 7} = \frac{20}{21}$$

4. 1

$$\frac{9}{12} \div \frac{3}{4} = \frac{9}{12} \times \frac{4}{3} = \frac{3 \times 3 \times 2 \times 2}{3 \times 2 \times 2 \times 3} = \frac{1}{1} = 1$$

5. $1\frac{1}{3}$

$$\frac{6}{15} \div \frac{9}{30} = \frac{6}{15} \times \frac{30}{9} = \frac{2 \times 3 \times 5 \times 3 \times 2}{3 \times 5 \times 3 \times 3} =$$

6. $\frac{7}{11}$

$$\frac{14}{11} \div 2 = \frac{14}{11} \times \frac{1}{2} = \frac{2 \times 7 \times 1}{2 \times 11} = \frac{7}{11}$$

$$\frac{4}{3} = 1\frac{1}{3}$$

7. $10\frac{2}{3}$

$\frac{16}{9} \div \frac{1}{6} = \frac{16}{9} \times \frac{6}{1} = \frac{16 \times 2 \times 3}{3 \times 3 \times 1} = \frac{16 \times 2}{3} =$

$\frac{32}{3} = 10\frac{2}{3}$

8. $1\frac{5}{16}$

$\frac{3}{8} \div \frac{2}{7} = \frac{3}{8} \times \frac{7}{2} = \frac{21}{16} = 1\frac{5}{6}$

9. 4

$4\frac{2}{5} \div 1\frac{1}{10} = \frac{22}{5} \times \frac{10}{11} = \frac{2 \times 11 \times 2 \times 5}{5 \times 11} = \frac{4}{1} = 4$

10. $\frac{7}{8}$

$\frac{35}{8} \div 5 = \frac{35}{8} \times \frac{5}{1} = \frac{5 \times 7 \times 1}{1 \times 8 \times 5} = \frac{7}{8}$

Comparing or Ordering Fractions

A point to remember when working with fractions: As the denominator gets larger, the value of the fraction gets smaller. In other words, 1/8 of a pizza is less than ¼ of it. ¼ of the pizza is smaller than ½ of it. This is known as "Ordering Fractions" or "Comparing Fractions". Another way to do this is to cross multiply the two fractions especially when the numerators are NOT equal because as the numerator gets larger the fraction gets larger.

4/5 and 2/3 or $\frac{4}{5}\ \frac{2}{3}$ you cross multiply the first numerator by the second denominator 4 x 3 = 12
and then the second numerator by the first denominator 2 x 5 = 10

If the two products are equal the fractions are equal.
If the first product (12) is larger, than the second product (10) then the first fraction is larger.
If the second product is larger, then the second fraction is larger.

If you are doing more than two fractions then you must find the least common denominator, as in addition and subtraction, and actually look at all the numerators.

1/4 and 1/2 and 1/8
All denominators are factors of 8. 1/4 = 2/8; 1/2 = 4/8; 2/8, 4/8, 1/8 so 1/2 is the largest 1/4 is snext largest and 1/8 is smallest.

Determine the Largest Fraction

1. $\frac{11}{12}$ or $\frac{1}{6}$ _____

2. $\frac{3}{4}$ or $\frac{5}{12}$ _____

3. $\frac{3}{5}$ or $\frac{1}{4}$ _____

4. $\frac{5}{6}$ or $\frac{5}{8}$ _____

5. $\frac{7}{22}$ or $\frac{11}{14}$ _____

6. $\frac{5}{12}$ or $\frac{6}{7}$ _____

Order These Fractions from Largest to Smallest

7. $\frac{7}{10}, \frac{1}{2}, \frac{2}{5}$ _____

8. $\frac{5}{9}, \frac{14}{36}, \frac{2}{3}$ _____

9. $\frac{7}{10}, \frac{7}{8}, \frac{3}{4}$ _____

10. $\frac{3}{7}, \frac{10}{21}, \frac{14}{147}$ _____

Answers

1. $\frac{11}{12}$

$\frac{11}{12}$ or $\frac{2}{12}$ so $\frac{11}{12}$ is larger

2. $\frac{3}{4}$

$\frac{3}{4}$ or $\frac{5}{12} = \frac{9}{12}$ or $\frac{5}{12} =$ so $\frac{3}{4}$ is larger

---

3. 3/5

$\frac{3}{5}$ or $\frac{1}{4} = \frac{12}{20}$ or $\frac{5}{}$ 20 so $\frac{3}{5}$ is larger

4. 5/6

$\frac{5}{6}$ or $\frac{5}{8}$ $5 \times 8 = 40$ and $5 \times 6 = 30$ so $\frac{5}{6}$ is larger

---

5. $\frac{11}{14}$

$\frac{7}{22}$ or $\frac{11}{14}$ $7 \times 14 = 98$

6. $\frac{6}{7}$

$\frac{5}{12}$ or $\frac{6}{7}$ $5 \times 7 = 35$

$6 \times 12 = 72$ so 6/7 is larger

---

7. $\frac{7}{10}, \frac{1}{2}, \frac{2}{5}$

$\frac{7}{10}, \frac{1}{2}, \frac{2}{5} =$

$\frac{7}{10}, \frac{5}{10}, \frac{4}{10}$ they are in order

8. $\frac{2}{3}, \frac{5}{9}, \frac{14}{36}$

$\frac{5}{9}, \frac{14}{36}, \frac{2}{3} =$

$\frac{20}{36}, \frac{14}{36}, \frac{24}{36}$ so $\frac{2}{3}$ is largest, $\frac{5}{9}$ is next, $\frac{14}{36}$ is smallest

---

9. $\frac{7}{8}, \frac{3}{4}, \frac{7}{10}$

$\frac{7}{10}, \frac{7}{8}, \frac{3}{4} =$

$\frac{56}{80}, \frac{70}{80}, \frac{60}{80}$ so $\frac{7}{8}$ is largest $\frac{3}{4}$ is next $\frac{7}{10}$ is Smallest

10. $\frac{10}{21}, \frac{3}{7}, \frac{14}{147}$

$\frac{3}{7}, \frac{10}{21}, \frac{14}{147} =$

$\frac{63}{147}, \frac{70}{147}, \frac{14}{147}$

Decimals

Decimals are not whole numbers. They are a part of a number and therefore have something in common with fractions. Fractions can be turned into decimals and decimals can be turned into fractions since they are both parts of a whole number.   For every fraction there is a decimal and for every decimal there is a fraction. Decimals always follow a "." (Period) but in math it is called a "DECIMAL POINT".

In whole numbers ones are always to the right, then tens, hundreds, etc.

10 = 1 ten and 0 ones.

In decimals the tenths place is to the right of the decimal point.

.1 is one tenth. .01 is one hundredth. .001 is one thousandths.   (notice the th added.)

NOTE: tens are whole numbers tenths are part of a number (decimal).

Name	decimal	fraction
3 tenths	.3	3/10
4 hundredths	.04	4/100
6 thousandths	.006	6/1000
8 ten thousandths	.0008	8/10000

Every time you add a zero you move one more place to the right in a decimal. To change the value of the decimal, the 0 is placed between the decimal point and the number. If the 0 is to the right of the decimal number it does not change the value of the decimal.

As the number of zeros increase between the decimal point and the number the value of the decimal decreases.

Changing a Fraction to a Decimal

To change a fraction to a decimal, divide the denominator into the numerator.

¾ is 3 divided by 4 =

4|3̄   Since 4 does not go into 3 add a decimal point and the first zero.

4|3̄.0   The decimal point is carried to the quotient (answer- above the line) and the necessary number of zeros can be added.

```
   .75
4|3.00
```

so ¾ is equal to .75

Changing a Decimal to a Fraction

To change a decimal to a fraction, count the number of places to the right of the decimal point and add that many zeros after a 1 in the denominator.

.63 is 63/100   1 and 2 zeros
.630 is 630/1000 which reduces to 63/100
.75 is 75/100 This can be reduced to ¾

Decimal/Fraction Converting Test and Answers

Decimals to Fractions and Fractions to Decimals

	Decimal	fraction			Decimal	fraction
1.	.36	_____		6.	.032	_____
2.	_____	6/25		7.	_____	202/250
3.	.6	_____		8.	.106	_____
4.	.275	_____		9.	_____	21/50
5.	_____	17/200		10.	.7	_____

Answers

1. 36/100, 9/25
   Multiply .36 by 100/100   100 x .36 = 36 leaves 36/100
   Reduce: 36/100   4 x 9 = 36   4 x 25 = 100   = 9/25

2. .24
   Multiply both by 4   4 x 6 = 24   4 x 25 = 100   24/100
   Move the decimal place 2 places to the left

3. 6/10, 3/5
   Multiply .6 by 100/100   100 x .6 = 60   leaves 60/100
   Reduce: 60/100   6 x 10 = 60   10 x 10 = 100 = 6/10
         6/10 2 x 3 = 6   2 x 5 = 10   = 3/5

4. 275/1000, 11/40
   Multiply .275 by 1000/1000   1000 x .275 = 275   leaves 275/1000
   Reduce: 275/1000   11 x 25 = 275   40 x 25 = 1000 = 11/40

5. .085
```
        .085
   200|17.000
       1600
       1000
       1000
```

6. 32/1000, 4/125
   Multiply .032 by 1000/1000   1000 x .032 = 275   leaves 32/1000
   Reduce: 32/1000   4 x 8 = 32 125 x 8 = 1000 = 4/125

7. .808
```
              .808
   250|202.000
         200 0
            2000
            2000
```

8. 106/1000, 53/500
   Multiply .106 by 1000/1000   1000 x .106 = 106   leaves 106/1000
   Reduce: 106/1000   2 x 53 = 106   2 x 500 = 1000   = 53/500

9. .42
```
        .42
   50|21.00
       20 0
         100
         100
```

10. 7/10
    Multiply .7 by 100/100   100 x .7 = 70   leaves 70/100
    Reduce: 70/100   7 x 10 = 70   10 x 10 = 100 = 7/10

Adding Decimals

To add decimals, line all numbers up under each other with the decimal point in the same place.

```
   3.245
+   .177
```

Add the same way as integers. Start to the far right number and add to the left carrying numbers just as in integers. The difference is to carry the decimal point down into the answer in the same column.

```
   3.245
+   .177
   3.422
```

If you are adding a number that has less decimal places in the top number than the bottom, simply add zeros to the top decimal digits. These zeros are called PLACEHOLDERS.

```
   1.24 becomes 1.240
+2.375          +2.375
                 3.615
```

Adding Decimals Test and Answers

Problems

1. 1.25 +0.80	2. 2.4 +0.95	3. 4.82 +3.77	4. 21.49 +12.25	5. 53.11 +24.26
6. 29.4 +36.7	7. 3.77 +5.44	8. 2.96 +3.27	9. 5.72 +9.122	10. 49.34 +54.45

Answers

1. 2.05	3. 8.59	5. 77.37	7. 9.21	9. 14.842
2. 3.35	4. 33.74	6. 66.10	8. 6.23	10. 103.79

Subtracting Decimals

To subtract decimals, line all numbers up under each other with the decimal point in the same place as in addition above.

Subtract the same way as integers. Start with the far right number and subtract and keep moving to the left carrying numbers just as in integers. The difference is to carry the decimal point down into the answer in the same column.

If you are subtracting a number from a number that has less decimal places in the top number than the bottom, simply add zeros to the top decimal digits as placeholders.

```
1.234   becomes     1.2340
- .3456             - .3456
                      .8884
```

Subtracting Decimals Test and Answers

Problems

1. 3.5 -1.75	2. 8.02 -2.64	3. .82 - .77	4. 40.49 -37.25	5. 15.11 -10.98
6. 18.89 - 6.28	7. 20.77 -15.58	8. 1.96 - .27	9. 3.72 -1.122	10. 29.83 -14.31

Answers

1. 1.75	3. .05	5. 4.13	7. 5.19	9. 2.598
2. 5.38	4. 3.24	6. 12.61	8. 1.69	10. 15.52

Multiplying Decimals

Multiplying by a Whole Number

```
  3.45
 x 21
  345
 690
 72.45
```

The multiplication is carried out the same as with integers.

Once the product is arrived at the decimal is taken into account. The number of decimal places is counted in the multiplicand (top number) and then the same number of places is counted off in the product starting from the right. The answer then becomes 72.45.

Multiplying Two Decimals

```
  2.54
 x .45
 1270
 1016
 1.1430 or 1.143
```

The multiplication is carried out the same as with integers.

Once the product is arrived at the decimal is taken into account. The number of decimal places is counted in the multiplicand (top number) and in the multiplier (bottom number), added together, then the same number of places is counted off in the product starting from the right. The answer then goes from 11430 to 1.1430 or dropping the last placeholder, 1.143.

Multiplying Decimals Test and Answers

Problems

1.	.5	2.	8.2	3.	42	4.	.75	5.	1.11
	x .7		x 2.6		x .007		x .37		x 10.9

6.	9.11	7.	8.41	8.	6.84	9.	1000	10.	7.5
	x .033		x 2.3		x .04		x .22		x .06

Answers

1. .35
```
     .5
  x .7
   35
```
bring down both decimal places counting from the right to the left = .35

2. 21.32
```
     8.2
  x 2.6
   492
  164
  2132
```
bring down both decimal places counting from the right to the left = 21.32

3. .294
```
      42
  X .007
   294
```
bring down the three decimal places counting from the right to the left = .294

4. .2775
```
     .75
  x .37
   525
  225
  2775
```
bring down the four decimal places counting from the right to the left = .2775

5. 12.099
```
    1.11
  x10.9
   999
  1110
  12099
```
bring down the three decimal places counting from the right to the left = 12.099

6. .30063
```
    9.11
  x .033
   2733
  2733
  30063
```
bring down the five decimal places counting from the right to the left = .30063

7. 19.343
```
     8.41
  x   2.3
   2523
  1682
  19343
```
bring down the three decimal places counting from the right to the left = 19.343

8. .2736

6.84
x .04
2736 bring down the four decimal places counting from the right to the left = .2736

9. 220

1000
x ,22
22000 bring down both decimal places counting from the right to the left = 220

10. .45

7.5
x .06
450 bring down the three decimal places counting from the right to the left = .45

Dividing Decimals

Dividing a Decimal by a Whole Number

```
      .11666
21|2.45000          The division is carried out the same as with integers.
   21                   The decimal place is carried to the quotient (answer) in the same place
    35                      as it occurs in the number.
    21
   140
   126
    140
    126
     140
     126   This is a repeating number; it will end the same always. The answer then needs to be rounded
           and can become .11667
```

Common fractions that end in repeating numbers are 1/3 and 2/3. As decimals these become .3333 and .6666. They are then often rounded to .33 and .67

Dividing a Whole Number by a Decimal

When this occurs the number of decimal places in the divisor is counted and the decimal point is eliminated and a decimal point is added to the end of the dividend and the same number of zeros is added.

.33|999   becomes   33|999.00

```
   32.727
33|999.00
   99
   ───
   90
   66
   ──
  240
  231
  ───
   90
   66
   ──
   24
```

Dividing two decimals

When this occurs, the number of decimal places in the divisor is counted and the decimal point is eliminated and the decimal point in the dividend is moved the same number of decimal places to the right. Zeros are added if necessary as placeholders.

.33|3.333   becomes   33|333.3

```
   10.1
33|333.3
   33
   ──
   33
   33
   ──
```

Dividing Decimals Tests and Answers

Problems

1. 8 | 0.424   2. 13 | 1.108   3. 14 | 4.289   4. 28 | 1.4   5. 5 | 0.45

6. 1.2 | 48   7. .4 | 24   8. .12 | 1212   9. .34 | 358   10. .05 | 955

11. 4.6 | 13.34   12. 3.7 | 2.8   13. 6.19 | .7218   14. .01 | .174   15. .17 | .0714

Answers

```
1.      . 053
    8 | 0. 424
        40
        ──
        24
        24
        ──
```

```
2.         .08523
      13 | 1.10800
           104
           ───
            68
            65
            ──
            30
            26
            ──
            40
            39
            ──
             1
```

```
3.          .30635
      14 | 4.28900
           42
           ──
           89
           84
           ──
           50
           42
           ──
           80
           70
           ──
           10
```

4.

```
     .05
28 | 1.40
     1 40
```

5.

```
    .09
5 | 0. 45
      45
```

6.

```
1.2 | 48   becomes         40
                     12 | 480.
                          48
```

7.

```
.4 | 240   becomes      60
                    4  240.
                       24
```

8.

```
.12 | 1212   becomes       10100
                      12  121200.
                          12
                            12
                            12
```

9.

```
.34 | 358   becomes       1052.941
                     34  35800.000
                         34
                          180
                          170
                           100
                            68
                            320
                            306
                             140
                             136
                               40
                               34
                                6
```

10.

```
.05 | 955   becomes       19100
                     5   95500.
                         5
                         45
                         45
                           5
                           5
```

11.

```
       .08523                        2.9
4.6 | 13.34       Becomes     46 | 133.4
      104                             92
         68                          414
         65                          414
          30
          26
           40
           39
            1
```

12.

```
3.7 | 2.8   becomes          .7567
                      37   28.0000
                           259
                            210
                            185
                             250
                             222
                              280
                              259
                               21
```

13.

```
6.19 | .7218   becomes          .116607
                         619   72.180000
                               619
                               1028
                                619
                                4090
                                3714
                                 3760
                                 3714
                                  4600
                                  4333
                                   267
```

14.

```
.01 | .174   becomes       17.4
                      1   17.4
                          1
                           7
                           7
                            4
                            4
```

15.

```
.17 | .0714   becomes         .42
                        17   07.14
                              6 8
                               34
                               34
```

Percents

The word percent is from the Latin "per centum" or "per hundred". Other ways of saying percent are: out of 100, parts per hundred. Percent is a special way of writing a fraction or a decimal. The denominator is ALWAYS 100. A percent has the % sign behind it.

Changing a Decimal to a Percent

Since the word means per 100, the decimal point is moved two (2) places to the right and the % sign is added. .05 is written as 5%. .05 becomes 5, the first zero is dropped and add the sign.
.25 is 25% .25 becomes 25 and add the sign.
If there are more than 2 decimal places the decimal point stays behind the second decimal place. .675 becomes 67.5%. Move the decimal point 2 places and add the sign behind the 5.
If a decimal only has one (1) place, a zero (0) is added for the second placeholder.
.2 is 20% add a zero behind the 2, this becomes 20 and add the sign.

Decimal to Percents Test and Answers

Change the Decimal to a Percent

	Decimal	%			Decimal	%
1.	.345	_____		6.	.0375	_____
2.	.04	_____		7.	.10	_____
3.	.27	_____		8.	.12 ½	_____
4.	.0075	_____		9.	.6	_____
5.	2.45	_____		10.	.927	_____

Answers

1. 34.5%   move the decimal 2 places right 34.5 and add the % sign 34.5%

2. 4%   move the decimal 2 places right 4 and add the % sign 4%

3. 27%   move the decimal 2 places right 27 and add the % sign 27%

4. .75%   move the decimal 2 places right .75 and add the % sign .75%

5. 245%   move the decimal 2 places right 245 and add the % sign 245%

6. 3.75%   move the decimal 2 places right 3.75 and add the % sign 3.75%

7. 10%   move the decimal 2 places right 10 and add the % sign 10%

8. 12 ½%   move the decimal 2 places right 12 1/2 and add the % sign 12 1/2%

9. 60%   move the decimal 2 places right 60 and add the % sign 60%

10. 92.7% move the decimal 2 places right 92.7 and add the % sign 92.7%

Changing a Percent to a Decimal

Since percent is part of 100, remove the % sign, move two places to the left and place a decimal point at that spot.

26% is .26 Remove the sign, move two places to the left and put the decimal point in front of the 2.

2% is .02 Remove the sign, move two places to the left, add a zero in front of the 2 and put the decimal point in front of the zero.   .02% is .0002 Remove the sign, move two places to the left, add 2 zeros in front of the02 and put the decimal point in front of the zero farthest to the left.

Percents to Decimals Test and Answers

Change the Percent to a Decimal

%	decimal
1. .01%	_____
2. 17%	_____
3. 7%	_____
4. 33 1/3%	_____
5. 425%	_____
6. 80%	_____
7. 99%	_____
8. 200%	_____
9. .003%	_____
10. 250%	_____

Answers

1. .0001   Remove the % sign .01 and move the decimal 2 places left .0001

2. .17   Remove the % sign 17 and move the decimal 2 places left .17

3. .07   Remove the % sign 7 and move the decimal 2 places left .07

4. .33 1/3 Remove the % sign 33 1/3 and move the decimal 2 places left .33 1/3

5. 4.25   Remove the % sign 425 and move the decimal 2 places left 4.25

6. .8 or .80 Remove the % sign 80 and move the decimal 2 places left .8 or .80

7. .99   Remove the % sign 99 and move the decimal 2 places left .99

8. 2 or 2.0 Remove the % sign 200 and move the decimal 2 places left 2 or 2.0

9. .00003   Remove the % sign .003 and move the decimal 2 places left .00003

10. 2.5   Remove the % sign 250 and move the decimal 2 places left 2.5

Changing a Percent to a Fraction

Since percent means "part of 100", remove the % sign and turn the number into a numerator with a denominator of 100.   Reduce the fraction if possible.   100% is

$\frac{100}{100}$ which is equal to 1   25% is $\frac{25}{100}$ which is equal to 1/4.

To change a percent that contains a fraction, change the entire number into the numerator with 100 as the denominator and then divide by the denominator.

8 ½% is $\frac{8\ 1/2}{100}$ this becomes $\frac{17}{2}$ times $\frac{1}{100}$ which equals $\frac{17}{200}$

To check the answer, divide 17 by 200.

Percents to Fractions Test and Answers

Change the Percent to a Fraction

	%	fraction		%	fraction
1.	30%	_____	6.	35%	_____
2.	4 1/2%	_____	7.	16 2/3%	_____
3.	12%	_____	8.	55%	_____
4.	97%	_____	9.	1%	_____
5.	24%	_____	10.	37 1/2%	_____

Answers

1. 3/10   Remove the % sign and place the number over 100 30/100, reduce if possible divide by 10 = 3/10

2. 9/200   Remove the % sign and place the number over 100 4 1/2/100, 4 ½ is 9/2 so 9/2 * 1/100 = 9/200

3. 3/25   Remove the % sign and place the number over 100 12/100, reduce if possible divide by 4 = 3/25

4. 97/100   Remove the % sign and place the number over 100 97/100

5. 6/25   Remove the % sign and place the number over 100 24/100, reduce if possible divide by 4 = 6/25

6. 7/20   Remove the % sign and place the number over 100 35/100, reduce if possible divide by 5 = 7/20

7. 1/6   Remove the % sign and place the number over 100 16 2/3/100, 16 2/3 = 50/3 so 50/3 * 1/100 = 1/6

8. 11/20   Remove the % sign and place the number over 100 55/100, reduce if possible divide by 5 = 11/20

9. 1/100   Remove the % sign and place the number over 100 1/100

10. 3/8   Remove the % sign and place the number over 100 37 1/2/100, 37 ½ = 75/2 75/2 * 1/100 = 75/200 = 3/8

Changing a Fraction to a Percent

The easiest way is to multiply the fraction by 100%.

To change 5/8 multiply 5/8 by $\frac{100\%}{1}$ this becomes 5/8 times $\frac{100\%}{1}$

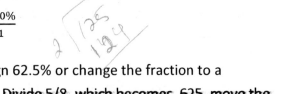

This becomes 500%/8 which becomes $\frac{125}{2}$, $\frac{125}{2}$ is 62.5 add the sign 62.5% or change the fraction to a decimal and the decimal to a % as was done earlier in this lesson. *Divide 5/8, which becomes .625, move the decimal point two places and add the sign 62.5%*

Fractions to Percents Test and Answers

Change the Fraction to a Percent

Fraction	%		Fraction	%
1. 3/10,000	_____		6. 18/25	_____
2. 7/8	_____		7. 1 1/10	_____
3. 4/25	_____		8. 1/50	_____
4. 3/50	_____		9. 11/100	_____
5. 11/25	_____		10. 1/5	_____

Answers

1. .03%

$$\frac{3}{10000} \times \frac{100\%}{1} = \frac{300\%}{10000} = \frac{3\%}{100}$$ move the decimal 2 places to the left and remove the 100 = .03%

2. 87.5%

$$\frac{7}{8} * \frac{100\%}{1} = \frac{700\%}{8} = 87.5\%$$

3. 16%

$$\frac{4}{25} * \frac{100\%}{1} = \frac{400\%}{25} = 16\%$$

4. 6%

$$\frac{3}{50} * \frac{100\%}{1} = \frac{300\%}{50} = 6\%$$

5. 44%

$$\frac{11}{25} * \frac{100\%}{1} = \frac{1100\%}{25} = 44\%$$

6. 72%

$$\frac{18}{25} * \frac{100\%}{1} = \frac{1800\%}{25} = 72\%$$

7. 110%

$$1\frac{1}{10} = \frac{11}{10}$$

$$\frac{11}{10} * \frac{100\%}{1} = \frac{1100\%}{25} = 110\%$$

8. 2%

$$\frac{1}{50} * \frac{100\%}{1} = \frac{100\%}{50} = 2\%$$

9. 11%

$$\frac{11}{100} * \frac{100\%}{1} = \frac{1100\%}{100} = 11\%$$

10. 20%

$$\frac{1}{5} * \frac{100\%}{1} \quad \frac{100\%}{5} = 20\%$$

Percent Problems

There are three parts to a percent question: "%" "whole" and "part"

There are three formulas to use to answer these questions:

1. Looking for PART

<u>Part = percent x whole</u>
  % of a number
"of" says multiply.

find 30% of 44   This is looking for a part of the whole.
   .3 x 44 = 13.2 change the percent to a decimal and multiply the decimal times the number.

You can change the number to a fraction and multiply also.
$\frac{30}{100} \times 44 = \frac{3}{10} \times 44 = \frac{3}{5} \times 22 = \frac{66}{5} = 13.5$ or 13.2

2. Looking for PERCENT

<u>Percent = part/whole</u>
x is what % of y x is the part y is the whole so it would be $\frac{x}{y}$

12 is what % of 36   12 is the part and 36 is the whole $\frac{12}{36}$ $33\frac{1}{3}\%$

3. Looking for WHOLE

<u>Whole = part/percent</u>

x % of what number is = to this number

the whole is "this number"   part is "what number" and percent is "$x\%$"

25% of what number is = 8   8 is the part, 25% is the percent so the problem is $\frac{8}{25\%} = \frac{8}{.25} = 32$
or .25 = $\frac{25}{100} = \frac{1}{4}$ 8 divided by $\frac{1}{4}$ it becomes 8 x 4 = 32

Percent Tests and Answers

Problems

1. Find 7% of 965
2. 9 is what % of 99
3. 87.5 % of this number is = 210
4. Find 75% 680
5. 75 is what % of 80
6. 5 % of this number is = 60
7. 1.5% of 753 =
8. 33 is what % of 44
9. 80 is 50% of what number
10. 80% of this number is = 304

Answers

1. 67.55
   Change the % to a decimal .07 then times the number .07 * 965 = 67.55

2. 9.1%
   Part is what % of whole $\frac{9}{99} = \frac{1}{11}$ = .0909 or 9.1%

3. 240
   210 is the part, 87.5% is the percent so the problem is $\frac{210}{87.5\%} = \frac{210}{.875} = 240$

4. 510
   Change the % to a decimal .75 then times the number .75 * 680 = 510

5. 93.75%
   Part is what % of whole $\frac{75}{80} = \frac{15}{16}$ = .9375 or 93.75%

6. 12000
   60 is the part, 5% is the percent so the problem is $\frac{60}{5\%} = \frac{60}{.005} = 12000$

7. 11.295
   Part = percent x whole 753 * 1.5% = 753 * .015 = 11.295

8. 75%
   Part is what % of whole $\frac{33}{44} = \frac{3}{4}$ = .75 or 75%

9. 160
   80 is the part, 50% is the percent so the problem is $\frac{80}{50\%} = \frac{80}{.5} = 160$

10. 380
    304 is the part, 80% is the percent so the problem is $\frac{304}{80\%} = \frac{304}{.8} = 380$

Ratio and Proportion

A **ratio** is the comparison of two numbers by division. It shows a relationship or that these two "items" have something in common.

5/6 means there are five of one thing and 6 of something else. Likewise, 5:6 means the same thing. The Slash or forward slash (/) and the colon (:) mean the same thing "is to".

An example: You have two items. One is 6 inches long and one is 18 inches long. What is the ratio?
6/18 Reduce this fraction and you get 1/3. Item one (6 inches) is 3 times as long as item two (18 inches). This is a 1 to 3 ratio (1/3 or 1:3)

A **proportion** is 2 equal ratios. 3/6=1/2 or can be written 3:6 :: 1:2 The = and :: mean equal to or "as".
6/18 = 1/3 is a proportion. 6/18 reduces to 1/3.
1/3 = 2/6 is also a proportion. 2/6 reduces to 1/3.

A proportion can be used to solve a problem when one of the four numbers is unknown. This type of problem is called an equation. In algebra this is called "solving for X."
X represents the unknown or the variable. Since we know that both sides are equal we can solve for X.

$\frac{6}{18} = \frac{x}{3}$ is the problem. Using the mathematical rule for a proportion you can cross multiply. This means 6 x 3 = 18 * X.   (The small x represents multiply.)

$\qquad$ 18 = 18 X

Now you want to move the numbers to one side and leave X by itself, so you divide both sides by 18. You now have X = 1 (both sides are equal.)

18/18 = 18X/18 = 18/18 =1 $\qquad$ 18X/ 18 =X $\quad$ X= 1

When working with a proportion you can add to, subtract from, divided by and multiply by "the same number" to both sides. This allows you to move numbers to one side and leave the X or variable alone on one side.

When representing the proportion as 3:6 :: 1:2. You call the 3 (first number) an "extreme", the second number (6) a "mean". You call the third number (1) a "mean" and the forth number (2) an "extreme".

When solving this problem, you multiply the means by the extremes. The extremes are the two outside numbers (3, 2) and the means are the two inside numbers (6, 1).

$\qquad$ 3:6 :: 1:2

$\qquad$ 6 x 1 = 3 x 2

$\qquad$ 6 $\ $ = 6

$$\frac{3}{6} = \frac{1}{2}$$

Conversions or Equivalents Formula Use

On the DET the formula is ALWAYS given. The test is trying to see if you can USE a formula not REMEMBER it. Conversions are NOT given. You need to remember these.

Length

1 centimeter = 0.3937 inch
1 inch = 2.54 centimeter
1 foot = 0.3048 meter, 30.48 cm
1 yard = 0.9144 meter, 91.4 cm
1 kilometer = 0.621 mile
1 meter = 39.37 inches
          1.094 yards
1 mile = 5,280 feet, 1.61 km
1 millimeter = 1.852 kilometers

Liquid Measurements

1 cup, measuring = 8 fluid ounces
                   $^1/_2$ liquid pint
                   240 ml
1 dram, fluid or liquid = $^1/_8$ fluid ounces
1 gallon (U.S.) = 3.785 liters
                  128 U.S. fluid ounces
1 liter = 1.057 liquid quarts
1 ounce, fluid or liquid (U.S.) = 29.574 milliliters
16 ounces = 2 cups = 1 pint = 480 ml
32 fluid ounces (2 pints = 1 quart) = 950 milliliters (.95 liter)
128 fluid ounces (4 quarts = 1 gallon) = 3.75 liters
1 tablespoon = 3 teaspoons
               $^1/_2$ fluid ounce
               15 ml
1 teaspoon = $^1/_3$ tablespoon = 5 ml

Dry Measurements

1 grain = 0.064798 gram
15.432 grains = 1 gram
1 kilogram = 2.205 pounds
1 microgram = 0.000001 gram
1 milligram = 0.015 grain, 1000 micrograms
1 gram = 1000 micrograms
1 ton = 2,000 pounds

Square Measurements

1 square inch = 6.4516 square centimeters
1 square foot = 0.09290304 square meters
1 square yard = 0.83613 square meter
0.38608 square mile = 1 square kilometer

Temperature Conversion

Fahrenheit to Celsius C= (F-32) x 5/9
Celsius to Fahrenheit F = 9/5 (C) + 32

Conversions Test and Answers

1. Change 42 inches into centimeters   _____
2. Change 3 ounces into milliliters   _____
3. Change 16 quarts into gallons   _____
4. Change 100 degrees F into degrees Celsius   _____
5. Change 1 mile into feet   _____
6. Change 3 grains into grams   _____
7. Change 2.5 square meters into square yards   _____
8. Change 10 degrees C into degrees F   _____
9. Change 3.5 lbs into kilograms   _____
10. Change 54 centimeters into inches   _____
11. Change 2 square meters into square feet   _____
12. Change 4 grains into milligrams   _____
13. Change 2 tablespoons into teaspoons   _____
14. Change 3 pints into ounces   _____
15. Change 45 milliliters into teaspoons   _____
16. Change 2 ounces into drams   _____
17. Change 8 cups into ounces   _____
18, Change 54 pounds into kilograms   _____
19. Change 4 yards into meters   _____
20. Change 37 degrees C to degrees F   _____

(handwritten note in margin:) in → cm   42 in $\frac{2.54\ Cm}{1\ in}$ =

Answers

1. 106.68
centimeter = 0.3937 inch
42 in / x cm = 0.3937 in / 1 cm
42*1 = 0.3937*x
42/.03937 = 106.68

2. 88.72
1 ounce, fluid or liquid (U.S.) = 29.574 milliliters
3 oz / x ml = 1 oz/29.574 ml
3*29.574 = 1*x
88.72 = 1x

3. 4
4 quarts = 1 gallon
16 quarts/x gallons = 4 quarts = 1 gallon
16*1 = 4*x
16/4= 4

4. 37.78
Fahrenheit to Celsius C= (F-32) x 5/9
Fill "knowns" into formula
C= (100-32) x 5/9
C= 68 x 5/9
C= 340/9 = 37.78

5. 5280
1 mile = 5,280 feet

6. 0.194394
1 grain = 0.064798 grams
3 grains/x grams = 1 grain/0.064798 grams
3*0.064798 = 1*x
0.194394 = 1x

7. 2.989
1 square yard = 0.83613 square meter
2.5 square meters/x square yard = .83613 square meter/ 1 square yard
2.5*1 = .83613*x
X= 2.5/.83613

8. 50
Celsius to Fahrenheit F = 9/5 (C) + 32
Fill "knowns" into formula
F = 9/5 (10) + 32
9/5 * 10 = 18 [(10 * 9)/5]
18 + 32 = 50

9. 1.588
1 kilogram = 2.205 pounds
3.5 lbs/ x kilograms = 2.205 lbs/ 1 kilogram
3.5*1 = x*2.205
3.5/2.205 = 1.588

10. 21.26
1 centimeter = 0.3937 inch
54 centimeters/ x inches = 1centimeter / 0.3937 inch
54*0.3937 = x*1
21.26 = 1x

11. 21.528
1 square foot = 0.09290304 square meters
2 square meters/x square feet =
  0.09290304 square meters/1 square foot
2*1 = x*0.09290304
0.09290304/2 = x = 21.528

12. 266.667
1 milligram = 0.015 grain
4 grains/ x milligrams = 0.015 grain/1 milligram
4*1 = x*0.015
X =4/ 0.015 = 259.196

13. 6
1 tablespoon = 3 teaspoons
2 tablespoons/ x teaspoons =
x tablespoons/ 3 teaspoons
2*3 = x*1
6 = x

14. 48
32 fluid ounces = 2 pints
3 pints/x ounces = 2 pints/ 32 ounces
3*32 = 2*x
96/2 = x = 48

15. 9
1 teaspoon = $^1/3$ tablespoon= 5 ml
45 milliliters/x teaspoons = 5 ml/ 1 teaspoon
45*1 = 5*x
45/5 = x = 9

16. 16
1 dram, fluid or liquid = $^1/8$ fluid ounces
Change 2 ounces/ x drams = $^1/8$ ounces/ 1 dram
2*1 = 1/8*x
2* 8 = x = 16

17. 64
1 cup, measuring = 8 fluid ounces
8 cups/ x ounces = 8 ounces/1 cup
8*x = 8
X = 8*8 = 64

18. 24.49
1 kilogram = 2.205 pounds
Change 54 pounds/ x kilograms = 2.205 pounds/ 1 kilogram
54*1 = 2.205*x
54/2.205 = x

19. 3.658
1 yard = 0.9144 meter
Change 4 yards/ x meters = 1 yard/0.9144 meter
4*1 = x*0.9144
X = 0.9144/4 = 3.658

20. 98.6
Celsius to Fahrenheit F = 9/5 (C) + 32
Fill 'knowns" into formula
Change 37 degrees C to degrees F
F = 9/5 (37) + 32
9/5 * 37 + 32 =
[(9*37)/5] + 32 =
6 [333/5= 66.6] + 32 = 98.6

Roman Numerals

To learn Roman Numerals you must memorize the basic Roman Numerals and then the basic rules in creating different numbers.

The basic Numerals and their corresponding numbers are:

I one (1)   L fifty (50)   M one thousand (1000)
V five (5)   C one hundred (100)
X ten (10)   D five hundred (500)

The I, V, X are easy to remember as they are used most often. The L, C, D, M is harder to keep in order. A little pneumonic could be "an <u>LCD</u> costs <u>M</u>oney".

No numerals can be repeated more than 3 times in a row (I, X, C, M). V, L and D cannot be repeated. To count the number, one less than the number in that placeholder, put the symbol that is less than it before it. E.g. 4 is IV, 9 is IX, 90 is XC.   (Subtraction rule)

To determine what a number is start on the left side of the symbols (letters) and add them if the symbol is equal to or less than it.
LXX is 50 + 10 + 10= 70
LXXI is 50 + 10 + 10 + 1 = 71

Adding   Subtracting
MMCCCLXXI is M + M   = 2000   MCMXLII   is   M   = 1000
              C + C + C   = 300   M − C   = 900
              L + X + X   =   70   L − X   =   40
                      I   =   1   II   =   2
                          2371   1942

Convert Roman Numerals and numbers   ## Answers

	Roman	Number			Roman	Number
1.	MMLXXXVI	_____		1.		2086
2.	CCCLX	_____		2.		360
3.	MCCLXI	_____		3.		1261
4.	CCCLXXXVII	_____		4.		387
5.	CLXXIX	_____		5.		179
6.	_____	35		6.	XXXV	
7.	_____	3366		7.	MMMCCCLXVI	
8.	_____	530		8.	DXXX	
9.	_____	1175		9.	MCLXXV	
10.	_____	3318		10.	MMMCCCXVIII	
11.	MMDCCLXI	_____		11.		2761
12.	DCCXVII	_____		12.		717
13.	_____	61		13.	LXI	
14.	_____	914		14.	CMXIV	
15.	MMDXCVII	_____		15.		2597

Word Problems

Word problems are mathematical problems using words instead of mathematical expressions. Word problems often have the following content: addition, multiplication, fractions, percent, formula solving, commission, interest, discount, sales tax and distance.

        To solve word problems follow these steps:

Step 1: What is the question?
        Be sure you know what you are being asked.

Step 2: What do I know?
        List the parts of the question that provides the information needed to answer the question.

Step 3: Is there a formula?
        If there is a formula given, plug the "knowns" into the formula.

Step 4: Can I use ratio and proportion?
        If there is no formula, can I use ratio and proportion? This is a common tool for solving word problems. (See discussion of ratio and proportion.)

A few math rules might help here.

The Associative property for addition says that if $(a + b) + c$ then $a + (b + c)$ equal the same number. In other words, as long as the numbers are all using the same operation (addition) they can be added in any order.

      (2 + 3) + 4 = 2 + (3 + 4)
        5   + 4 = 2 +   7   both = 9

The Associative property for multiplication says that if $(a \times b) \times c = a \times (b \times c)$. In other words, as long as the numbers are all using the same operation (multiplication) they can be multiplied in any order.

      (2 x 3) x 4 = 2 x (3 x 4)
        6   x 4 = 2 x   12
         24   =   24   both = 24

Word problems can contain more than one set of mathematical expressions. These expressions may be in parentheses ( ).

    1. When working with a problem that contains the parentheses solve the problem within the parentheses first.

      10 - (3 x 2) = 10 - 6 = 4

      24 / (2 x 3) = 24/ 6 = 4

    2. If there are no parentheses and you have mixed operations (addition and multiplication, etc.) work from left to right. Multiply and divide first then add and subtract.

      3 + 6 x 2 =   6 x 2 = 12   12 + 3 = 15

      2 x 4 - 6/2 =   2 x 4 = 8   6/2 = 3   8-3 = 5

Using ratio and proportion to solve for X.

500 grams of peanut butter is $.90.
350 grams would be how much?

	500 gm/$.90 = 350 gm/$X	or	500 gm : $.90 :: 350 gm : $X
Cross multiply:	500 gm x $X = $.90 x 350 gm or		500 gm x $X = $.90 x 350 gm
	500 X = 31500		500 X = 31500
Divide both sides by 500	X = 31500/500		X = 31500/500
	$.63		$.63

Finding percent

Ralph got 18 out of 25 questions correct. What percent did he get correct?

Turn this into a fraction: 18/25

Now make it a proportion: % is something over 100
Make the unknown Q

	18/25 = Q/ 100		18 : 25 :: Q : 100
Cross multiply:	18 x 100 = 25 x Q	or	18 x 100 = 25 x Q
	18 x 100 = 25 Q		18 x 100 = 25 Q
Divide both sides by 25	x = 1800/25		x = 1800/25
	.72		.72

Move decimal point 2 places to make it a percent (x 100) = 72%

Commission

Commission is a percent of a sum. It usually relates to sales.

If Mary makes a 12% commission and she sold $340.00 worth, how much commission did she receive?

The problem is 12% of $340.00   or   .12 of $340.00
"Of" means times, multiplication.

.12 x $340 = $40.80

It could be written $\frac{12}{100}$ x $340 = $\frac{\$4080}{100}$ = $40.80

The commission Mary received was $40.80.

Discounts

This is when an item is reduced by a certain percent (%). It usually relates to sales.

A $250.00 item is reduced by 15%. A) What is the discount? B) What is the discounted price?

A)

Discount = price   x %discount

      = $250.00   x 15%   15% is either .15 or 15/100

      = $250.00   x .15

      = $37.50

handwritten: $.15 (250) = 37.50   250   37.50 = 212.50

B)

Discounted price = original price - discount

             = $250.00   - $37.50

                $212.50

Be sure you know what you are being asked in this type of problem "discount" or "discounted price"!

Sales Tax

Sales tax is similar to commission. Sales tax is a percent of original cost.
Again be careful you know what you are being asked: "amount of sales tax" or "cost of item with the sales tax".

Sally bought a $.99 drink. Sales tax is 7%. A) What is the tax on her drink? B) How much did she pay for her drink?

handwritten: 0.7(.99) = 0.0693 = 0.07   .99 + .07 = 1.06

A)

Tax = cost x %tax

      = $.99   x 7%   7% is either .07 or 7/100

      = $.99   x .07

      = $.0693 which is $.07   Cents is only two decimal places.

B)

Cost = original cost + tax

       = $.99   + $.07

           $1.06

Interest

Interest like commission is a percent of a sum of money. Interest can be paid to a person or paid to a lender.

Tom has $50.00 in a savings account. The bank told him they just paid him 5% interest. How much did they pay him?

handwritten: .05 (50) = 2.50   =

Interest = $ amount x % interest

       = $50.00   x 5%   5% is either .05 or 5/100

       = $50.00   x .05

          =$2.50

How much money does he now have?

Total money = original amount + interest

    = $50.00   + $2.50

                $52.50

If Tom had been <u>charged</u> 5% interest, how much interest would he pay? This is the same problem but he would PAY $2.50 or he would owe $52.50.

Again be SURE you know what you are being asked.

Distance

Distance is how far someone traveled in a certain amount of time. The formula is

distance = speed x time

Speed is a "specified distance" per a "specified time". The specified distance can be expressed in steps, feet, or miles. The specified time can be expressed in seconds, minutes or hours. You travel in a car by miles per hour. You might walk feet per second. The final "distance" label (feet, etc.) must match the speed label (feet, etc.).

Remember there are 60 seconds in a minute and 60 minutes in an hour.

There are 12 inches in a foot and 5280 feet in a mile.

Philip ran to his friend's house. Philip traveled at 54 feet per minute. If he ran for **35** minutes, how far away did his friend live?

$$\frac{54 ft}{1 min} \quad \frac{x}{35 min}$$

Distance = speed x time

    = 54 ft/ 1 min x 35 minutes   all labels are equal!

    = 54 x 35/1 $= 54 (35) \div 1 = 1890 ft$

      1890 ft

If I wanted to know how many miles away his friend lived, I would divide 1890 by 5280, which would equal .36 of a mile.

ft → miles

$$1890 ft \quad \frac{1 mile}{5280 ft} = 0.3579$$

$$= 0.36 \ miles$$

Word Problems Test

1. Carl has twice as many pieces of candy as Bobby. Mike has 10 pieces of candy. Carl has 14 more pieces than Mike has. How many pieces of candy does Bobby have?

A. 12

B. 24

C. 42

D. 20

(handwritten: Carl 24   Bobby 12   mike 10)

2. Kathy has traveled 328 miles in 4 hours. For Kathy to reach her destination, she must travel another 574 miles. If she stays at the same rate of travel, how long will it take her to get there?

A. 10 hours

B. 14 hours

C. 7 hours

D. 5 hours

(handwritten: 328/4   574/x   4(574) ÷ 328)

3. The red light changes 3 times a minute. How long will it take for the light to change 633 times?

A. 1899 minutes

B. 124 minutes

C. 368 minutes

D. 211 minutes

(handwritten: 3/1 min   633/x   (1) 633 ÷ 3 = 211)

4. Jason needs his truck towed 235 miles. Because of Jason's auto club membership, the tow truck company will tow him 124 miles free and $1.50 each mile afterwards. How much will it cost for Jason to have his truck towed?

A. $538.50

B. $166.50

C. $186.00

D. $318.00

(handwritten: 235 - 124, 111 × 1.50 =)

5. Casie is selling fruit to pay for her high school band trip. The total pay off of her trip is $1,346.50. After she had sold all of her fruit, her trip was paid in full with a remainder of $487.36. How much did Casie raise for her trip?

A. $673.25

B. $859.14

C. $1,833.86

D. $917.86

(handwritten: 1,346.50 + 487.36 = 1833.86)

6. Ashley went birthday shopping for her son, Tyler. She bought three toys at $14.84, two toys at $19.53, and six toys at $3.86. How much did Ashley spend on her son's birthday presents?

A. $102.88

B. $87.21

C. $91.90

D. $106.74

(handwritten: 3(14.84) + 2(19.53) + 6(3.86)   44.52 + 39.06 + 23.16)

7. Mya is selling balloons to raise money for the children's hospital. Her mother agreed to buy eight balloons for every four Mya sells. If Mya sold 54 balloons alone, how many did her mom buy?
A. 423 balloons
B. 110 balloons
C. 108 balloons
D. 244 balloons

$$\frac{8}{4} = \frac{x}{54}$$

$$8(54) \div 4$$
$$= 108$$

8. William is walking down the street. Every two minutes he takes 76 steps forward and 22 steps back. If he continues to walk at this rate, how long will it take him to walk one mile? Round your answer.
Every step is equal to 2 feet.
There are 5,280 feet in a mile.
A. 98 minutes
B. 49 minutes
C. 102 minutes
D. 73 minutes

$$\frac{2\text{min}}{54} = \frac{1\text{min}}{27 \times 2} \quad \frac{1\text{min}}{54\text{ft}}$$

$$54\overline{)5280}$$

9.

Crayons	Pencils	Erasers	Paper	Folders	3-Ring Binder	Index Dividers
$0.56 box	$0.14 each	$0.22 each	$0.89 pack	$0.37 each	$1.25 each	$0.75 each

James starts his new semester in school tomorrow. He has some supplies to buy before he goes to school. All together, James has three classes. Each class requires him to have two boxes of crayons, five pencils, and five erasers, three packs of paper, four folders, two binders and two index dividers. How much did Jason spend?
A. $11.07
B. $12.19
C. $33.21
D. $44.33

$$2x(.56) + 5(0.14) + 5(0.22) + 3(0.89) + 4(0.37)$$

10. Mark is a mechanic. For every vehicle he repairs, Mark makes 9.9% commission. This month, the total of repaired vehicles done by Mark totaled $139,000. What was Mark's commission from these vehicles?
A. $137.61
B. $13,761.00
C. $1,376.10
D. $137,610.00

$$.099 \text{ of } 139\ 000$$
$$= 13761.60$$

$$\frac{.099}{1\text{ veh}} = \frac{x}{139,000}$$

11. An Art store is having a sale. Every item in the store is marked down 40%. Whatever does not sell gets marked down an additional 25%. If the kit of paint tubes did not sell and the original price was $60.00, what is the price of the kit now?
A. $21.00
B. $36.00
C. $27.00
D. $9.00

$$.40 \text{ of } 60 = 24 \qquad \begin{array}{r} 60 \\ -24 \\ \hline =36 \end{array}$$

$$.25 \text{ of } 36 = 9 \qquad \begin{array}{r} 36 \\ -9 \\ \hline = 27. \end{array}$$

12. Lesley has 120 sentences to write for school. If she completes 30% of the sentences in one and a half hours, how long will it take Lesley to complete all of her sentences?

A. 4.5 hours

B. 5 hours

C. 5.5 hours

D. 6 hours

$$.30 \text{ of } 120 = \frac{36}{1.5 \text{ ws}} = \frac{120}{x}$$

13. A lady walking passes a yellow house at 5:07pm. At 5:52pm the lady passes another yellow house. If the lady is walking at 7mph, how far apart are the yellow houses?

*Distance = (Rate) (Time)

A. 3.15 miles

B. 5.25 miles

C. 1.33 miles

D. 2.21 miles

$$\frac{7m}{60 \text{ min}} = \frac{x}{45 \text{ min}} = 7(45) \div 60$$

$$5.25 \text{ miles}$$

14. Three friends agreed to split the cost of their trip. They each paid $474.32. What was the total cost of the trip?

A. $948.64

B. $1,422.96

C. $1,897.28

D. $1,581.00

15. Michelle has $49.43 saved in her account, and $125.95 saved from a yard sale. How much money does Michelle have all together?

A. $176.35

B. $198.43

C. $184.93

D. $175.38

16. What is the price difference between a $178,000 beach house and a $140,000 town house?

A. $38,000

B. $42,000

C. $36,000

D. $60,000

$$\begin{array}{r} 178,000 \\ - 140,000 \\ \hline 38,000 \end{array}$$

17. Sean has a boat with a 75 gallon tank. If gas is $2.50 a gallon, how much will it cost for Sean to fill up his boat when his tank is empty?

A. $186.25

B. $187.50

C. $190.00

D. $185.75

$$2.50 (75)$$

18. In the senior class at Rosedale High, 72 out of 183 students drive to school. What percent of the students drive to school?

A. 39%

B. 43%

C. 11 %

D. 27%

$$\frac{72}{183} = \frac{183}{100} = \frac{72}{x}$$

19. Malorie burns 400 calories per hour walking. Her goal is to burn 2400 calories. How long will it take her to burn those calories?

A. 4 hrs

B. 6 hrs

C. 8.5 hrs

D. 9 hrs

$$\frac{400}{1hr} = \frac{2400}{x}$$

20. Alan made it to Myrtle Beach in 4 hours covering 328 miles. What was Alan's average speed?

A. 82 mph

B. 75 mph

C. 94 mph

D. 68 mph

$$Speed = \frac{d}{time} \qquad \frac{328 miles}{4} = 82 miles$$

21. Mrs. Kinman is planning a trip for her second grade class. For every 7 students, she needs 1 chaperone. If there are 28 students in her class, how many chaperones will she need for her trip?

A. 7

B. 5

C. 4

D. 9

$$\frac{7}{1} \qquad \frac{28}{x} = 4$$

22. Edward needs 84 half pound servings of crab legs. How many ounces does he need?
* 16 oz = 1 Lb

A. 672 oz

B. 725 oz

C. 431 oz

D. 568 oz

$$\frac{84}{8 oz} \qquad 84(8) = 672 oz$$

23. Each week Sally receives $25.00 in allowance. How long will it take her to get $550.00?

A. 18 weeks

B. 22 weeks

C. 20 weeks

D. 16 weeks

$$\frac{\$25}{1 week} = \frac{550.00}{x} \qquad (1)550 \div 25 = 22$$

24. Tom's house payment is $565.00 a month. How much does it cost him a year?

A. $3,390.00

B. $6,870.00

C. $7,680.00

D. $6,780.00

$$\frac{565}{1m} \qquad \frac{x}{12m} =$$

25. The ratio of cats to dogs at the local pound is 7:8. If there are 72 dogs at the pound, how many cats are there?

A. 74

B. 143

C. 58

D. 63

$$\frac{7 cats}{8 dog} = \frac{x}{72 dog} = 7(72) \div 8 = 63$$

Word Problem Answers

1. Correct answer: A

       A. What are you being asked? How many pieces of candy does Bobby have?

       B. What do we know?

              1. Carl has twice as many pieces of candy as Bobby.

              2. Mike has 10 pieces of candy.

              3. Carl has 14 more pieces than Mike has.

       C. What do we need to do?

              1. Find out how many pieces of candy Carl has (Mike +14)

              2. Find out how many pieces of candy Bobby has (Carl = Bobby x 2)

Carl= Mike +14   Mike = 10 so Carl = 24

Carl= Bobby x 2   Carl = 24 so 24=Bobby x 2

Divide both sides by 2   24/2= Bobby x 2/2   12= Bobby

              24/2= 12   2/2 goes away and leaves Bobby

Bobby has 12 pieces of candy

2. Correct answer: C

       A. What are you being asked? If she stays at the same rate of travel, how long will it take her to get there?

       B. What do we know?

              1. Kathy has traveled 328 miles in 4 hours.

              2. For Kathy to reach her destination, she must travel another 574 miles.

       C. Is there a formula to use?

              Distance = speed x time traveled

Method 1:   Step 1: Determine her rate of speed

              speed= miles/hour

                    328 miles/4 hours = 82 miles/hour

              Step 2: Plug available numbers in formula

              Distance = speed x time traveled

              574 miles = (82 miles/hour) x N   N = time to get there

              Step 3: Divide both sides by 82 miles/ hour   574/82 = N   N = 7 hours

Method 2:   ratio and proportion

              Step 1: 328 miles in 4 hours = 574 miles in N hours

              Step 2: cross multiply

                    328 miles x N hours = 574 miles x 4 hours

              Step 3: 328 x N = 2296

              Step 4: Divide both sides by 328   N = 7 hours

It will take Kathy 7 hours to reach her destination.

3. Correct answer: D
   A. What are you being asked? How long will it take for the light to change 633 times?
   B. What do we know?
       1. The red light changes 3 times a minute.
   C: ratio and proportion
       Step 1: 3 times in 1 minute = 633 times in N minutes
       Step 2: cross multiply
           3 times x N minutes = 633 times x 1 minute
       Step 3: 3 x N = 633
       Step 4: Divide both sides by 3   N = 211 minutes
It will take 211 minutes to change 633 times.

4. Correct answer: B
   A. What are you being asked? How much will it cost for Jason to have his truck towed?
   B. What do we know?
       1. Jason needs his truck towed 235 miles.
       2. Because of Jason's auto club membership, the tow truck company will tow him 124 miles free and
       3. $1.50 each mile afterwards.
   C. Method:
   Step 1: Subtract the amount of miles that will be paid for from the total miles. 235 - 124 = 111 miles. Jason will have to pay for 111 miles.
   Step 2: Cost= Miles x $150   111 miles x $1.50 = $166.50
It will cost Jason $166.50 to get his truck towed.

5. Correct answer: C
   A. What are you being asked? How much did Casie raise for her trip?
   B. What do we know?
       1. The total pay off of her trip is $1,346.50.
       2. After she had sold all of her fruit, her trip was paid in full with a remainder of $487.36.
   Method:
   Step 1: Total sold = cost + remainder
           N $1346.50 + $487.36
           $1833.86
The total amount Casie made was $1,833.86

6. Correct answer: D
   A. What are you being asked? How much did Ashley spend on her son's birthday presents?
   B. What do we know?
       1. She bought three toys at $14.84
       2. two toys at $19.53
       3. and six toys at $3.86.
   C. Method:
       Step 1: Cost= 3 toys ($14.84) + 2 toys ($19.53) + 6 toys ($3.86)
       Step 2: Cost= $44.52 + $39.06 + $23.16 = $106.74
Ashley spent $106.74 on the 11 toys.

7. Correct answer: C
      A. What are you being asked? How many did her mom buy?
      B. What do we know?
            1. Her mother agreed to buy eight balloons for every four Mya sells.
            2. If Mya sold 54 balloons alone
      C. Method:
            ratio and proportion
            Step 1: 54 balloons /4 balloons = N balloons x
            Step 2: cross multiply
                54 balloons x 8 balloons = N balloons x 4 balloons
            Step 3: 54 x 8 = 432   N x 4= 4N
            Step 4: Divide both sides by 4   N = 108 balloons
Mya's mother bought 108 balloons.

8. Correct answer: A
      A. What are you being asked? If he continues to walk at this rate, how long will it take him to walk one mile?
      B. What do we know?
            1. Every two minutes he takes 76 steps forward and 22 steps back.
            2. 1 mile = 5,280 feet. 1 step = 2 feet.
      C. Is there a formula to use?
            Distance = speed x time traveled

Method 1:   Step 1: Determine his rate of speed
            speed= steps/minute
                76 forward - 22 back/2 minutes = steps/minute
                54 steps/2 minutes = 27 steps/minute
            Step 2: 1 step= 2 feet therefore 27 steps = 2feet x 27 = 54 feet/minute
            Distance is 1 mile = 5280 feet
Plug available numbers in formula
            Distance = speed x time traveled
            5280 feet = 54feet/minute x N   N = time to get there
            Step 3: Divide both sides by 54 feet/ minute 5280/54 = N
            N = 97.78 minutes rounded to 98 minutes
Method 2:   ratio and proportion
            Step 1: (76 steps - 22 steps) x 2 feet in 2 minutes = 1 mile (5280 feet) in N minutes
            Step 2: cross multiply
                  (54 x 2) feet x N minutes = 5280 feet x 2 minutes
            Step 3: 108 feet x N minutes = 10560 feet
             Step 4: Divide both sides by 108   N = 97.78 minutes rounded as requested to 98 minutes
He will walk 1 mile in 98 minutes.

9. Correct answer: C
    A. What are you being asked? How much did Jason spend?
    B. What do we know?

Crayons	Pencils	Erasers 2(.75)	Paper	Folders	3-Ring Binder	Index Dividers
$0.56 box	$0.14 each	$0.22 each	$0.89 pack	$0.37 each	$1.25 each	$0.75 each

    1. All together, James has three classes.
    2. Each class requires him to have

        two boxes of crayons   four folders
        five pencils   two binders
        five erasers   two index dividers
        three packs of paper

C. Method:
Step 1: Multiply each item by the number of items needed:
$2(.56) + 5(.14) + 5(.22) + 3(.89) + 4(.37) + 2(1.25) + 2(.75) =$

$\$1.12 + \$.70 + \$1.10 + \$+ 2.67 + \$1.48 + \$2.50 + \$1.50 = \$11.07$

Step 2: Multiply total cost by 3 classes $11.07 (3) = $33.21.
James spent $33.21

10. Correct answer: B
    A. What are you being asked? What was Mark's commission from these vehicles?
    B. What do we know?
        1. For every vehicle he repairs, Mark makes 9.9% commission.
        2. This month, the total of repaired vehicles done by Mark totaled $139,000.
    C. Method 1: Commission = % of commission x sales
        C   = 9.9% x $139,000.00
                = 0.099 x $139,000.00
        $13,761.00
Method 2: Commission/Sales = %/100
        C/$139,000.00 = 9.9/100
        C x 100 = $139,000.00 x 9.9
        C= $1,376,100/100 = $13,761.00
Mark will make $13,761.00 commission.

11. Correct answer: C
        A. What are you being asked? What is the price of the kit now?
        B. What do we know?
                1. Every item in the store is marked down 40%.
                2. Whatever does not sell gets marked down an additional 25%.
                3. The original price was $60.00
        C. Method:
        Step 1: first discount (40%)
                Sale price = orig price - discount
                        = $60.00 - ($60.00 x .4)   (40 % = .4 or 40/100)
                $36.00
        Step 2: second discount
                Sale price = sale price - discount
                        = $36.00 - ($36.00 x .25)   (25 % = .25 or 25/100)
                $27.00
The kit of paint tubes is $27.00.

12. Correct answer: B
        A. What are you being asked? How long will it take Lesley to complete all of her sentences?
        B. What do we know?
                1. Lesley has 120 sentences to write for school.
                2. If she completes 30% of the sentences in one and a half hours.
        C: ratio and proportion
                Step 1: 30% (120 sentences) in 1 ½ hour = 120 sentences in N hours
                Step 2: cross multiply
                      30% (120 sentences) x N hours = 120 sentences x 1 ½ hours
                                  (30% = .3 or 30/100)
                Step 3: 36 sentences   x N hours = 180 sentences/hour
                Step 4: Divide both sides by 36   N = 5 hours
Lesley would take 5 hours to complete all of her sentences.

13. Correct answer: B
        A. What are you being asked? How far apart are the yellow houses?
        B. What do we know?
                1. A lady walking passes a yellow house at 5:07pm.
                2. At 5:52pm the lady passes another yellow house.
                3.   If the lady is walking at 7mph
        C. Is there a formula to use?
                Distance = speed x time traveled or Distance = (Rate) (Time)
Method 1:   Step 1: Determine her time
                time traveled = 5:52 p.m. - 5:07 p.m. = 45 minutes
                Step 2: Plug available numbers in formula
                Distance = speed x time traveled
                Convert time traveled into hours by dividing the minutes by 1 hour (60 minutes)
                      D = (7 miles/hour) x (45 minutes/60 minutes)
                Step 3: D = 5.25 miles
The two yellow houses are 5.25 miles apart.

14. Correct answer: B
    A. What are you being asked? What was the total cost of the trip?
    B. What do we know?
        1. Three friends agreed to split the cost of their trip.
        2. They each paid $474.32.
    C. Method:
        Cost = number of friends x individual cost
        C   = 3 x $474.32
        C   = $1422.96
The total cost of the trip was 41422.96

15. Correct answer: D
    A. What are you being asked? How much money does Michelle have all together?
    B. What do we know?
        1. Michelle has $49.43 saved in her account
        2. $125.95 saved from a yard sale.
    C. Method:
    Add the 2 amounts together
    $49.43 + $125.95 = $175.38.
Michelle has $175.38 all together.

16. Correct answer: A
    A. What are you being asked? What is the price difference?
    B. What do we know?
        1. between a $178,000 beach house and a $140,000 town house?
    C. Method:
    Subtract $178,000 from $140,000 and you get $38,000.
The price difference is $38,000.00

17. Correct answer: B
    A. What are you being asked? How much will it cost for Sean to fill up his boat when his tank is empty?
    B. What do we know?
        1. Sean has a boat with a 75 gallon tank.
        2. If gas is $2.50 a gallon
    C. Method:
        Multiply cost of a gallon by number of gallons purchased.
            $2.50 by 75 = $187.50
It will cost Sean $187.50 to fill up his boat.

18. Correct answer: A
    A. What are you being asked? What percent of the students drive to school?
    B. What do we know?
        1. In the senior class at Rosedale High, 72 out of 183 students drive to school.
    C. Method:
        number of student driving/total number of students x 100 = % driving
            72/183 x 100 =
          .39   x 100 = 39%
39% of the senior class drives to school.

19. Correct answer: B
    A. What are you being asked? How long will it take her to burn those calories?
    B. What do we know?
        1. Malorie burns 400 calories per hour walking.
        2. Her goal is to burn 2400 calories.
    C: ratio and proportion
        Step 1: 400 calories in 1 hour = 2400 calories in N hours
        Step 2: cross multiply
            400 calories x N hours = 2400 calories x 1 hour
        Step 3: Divide both sides by 400   N = 6 hours
It will take Malorie 6 hours to burn those calories.

20. Correct answer: A
    A. What are you being asked? What was Alan's average speed?
    B. What do we know?
        1. Alan made it to Myrtle Beach in 4 hours
        2. Covering 328 miles.
        C. Is there a formula to use?
        Distance = speed x time traveled or Distance = (Rate) (Time)
Method 1:   Step 1: Plug available numbers in formula
        Distance = speed x time traveled
        328 miles = speed x 4 hours
        Step 2: Divide miles (328) by time (4) to find rate.
        328/4 = 82 miles/ hour
Alan's average speed was 82 miles/ hour.

21. Correct answer: C
    A. What are you being asked? How many chaperones will she need for her trip?
    B. What do we know?
        1. For every 7 students, she needs 1 chaperone.
        2. If there are 28 students in her class
    C. ratio and proportion
    Step 1: 7 students/ 1 chaperone = 28 students/ N chaperones
    Step 2: cross multiply: 7 students x N chaperones = 28 students x 1 chaperone
        7N = 28
    Step 3: Divide both sides by 7
        N = 4 chaperones
4 is the number of chaperones needed.

22. Correct answer: A
    A. What are you being asked? How many ounces does he need?
    B. What do we know?
        1. Edward needs 84 half pound servings of crab legs.
        2. 16 oz= 1 Lb
    C. ratio and proportion
    Step 1: 1 Lb/ 16 oz = ½ Lb / N oz
    Step 2: cross multiply 1 Lb x N oz = 16 oz x ½ Lb
        1 N = 16 x ½ = 8 oz
    Step 3: Multiply # of servings x 8 oz
        84 x 8 oz = 672 oz
He needs 672 ounces.

23. Correct answer: B
    A. What are you being asked? How long will it take her to get $550.00?
    B. What do we know?
        1. Each week Sally receives $25.00 in allowance.
        2. $550.00 total
    C. ratio and proportion
    Step 1: 1 week/ $25.00 = N weeks / $550.00
    Step 2: cross multiply 1 week x $550.00 = $25.00 x N weeks
        $550.00 = $25.00 N weeks
    Step 3: Divide both sides by $25.00
        $550.00/$25.00 = 22 weeks
It will take Sally 22 weeks to save $550.00.

24. Correct answer: D
    A. What are you being asked? How much does it cost him a year?
    B. What do we know?
        1. Tom's house payment is $565.00 a month.
        2. There are 12 months in a year.
    C. Multiply $565.00 by 12 = $6,780.00
It will cost him $6,780.00 a year.

25. Correct answer: D
    A. What are you being asked? How many cats are there?
    B. What do we know?
        1. The ratio of cats to dogs at the local pound is 7:8.
        2. If there are 72 dogs at the pound
    C. ratio and proportion
    Step 1: 7 cats/ 8 dogs = N cats / 72 dogs
    Step 2: cross multiply 7 cats x 72 dogs = N cats x 8 dogs
        504 = 8N
    Step 3: Divide both sides by 8
        504/8 = 63 cats
There are 63 cats.

Blank

Please Note:

Science is an Optional Test

Check with Your School to See
If This Is Part of Your Entrance Test

This Section Includes
General Science
Biology
Chemistry
Physical Science

Blank

Comprehensive Review for General Science

Science is not a single subject nor is it a specialized field of interest. Science is much more; it is interconnected in every aspect of life just as in life everything somehow is interconnected and overlaps with something else. Nothing in this world or universe is completely independent of itself. Science includes biology, chemistry, physics, geology, astronomy, medicine and mathematics. Science also is interconnected to other parts of life, such as philosophical theories developed by philosophers who were some of the first to develop the theories and understandings of science. In our world today, science is also surprisingly interconnected in theology, religion, art, literature, music and everything our world is today.

Therefore, with a basic understanding of the life sciences, you understand the interrelationships that exist and come together for a search of knowledge and understanding of humans and our environment. Science is a part of our life and so is the scientific method, principles, and processes. In all forms of science, it is perception or the act of awareness and understanding that is the scientist's goal. Scientists make observations, perform experiments, make comparisons, find relationships observe and note differences and likenesses, ask questions, find answers, make theories and form conclusions from their findings. Scientists have developed the scientific method, and it is used in various areas of our world and in various types and levels of research and investigations.

There are three basic sciences that are the foundation to science, which are biology, chemistry and physics. Chemistry is considered to be the fundamental and central science, and both biology and physics are interconnected and overlap with chemistry. These three sciences form the foundation from which all other sciences evolve. We refer to these sciences as applied sciences. Chemistry is an experimental science, being that we know what we know to be true because it has been observed to be true. It is from the facts or experimental observations that the theories have evolved to explain the facts; therefore we can predict results of experiments that have not yet been performed based on these facts. Natural phenomena are explained and attempted to be understood by these experiments and theories and are directly related to each other.

In Science, as well as in the entire world, there are two types of data, qualitative and quantitative. Qualitative data is the non-numerical form of data that is in words, pictures, images, objects and sounds. It is the information that is descriptive that forms patterns of groupings of these things. Quantitative, on the other hand, is the numerical data that can be presented as numbers, percents, fractions, figures and even formulas. Science is interrelated to other things, for example, mathematics and statistics. Qualitative data is for example, birds, red and blue, living in the eastern region of the US. The quantitative data for this qualitative data would be the numbers that coincide with the color of the birds, how many are red or blue and those that live in the eastern region of the US. From this, Scientists will use the data that has been collected from their observations and experiments, put together qualitatively and quantitatively, and with the use of statistics will form conclusions from the data for their theories and provide facts.

Scientific Method

The scientific method is a set of techniques used in science to investigate natural phenomena it provides an objective framework to ask scientific questions and to analyze the data to reach a conclusion about that question.

Steps of the Scientific Method

- The goals of the scientific method are uniform; however the method itself is not necessarily formalized across all forms of science. It is usually a series of steps but the exact number and their nature do vary.
- The scientific method is not concrete but is meant to be an ongoing cycle to be applied with intelligence, imagination, and creativity.
- It is not uncommon for some of the steps to be done simultaneously, or out of order or even repeated but the general sequence is as follows:
  - Ask a question
    - Determine a natural phenomenon (or group of phenomena) that you are curious about and would like to explain or learn more about, then ask a specific question to focus your inquiry.
  - Research the topic
    - This step involves learning as much about the phenomenon as you can, including studying the previous studies of others in the area.
  - Create a hypothesis
    - Using the knowledge you have gained, formulate a hypothesis about a cause or effect of the phenomenon, or the relationship of the phenomenon to some other phenomenon.
  - Test the hypothesis
    - Plan and carry out a procedure for testing the hypothesis (an experiment) by gathering data.
  - Analyze the data
    - Use proper mathematical analysis to see if the results of the experiment support or refute the hypothesis.

If the data does not support the hypothesis, it must be rejected or modified and re-tested.
Frequently, the results of the experiment are compiled in the form of a lab report (for typical classroom work) or a paper (in the case of publishable academic research). It is also common for the results of the experiment to provide an opportunity for more questions about the same phenomenon or related phenomena, which begins the process of inquiry over again with a new question.

Key Elements of the Scientific Method

- We use the scientific method to get results that accurately represent the physical processes taking place in the phenomenon in the experiment.
- To insure that the results are valid to the natural world there needs to be the following :
  - **objective**
    - The scientific method intends to remove personal and cultural biases by focusing on objective testing procedures
  - **consistent**
    - The laws of reasoning should be used to make hypotheses that are consistent with broader, currently known scientific laws
    - When the hypothesis is to test one part of a broader law it should be composed only to challenge one law at a time

- **observable**
  - The hypothesis presented should allow for experiments with observable and measurable results.
- **pertinent**
  - All steps of the process should be focused on describing and explaining observed phenomena.
- **parsimonious**
  - Only a limited number of assumptions and hypothetical entities should be proposed in a given theory
- **falsifiable**
  - The hypothesis should be something which can be proven incorrect by observable data within the experiment, or else the experiment is not useful in supporting the hypothesis.
- **reproducible**
  - The test should be able to be reproduced by other observers with trials that extend indefinitely into the future.

Hypothesis, Model, Theory & Law

The words; hypothesis, model, theory, and law, in science have very exact meanings.

Hypothesis

Perhaps the most difficult and intriguing step is the development of a specific, testable hypothesis.
A useful hypothesis enables predictions by applying deductive reasoning.
It is a **limited statement** regarding the cause and effect in a specific situation, which can be tested by experimentation and observation or by statistical analysis of the probabilities from the data obtained. The outcome of the test hypothesis should be currently unknown, so that the results can provide useful data regarding the validity of the hypothesis.
Sometimes a hypothesis is developed that must wait for new knowledge or technology to be testable.

Model

A *model* is used for situations when it is known that the hypothesis has a limitation on its validity.

Theory & Law

A *scientific theory* or *law* represents a hypothesis (or group of related hypotheses) which has been confirmed through repeated testing.
A law uses a handful of fundamental concepts and equations to define the rules governing a set of phenomena.

Significant Figures

When making a measurement, a scientist can only reach a certain level of precision, limited either by the tools being used or the physical nature of the situation. The most obvious example is measuring distance.

Consider what happens when measuring the distance an object moved using a tape measure (in metric units). The tape measure is likely broken down into the smallest units of millimeters. Therefore, there's no way that you can measure with a precision greater than a millimeter. If the object moves 87.245365 millimeters, we can only tell for sure that it moved 87 millimeters, 8.7 centimeters or 0.087 meters.

The number of meaningful numbers in a measurement is called the number of *significant figures* of the number. The 87 millimeter answer would provide us with 2 significant figures in our measurement.

Zeroes & Significant Figures

Consider the number 4,300.
If the number is written as 4,300.0, it would have five significant figures.
The decimal point and following zero is only added if the measurement is precise to that level.
A decimal point at the end of a whole number indicates significant figures.

One significant figure	Two significant figures	Three significant figures
5	2.5	4.35
800	0.0098	0.00780
0.00004	78,000	88,600
	6.0	4.00
		500.

Mathematics with Significant Figures

- ✏ Scientific figures provide some different rules from mathematics.
- ✏ The key in using significant figures is to be sure that you are maintaining the same level of precision throughout the calculation.
- ✏ In scientific work you frequently round based on the significant figures involved.
- ✏ When adding or subtracting scientific data, it is only the last digit (the digit the furthest to the right) that matters. For 8.347 + 6.6543454 + 5.3
- ✏ The first term in the addition problem has four significant figures, the second has eight, and the third has only two. The precision is determined by the shortest decimal point. You will round to the tenths place (the first place after the decimal point), because while two of your measurements are more precise the third can't tell you anything more than the tenths place, so the result of this addition problem can only be that precise as well.
- ✏ When multiplying or dividing scientific data the number of significant figures do matter.
- ✏ Multiplying significant figures will always result in a solution that has the same significant figures as the smallest significant figures you started with.
- ✏ 4.345 x 4.2
- ✏ The first number has four significant figures and the second factor has two significant figures.
- ✏ Your answer ends up with two significant figures.
- ✏ Get your answer *then* round your solution to the correct number of significant figures. The precision in the multiplication will insure for you not to give a false level of precision in your final answer.

- *Exponential numbers (i.e. 10^5, 10^{-8}, etc.). In order to use this* scientists use *scientific notation*. The significant figures are listed, and then multiplied by ten to the necessary power. The speed of light is written as: 2.997925×10^8 m/s.
- There are 7 significant figures and this is much better than writing 299,792,500 m/s.
- The speed of light is frequently written as 3.00×10^8 m/s, in which there are only three significant figures.
- Very small numbers are written in scientific notation with a negative exponent instead of the positive exponent.

The Limits of Significant Figures

Significant figures are a basic means that scientists use to provide a measure of precision to the numbers they are using.
The rounding process does allow for a measure of error in the numbers.
The correct use of significant figures will be the level of precision.

The trouble is almost entirely remembering which rule is applied at which time.
When do I add exponents and when do I subtract them?
When do I move the decimal point to the left and when to the right?
You can't directly add centimeters and meters.
Just slow down, be careful, and think about what you're doing.

Metric Conversion Chart

US Units	Multiplied By	Equals Metric Units	Metric Units	Multiplied By	Equals US Units
Length					
Inches	2.5400	Centimeters	Centimeters	0.3937	Inches
Feet	0.3048	Meters	Meters	3.2808	Feet
Yards	0.9144	Meters	Meters	1.0936	Yards
Miles	1.6093	Kilometers	Kilometers	0.6214	Miles
Area					
Square inches	6.4516	Square centimeters	Square centimeters	0.1550	Square inches
Square feet	0.0929	Square meters	Square meters	10.7640	Square feet
Square yards	0.8361	Square meters	Square meters	1.1960	Square yards
Acres	0.4047	Hectares	Hectares	2.4710	Acres
Volume					
Cubic feet	0.0283	Cubic meters	Cubic meters	35.3144	Cubic feet
Cubic yards	0.7646	Cubic meters	Cubic meters	1.3079	Cubic yards
Gallons	3.7854	Liters	Liters	0.2642	Gallons
Weight					
Foot-pounds	1.3830	Newton-meters	Newton-meters	0.7380	Foot-pounds
Pounds	0.4536	Kilograms	Kilograms	2.2046	Pounds
Foot-pounds	1.3830	Newton-meters	Newton-meters	0.7380	Foot-pounds

Length

The standard unit of length in the metric system is the meter. Other units of length and their equivalents in meters are as follows:

1 millimeter = 0.001 meter
1 centimeter = 0.01 meter
1 decimeter = 0.1 meter
1 kilometer = 1000 meters

We symbolize these lengths as follows:
1 millimeter = 1 *mm*
1 centimeter = 1 *cm*
1 meter = 1 *m*
1 decimeter = 1 *dm*
1 kilometer = 1 *km*

For reference, 1 meter is a little longer than 1 yard or 3 feet. It is about half the height of a very tall adult. A centimeter is nearly the diameter of a dime, a little less than half an inch. A millimeter is about the thickness of a dime.

Volume

The standard unit of volume in the metric system is the liter. One liter is equal to 1000 cubic centimeters in volume. Other units of volume and their equivalents in liters are as follows:

1 milliliter = 0.001 liter
1 centiliter = 0.01 liter
1 deciliter = 0.1 liter
1 kiloliter = 1000 liters

We symbolize these volumes as follows:
1 milliliter = 1 *ml*
1 centiliter = 1 *cl*
1 deciliter = 1 *dl*
1 liter = 1 *l*
1 kiloliter = 1 *kl*

From these units, we see that 1000 milliliters equal 1 liter; so 1 milliliter equals 1 cubic centimeter in volume. For reference, 1 liter is a little more than 1 quart. One teaspoon equals about 5 milliliters.

Mass

The standard unit of mass in the metric system is the gram. Other units of mass and their equivalents in grams are as follows:

1 milligram = 0.001 gram
1 centigram = 0.01 gram
1 decigram = 0.1 gram
1 kilogram = 1000 grams

We symbolize these masses as follows:
1 milligram = 1 *mg*
1 centigram = 1 *cg*
1 decigram = 1 *dg*
1 gram = 1 *g*
1 kilogram = 1 *kg*

For reference, 1 gram is about the mass of a paper clip. One kilogram is about the mass of a liter of water.

Time

The following conversions are useful when working with time:
1 minute = 60 seconds
1 hour = 60 minutes = 3600 seconds
1 day = 24 hours
1 week = 7 days
1 year = 365 1/4 days (for the Earth to travel once around the sun)
In practice, every three calendar years will have 365 days, and every fourth year is a "leap year", which has 366 days, to make up for the extra quarter day over four years. The years 1992, 1996, 2000, and 2004 are all leap years. This gives us a total of 52 complete 7 day weeks in each calendar year, with 1 day left over (or 2 in a leap year).
The year is divided into 12 months, each of which has 30 or 31 days, except for February, which has 28 days (or 29 days in a leap year).

Temperature

Temperature is expressed in degrees Celsius in the metric system. The boiling point of water (at sea level) is 100°Celsius, or 100°C. The freezing point of water (at sea level) is 0° Celsius. A hot day is about 30° Celsius.

Decimals in measurement

We use decimals to specify units of measurement when we need more precision about length, volume, mass, or time. For example, when specifying the height of a person 1.63 meters tall, to say that person is 1 or 2 meters tall doesn't give us a very good idea of how tall that person really is.
The prefixes for the different units of length, volume, and mass in the metric system obey the following rules:

Prefix	Multiply by
milli-	0.001
centi-	0.01
deci-	0.1
deka-	10
hecto-	100
kilo-	1000

So for example:
1 *hecto*meter = 100 meters
1 *centi*gram = 0.01 gram
3 *milli*liters = 3 × (0.001 liters) = 0.003 liters
0.9 *kilo*meters = 0.9 × (1000 meters) = 900 meters

Blank

Cells

Plants

Protists

Animals

Blank

Comprehensive Review for Biology

Biology is the study of life and all living things. The cell is the foundation of biology as the atom is the foundation of Chemistry and matter is the foundation of Physics or Physical Science.

All living things are similar yet different. For this purpose scientists look at likenesses, differences, function, structure, development and then form classifications. This is where scientists have formed a perceived order where disorder appears to exist. It is through systematics that there has been order and reason brought to how living organisms have been able to be classified with the intention to understand the groupings and the relationships amongst these organisms. A modern Taxonomy was established, a classifying system that starts at the highest level at Kingdom with three distinct ones. The Three Kingdoms are Plantae', Animalia, and Protista. From this all things are then further classified. The Taxonomy system is as follows: Kingdom, Phylum, Class, Order, Family, Genus, and finally Species. The Protists Kingdom or Kingdom Protista is all of the microorganisms we usually call protozoans or at one time were in the Animal Kingdom as Protozoa for first animals. Bacteria and Viruses also fall into this Kingdom of Protista.

Cells

Cells are the smallest fundamental unit of all living things. They are actually the smallest structured unit of any and all living things called organisms and are made up of only one single cell. One biological cell is all that is needed to create an organism. Organisms are either one celled or many celled. A bacterium or a paramecium are each a one celled organism yet they are microscopic. Fungi, algae, protozoan's and amebas are all examples of one celled organisms that are self functioning and can self reproduce. The cell is microscopic in size but the shape of a cell varies greatly. They can be flat, rectangular, thread like, circular, irregular, or even change shape.

Animal Cell Structure and Components

The cell in general will be discussed and is described using the animal cell. In a later section there is a complete description of the plant cell. The cell is composed of three main parts; the plasma membrane, the cytoplasm, and the nucleus. The plasma membrane is the membrane that surrounds the cell that encloses the cytoplasm and forms the outer boundary.

- Plasma Membrane
  - Cell Membrane or the plasma membrane, is a semi-permeable structure consisting mainly of 2 layers of phospholipids (fat) molecules and proteins, to form a fluid framework. Cholesterol also is a component of the plasma membrane to help stabilize the phospholipids to prevent breakage of the membrane. It is the outer layer of a cell and assists in the movement of molecules in and out of the cell. It also serves as a gateway and a communication device.
- Cytoplasm is "living matter", it is a living material only found in cells. It is the interior environment between the plasma membrane and the nucleus. The cytoplasm is a liquid with numerous small structures that function in the cell as a group of small organs referred to as organelles.
  - Organelles
    - Mitochondria – is considered the power plant of the cell. It is made up of two membranous sacs, one inside the other that composes a mitochondrion. The inner membrane forms folds within its fragile walls. The mitochondria continuously have complex energy releasing chemical reactions that supply most of the power for the work of the cell.

- Enzymes – are molecules that promote specific chemical reactions found in the mitochondria. It uses oxygen to break down glucose and other nutrients to release energy for work of the cell. This is aerobic respiration or cellular respiration.
- Golgi apparatus – chemical processing and packaging center is made up of tiny, flattened sacs stacked on each other near the nucleus. Vesicles are tiny little sacs or bubbles that break off the smooth endoplasmic reticulum and carry chemicals to the sacs of the Golgi apparatus. The vesicles fuse with Golgi sacs so the contents can mingle. The Golgi apparatus processes chemically the molecules from the Endoplasmic Reticulum, packages them into vesicles that break away, fuse to the plasma membrane, it opens to the outside and expels its contents mucus is an example of its product.
- Endoplasmic Reticulum (or ER) there are two forms of ER; smooth and rough ER is a system made of membranes that contain sacs and canals that wind throughout the cells cytoplasm as a network. Rough ER receives and transports newly made proteins and have Ribosomes attached to the outer surface. As Ribosomes make proteins and attach to the rough ER and drop their protein into the interior of the ER, they are then transported to areas for chemical processes to take place. Smooth ER makes new membranes. This area is so full of proteins they don't attach, that is why it is smooth in texture. The Smooth ER is where fats, carbohydrates, and proteins are manufactured to make up the cellular membrane material for a new membrane for the cell.
- Lysosomes are sacs that contain digestive enzymes. They are membranous walled organelles and are like small sacs in an active stage. They are considered "digestive bags" or suicide bags. They also digest and destroy microbes that invade the cell so it acts as a protector but sometimes kill the cells instead of protecting it. Paradoxically!
- Ribosomes are protein factories and make enzymes and other protein compounds for the cell. They may be freely found throughout the cells cytoplasm or found temporally attached to the rough endoplasmic reticulum.
- Centrioles are rod shaped structures and are paired organelles and exist in every cell. They are part of the cells reproduction and lie at right angles to each other near the nucleus.
- Cilia are found on the exposed or free are surfaces of some cells and are fine hair like extensions. These hairs like extensions are capable of moving together in a wave like fashion over the cells surface. Often they have highly specialized functions.
- Flagella are projections extending from the cell surface and are also capable of movement. Flagellum is single flagella and is much larger than cilia.

- Nucleus – is the brain of the cell. It contains all of the genetic information that controls every process in a cell. The nucleus appears to be a very simple structure, a small sphere in the central part of the cell. It is not simple; it is complex and has a critical role in the cells very existence. The nucleus is surrounded by two membranes called a nuclear envelope. Inside this membrane, the nucleus contains a special cell material called the nucleoplasm. The nucleus, like the cell, has specialized structures which are as follows: nuclear envelope, nucleoplasm, nucleolus, and chromatin granules. The nucleolus is the programming for the protein formation and programs the formation of Ribosomes in the nucleus to then migrate out of the nucleus into the cytoplasm and produce protein.
  - Chromatin granules – are the threadlike structures that are proteins and genetic material called DNA. DNA or deoxyribonucleic acid is the chemical "blue print" of the body with all of the genetic material. During cell division DNA molecules become tightly coiled and look like short, rod like structures called chromosomes.

The Cell Wall is a structure that is found in plants and prokaryotes. It provides structure and protection. Cells become specialized to perform a particular function within an organism. This is usually characteristic of a cell in a multi-cellular organism like humans. The same cells work together to provide a specific function or perform a common cause. An example would be nerve cells or skin cells where each has a specific purpose. Nerve cells are part of the nervous system and help to transport messages back and forth to the brain, where skin cells are for protection against pathogens and for waterproofing and containment of the tissues and are part of the integumentary system in the human body.

Cell Functions and Processes

ADP & ATP

The breakdown of materials in a cell is required to take complex molecules and become more simple molecules which then can be used as needed by the cell or to form other different molecules. ATP is Adenosine TriPhosphate and is the energy used by the cell and /or organisms for its cellular operations. ATP is broken down into ADP; energy is released from the bond of the molecules being broken as an exothermic process. AS ATP is used ADP is cycled to build ATP back up so it can be used as energy. Glucose, a sugar, is used in the processes to make ATP. This is a reason that glucose in the cell is such a basic necessity. It can be transformed into a form of energy for the cells use.

Respiration

Respiration is the process where glucose is broken down to be used by the cell. Both plant and animal cells create ATP through respiration. Through a series of processes, glucose with other enzymes release energy as ATP. In plants, glucose is acquired by photosynthesis for the respiration process. When oxygen is present, cell respiration occurs in three steps in different parts of the cell. These steps are glycolysis, The Krebs's Cycle, and the cytochrome system. This type of respiration is aerobic or requires the presence of oxygen.

- Glycolysis
    - takes place in the cytoplasm
    - hydrogen is removed from the glucose (oxidation)
    - the hydrogen is transported to the cristae of the mitochondria
- The Krebs's Cycle
    - takes the pyruvic acid from glycolysis
    - Consists of three main actions:
        - There is an infinite cycle of the carbon from the pyruvic acid which binds with another carbon compound that is always present
        - Carbon Dioxide (CO^2) is released, because Oxygen (O^2) is present in the respiration (aerobic Respiration) so it combines with the carbon from the carbon compounds
            - This is the reason animal's (Animal Kingdom) breathing is the intake of oxygen and the expulsion of carbon dioxide.
        - Enzymes oxidize the carbon compounds
            - The hydrogen is transported to the cristae of the mitochondria of the cell.
- The Cytochrome System
    - also called the hydrogen carrier system
        - This is where the hydrogen has been transported to the cristae of the mitochondria
        - Here the hydrogen acceptors get the hydrogen and then the coenzemes are then oxidized releasing hydrogen and energy
        - As a byproduct of respiration water is formed.

Movement of Substances In or Out of the Cell

Each cell has a cell membrane which is a selectively permeable membrane and it only allows certain things in and out of the cell. There are various methods that are used for exchange of materials. There are three methods in which ions are transported through the cell membrane into the cell: active transport, passive transport and simple diffusion. The cell continuously has heavy traffic in both directions across the cell membrane. This includes water, food, gases, wastes, and other substances in and out of the cell that are a result of a number of processes. These processes are considered transport process. There are two general transport processes; passive transport and active transport. Simply put, passive transport does not require the expenditure of energy by the cell where active transport does require energy to be used.

- ℘ The passive transport processes
  - ങ Passive transport processes don't require any cellular energy to move molecules from areas of high concentration to areas of low concentration until the two sides reach equilibrium. This is also considered the movement "down a concentration gradient".
  - ങ These processes include:
    - ℔ Diffusion
      - ℵ Osmosis
      - ℵ Dialysis
    - ℔ Filtration
      - ℑ Diffusion
        - δ Is the passive transport process where no energy is used and the substance scatters evenly throughout the available space? The substances diffuse across the membrane rapidly and bidirectionally. This is a movement down a concentration gradient for both sides so there is equilibrium, the balancing of the concentrations of the two solutions over time.
        - δ Osmosis and Dialysis are forms of diffusion but are specialized. Both occur across a selectively permeable membrane. Osmosis the diffusion of water and Dialysis is the diffusion of solutes, dissolved particles in water across a selectively permeable membrane.
        - δ Filtration is the movement of both water and solutions through a membrane by hydrostatic pressure, force of a fluid pushing on one side of the membrane that is greater than the other. Filtration always occurs down a hydrostatic pressure gradient with two fluids with unequal hydrostatic pressure gradient and separated by a membrane. Water, and diffusible solutes or particles filter out of the solution with the higher hydrostatic pressure into the one with the lower hydrostatic pressure.
  - ങ Active transport requires energy to move substances and it acquires the energy from a specific important chemical substance called ATP, Adenosine Triphosphate. ATP is produced from the cell's mitochondria where the energy is produced from nutrients and releases energy to do work. Active transport processes moves substances from areas of low concentration to areas of high concentration. It is an uphill movement or "up a concentration gradient". Active transport can only take place through living membranes and only in living cells.
    - ℘ Active transport processes include:
      - ℵ on pumps
      - ℵ Phagocytosis
      - ℵ Pinocytosis

- Ion pumps are protein structures in the cell membrane called carriers. They use energy from ATP to move "up a concentration gradient". Some ion pumps work with other carriers so that glucose or amino acids are transported along with ions.
    - Sodium potassium pump and calcium pumps are examples of ion pumps.
- Phagocytosis is the process when a cell permits a substance or objects to be engulfed and eats the foreign material. The cell membrane forms a pocket around the material to be moved into the cell.
- Pinocytosis is the process when active transport is used to get fluids or dissolved substances into the cell. This is when the cell actually drinks.

Cell Reproduction

All human and animal cells don't live forever and therefore cell reproduction is required. The cell reproduction process is called mitosis. The nucleus of a cell contains two nucleic acids, DNA and RNA, and is crucial in the protein synthesis for reproduction.

Genes

A gene is a specific segment of base pairs in a chromosome. As stated before all types of base pairs are the same in chromosomes but the sequence of the base pairs is not always the same. This is extremely important because the sequence in each gene of each chromosome is what makes and determines the inherited traits. Humans have forty-six chromosomes in each body cell and the nuclear body DNA is the total genetic information package also called a genome. Each parent of a human gives twenty-three pairs of chromosomes that come together to form a new cell that becomes a new human. Yet no two humans inherit exactly the same traits. Genetic code is the storage of information in each gene.

DNA

DNA is arranged in a double helix structure where spirals of DNA are intertwined. a nucleotide is the building blocks of DNA and are called the unpaired base pair. There are only 4 types and they can only be paired a specific way called the complimentary base pairing. These nucleotides are adenine, thymine, cytosine, and quinine. DNA is placed on a double Helix and the nucleotides are situated in adjacent pairs on the double helix. The only way the nucleotides can pair up are adenine with thymine and quinine with cytosine.
Cells do not live forever so they must pass their genetic information on to new cells and replicate their DNA to be passed on. In DNA replication certain parts of the DNA, the genes have to be replicated and copied.

Cell Division

Cell reproduction requires mitosis (division of the nucleus and the cytoplasm), the result of two identical daughter cells with the same original cells genetic material. Prior to cell division is a period called interphase. The cell is in resting state only in relation to active cell division yet it is active in all other aspects. There are four stages of cell reproduction that are:
1. Prophase
2. Metaphase
3. Anaphase
4. Telophase

- Prophase
  - In the nucleus:
    - Chromatin granules become organized
    - Chromosomes become visible
    - Two strands from the chromosomes have formed called the chromatids.
    - Nuclear membrane is gone and the genetic material is free.
  - In the cytoplasm:
    - Centrioles move away from the nucleus.
    - Spindle fibers are formed.
- Metaphase
  - Chromosomes have aligned across the center of the cell.
  - Centrioles have migrated to the cells opposite ends.
  - Spindle fibers have attached to chromatids.
- Anaphase
  - The chromatids break apart and are separated and called chromosomes.
  - The chromosomes move towards the opposing ends of the cell towards the Centrioles of the cell along the spindle fibers.
  - A cleavage furrow appears and begins to divide the cell into two equal parts.
- Telophase
  - The cell division completes forming two identical daughter cells.
  - In the daughter cells the nucleus appears.
  - The nuclear envelope, nucleoplasm and nucleus appear.
  - The cytoplasm and organelles equally divide to surround the nucleus.
  - The two daughter cells become fully functional individual cells and go into interphase.

Cell Division and the Results

- Due to cell division the new identical cells replace cells that have become less functional, damaged, or destroyed. Mitosis in humans is usually during periods of body growth and takes place in groups of similar cells to form into tissues.
- If for some reason mitosis is unable to be continued by the body extra cells develop an abnormal mass of these proliferating cells called a neoplasm. There are two types of neoplasm growths, benign tumors or dangerous malignant tumors. Benign tumors are relatively harmless growths where dangerous malignant growths are cancerous growths.

Threats to the Cell

All organisms primary goal is survival. Organisms are meant to survive and reproduce. Viruses are tiny micro-organisms that are unable to replicate on their own so they are called obligate parasites. They have both living and non living characteristics. Viruses can be spread by being airborne, blood borne, fluid borne or contamination. The virus cell, before it reproduces in its host and dies, alters its genetic makeup of the cell to start coding for the materials it will need to replicate itself. With the cell altering its genetics more viruses can be produces which can affect more cells and continues its existence and its species.

Defenses

For defense organisms have to find something as a defense against these antigens such as, viruses, bacteria, diseases and fungi.

- There are the first line and second line of defenses
    - First Lines of Defense
        - These are directly in contact with the external environment
    - Second Line of Defenses
        - These are found within the body to deal with the antigen
            - Interferons are a protein released by a cell attacked by an antigen.
                - Interferons also attach to other cell receptors to communicate to begin coding for antiviral proteins which protect the cell by shutting it down.
            - White Blood cells are a means to attack these antigens in animals and humans. White blood cells create antibodies and certain antibodies are synthesized when an antigen is present. A white Blood Cell that produces a specific immune response is called a lymphocyte.
            - Cells also use phagocytosis. They use digestive enzymes to break down the antigen.
        - Immunity
        - Active immunity
            - Active immunity is when vaccines are used to expose the body to a particular antigen.
                - Vaccines are a particular antigen that is dead or severely weakened
                - The vaccine is administered into the body and the body then destroys the pathogens and stores some T-cells as memory.
                - T-cells are specific cells coded for a particular antigen and can be used whenever the body needs it.
                - Vaccines are artificially acquiring immunity where a naturally acquired immunity is a result of a genuine attack by a pathogen.
        - Passive Immunity
            - Passive Immunity is when immunity is acquired as a result of a genetic trait or traits that are passed on to the offspring to protect the offspring from a pathogenic threat.

Blank

Plants

Plant Cell Structure and Components

Plant's Structure and Components

Plant Cell Functions and Processes

Plant Cells and Animal Cells Differences

The Implications and Importance of Plants to Humans

Blank

Plant Cell Structure and Components

In plants the younger parts of the cells shape is generally round where in older parts they are more boxlike and as they become packed together can have up to 14 sides. A plant cell is bounded by a cell wall and the living portion of the cell is within the walls. The living portion of the cell is divided into two portions: the nucleus, or central control center; and the cytoplasm, a fluid in which membrane bound organelles are found.

- Cell Wall
    - A plant cell is bounded by a cell wall and the living portion of the cell is within the walls. Between adjacent plant cells and the primary cell's walls there is a pectic middle lamella. There is a secondary cell wall which is just inside of the primary wall. Both cellular walls consist mainly of cellulose, but the secondary cell wall may contain lignin and other substances. A flexible plasma membrane is the outer boundary of the protoplasm (cytoplasm and nucleus) and controls what enters and leaves the plant cell.

- Nucleus
    - A plant cell's nucleus is bound by a nuclear envelope with pores. The pores allow for movement of substances in and out of the nucleus. Within the nucleus is a number of chromosomes. The number present is specific to the organism. The nucleus is in the center of most cells and is responsible for storing and transmitting genetic information. The nucleus is surrounded by a selective nuclear envelope. Within the nucleus, DNA and proteins form a network of threads called chromatin. The chromatin becomes vital at the time of cell division as it becomes tightly condensed thus forming the rod like chromosomes with the enmeshed DNA. Within the nucleus is a filamentous region called the nucleolus which is not bound by a membrane.

- Cytoplasm
    - fluid in which membrane bound organelles are found
    - Organelles
        - A plant cell has a number of organelles. They are: Ribosomes, endoplasmic reticulum, Golgi apparatus, endosomes, mitochondria, Lysosomes, peroxisomes, cytoskeleton, chloroplasts, and vacuoles.
            - Ribosomes are the sites where protein molecules are synthesized from amino acids. Some Ribosomes are found bound to granular endoplasmic reticulum, while others are free in the cytoplasm.
            - The endoplasmic reticulum (ER) a network of membranes enclosing a singular continuous space. Rough ER gives the exterior surface a rough or granular appearance and is involved in packaging proteins for the Golgi apparatus. Smooth ER lacks is the site of lipid synthesis.
            - The Golgi apparatus is a membranous sac that changes and sorts proteins into secretory/transport vesicles and then delivers them to other cell organelles and the plasma membrane. The Golgi apparatus is usually located near the nucleus.
            - Endosomes are present to sort and direct vesicular traffic by pinching off vesicles or fusing with them. Endosomes are located between the plasma membrane and the Golgi apparatus. Endosomes are membrane-bound tubular and vesicular structures.
            - Mitochondria are the site of various chemical processes involved in the synthesis of energy packets, ATP. The mitochondria has two membranes, the

outer membrane is smooth, and the inner is folded into tubule structures called cristae. Mitochondria contain small amounts of DNA containing the genes for the synthesis of some mitochondrial proteins and the DNA only comes from the mother.

- Lysosomes are bound by a single membrane and contain highly acidic fluid that acts as digesting enzymes to break down bacteria and cell debris. They are part of the immune system of a cell.

- Peroxisomes consume oxygen and work to drive reactions that remove hydrogen from various molecules and are important for maintaining the chemical balances within the cell.

- The cytoskeleton is a group of filament like proteins that maintain and change cell shape and produce cell movements in animal and bacteria cells. In plants, it is responsible for maintaining the plants structures. It also forms tracks along which cell organelles move like a little highway inside the cell. There are three types of filaments.

  - Microfilaments are the thinnest and most abundant of the cytoskeleton proteins and can be assembled and disassembled as needed.

  - Intermediate filaments are slightly larger in diameter and are mostly in regions that are subjected to stress; these filaments are not capable of rapid disassembly once assembled.

  - Microtubules are hollow tubes composed of a protein called tubulin. They are found in the axons and long dendrite projections of nerve cells. These filaments are the thickest and most rigid yet are capable of rapid assembly and disassembly.

- Plastids are chloroplasts, chromoplasts or leucoplasts.

  - Chloroplasts have a matrix called the stroma. Enzymes are found in the stroma as well as grana—stacks of coin-shaped discs, called thylakoids, which is where photosynthesis takes place. Chloroplasts contain their own DNA yet rely on proteins from the nucleus.

- Vacuoles contain cell sap which is composed of dissolved substances and may include pigments. They are bound by a special membrane, called the tonoplast.

Plant's Structure and Components

Plant Organs

Plants are composed of three major organ groups: roots, stems and leaves. These organs are comprised of tissues working together for a common function. Tissues are made up of cells which are made of elements and atoms. Plant tissues are characterized and classified according to their structure and function and the organs that they form will be organized into patterns within a plant. There are three basic tissue patterns found in roots and stems which serve to delineate between woody dicot, herbaceous dicot and monocot plants.

- Meristematic Tissues are cells that are constantly dividing to produce new cells, they are called meristems. The new cells are small, six-sided boxy structures with a number of tiny vacuoles and a larger nucleus. The tissues that do not actively produce new cells are called nonmeristematic tissues. These are cells produced by the meristems and have formed into various shapes and sizes depending on their intended function in the plant. The tissues can be the same type or mixed and be considered simple tissues or complex tissues.

- Simple Tissues have three basic types named for the cell type that makes up its composition.

    - Tarenchyma tissue: These cells are the most abundant of all cell types with thin walls and with large vacuoles and various secretions. Some types of secretions are starch oils, tannins, and crystals. Some of the cells also have chloroplasts and form leaves called chlorenchyma for photosynthesis. The cells without chloroplasts form tissues that are used for food and water storage. These cells and tissues are what make up most of the edible parts of all fruits.

    - Collenchymas Tissue have cells that have living protoplasm and have a thickness to the cell walls, lie just below the epidermis and are elongated. The thick cell walls are still very pliable and yet strong. This tissue provides flexible support for plants, leaves and flowers. A good example of this type of tissue is the strings in celery.

    - Sclerenchyma Tissue: This tissues has cells with a secondary wall that is thick, tough and imbedded within lignin and are usually dead and are for structure and support.

    - Secretory cells are usually derive,ed from parenchyma cells and can function on their own or as a tissue. Due to cellular processes that take place they can leave behind substances that can accumulate in the cell and can be damaging. These substances are either isolated or moved outside of the plant body. Most of the substances are waste products but some can be of great value to humans commercially such as pine resin, nectar, oils in citrus, latex, perfumes, plant hormones and opium as well as medicines.

- Complex Tissues are tissues composed of more than one cell type. Xylem and phloem are the two most important complex tissues in a plant. Their primary function is to transport of water, ions and soluble food substances throughout the plant. Some other complex tissues include the epidermis and the perineum.

    - The epidermis forms a protective covering for all plant organs and allows the movement of water and gases in and out of the plant.
    - The perineum is mostly cork cells and forms the outer bark of woody plants.

Stems

A woody twig, or stem, is an axis with leaves attached. The leaves are arranged in various ways around and on the axis either alternately arranged, oppositely arranged, or whorled (found in groups of three or more.) The areas where the leaves attach to the stem are called nodes and the area between two nodes is called the internodes. The leaf is attached to the stem at the node by a stalk called the petiole. In the angle formed between the petiole and the stem you will find the axillary bud. This bud can become either new branches or they will form into flowers for the next season. Most buds are protected by bud scales which fall off as bud tissue begins to grow. At the tip of a twig there is a terminal bud, it is larger than an axillary bud and it is intended to extend the twig's length during the growing season. A terminal bud has bud scales on it and when it falls of it leaves a scar on the twig. You therefore can calculate the age of the twig by counting the bud scars.

Trees and shrubs that lose their leaves every year, deciduous plants, have characteristic leaf scars with dormant axillary buds directly above them. Tiny bundle scars can be found in the leaf scar and mark the location of food and water conducting tissues. These tiny bundle scars, based on the arrangement and their shape, can identify deciduous trees when the leaf structures are absent.

Monocots/Dicots

The two main divisions of flowering plants is monocots and dicots. A seed leaf, cotyledons function is storing food for the seedling. A monocotyledon (monocot) plant forms from seeds that have one embryonic seed leaf where a dicotyledon (dicot) plant forms from seeds that have two embryonic seed leaf. Cone bearing trees usually have multiple cotyledons in their seed structure.

Monocots:	Dicots:
One seed leaf—cotyledon	Two seed leaves—cotyledon
Flower components in threes or multiples of three	Flower components in fours or fives or multiples of fours or fives
Leaf veins are parallel	Leaf veins are branching and networked
No vascular or cork cambiums	Vascular cambium present, usually cork cambium present
Vascular bundles are scattered throughout the stem	Vascular bundles are arranged in a ring in the stem
One aperture (thin spot) in pollen grains	Three apertures in pollen grains

Roots

Dicots are nearly all flowering trees and shrubs, and about 75% of all flowering plants. Monocots are primarily herbaceous with little or no woody growth they include bulb producing plants, grasses, orchids and palms. Most dicot plants have taproot systems while monocot plants have fibrous root systems. The embryo root, called the radicle, grows and develops into the first root after seed germination. The radicle may thicken into a taproot with many branching roots, or it may develop into many adventitious roots which develops the fibrous root system. There are many plants that have a combination system meaning there is a primary taproot with many branching fibrous roots attached. Root hairs increase the contact surface area of the root system which allows for a larger amount of exchange with the surrounding soil.

Soil

The soil is where most plants grow, there are exceptions to this but not necessary to be discussed at this level. The resources that are available in the soil is what determines the life of a plant. The difference between the survival and death of a plant is directly related to the soil type and its quality. Soil is an integrate part to the earth and is vital to the existence of nearly all living things.

The environment is constantly changing. Due to this, soil and plants have a dynamic exchange with both living and nonliving things. This is the same kind of relationship that we have with plants because of the oxygen we breathe and the carbon dioxide the plants need to function. Soil is a composition of minerals and organic matter where there are pores or small spaces where air and water fill the space.

There are thousands of types of soil. Soil is classified by it's unique composition which is based on various factors acting upon the soil sample. These factors include climate, parent material, local topography, vegetation, living organisms, and time. Parent material is from the weathering of igneous, sedimentary and metamorphic rock. These three rock types are the basis for all soil formation and development. Minerals available in a soil directly relate to plant growth rates and the quality of the plant. Plants have essential elements required to even exist. These minerals are as follows: Carbon, Hydrogen, Nitrogen, Oxygen, Phosphorous, Potassium, Nitrogen, Sulfur, Calcium, Iron, Sodium, Magnesium, Chlorine, Copper, Manganese, Cobalt, Zinc, Molybdenum and Boron being the most common. Each plant however requires its own unique combination of some or all of these minerals and some even require some other minerals. When an element or mineral in the soil is lacking, a deficiency is present and the plant in that soil that needs that deficient element or mineral added or it will have specific characteristic symptoms of that deficiency.

Plant Leaves

Leaves are solar energy converters. They capture light energy and through the process of photosynthesis they are able to trap energy in the form of sugar molecules that are constructed from carbon dioxide and water (both found in the atmosphere). All the energy required by living organisms is ultimately dependent upon photosynthesis. Leaves are able to twist on their petioles, stalks, in order to maximize sun exposure and photosynthetic activity. Leaves are covered with a thin layer of epidermal cells which permit light to enter the interior of the leaf, yet protect the cells from physical damage. In addition to photosynthesis, leaves are involved in other vital plant functions. Respiration is a metabolic process which produces waste products. These products are deposited outside the plant when the leaves are shed. Leaves are also important to the movement of water absorbed by the roots and transported throughout the plant. The water that reaches the leaves mostly evaporates into the atmosphere via transpiration. Leaves are complex plant organs upon which life depends.

There are three major parts in a leaf: epidermis, mesophyll and veins. The epidermal layer is the surface of the leaf and is one cell thick. On the underside of the leaf the epidermis is interrupted by stomata. The epidermal cells look like jigsaw puzzle pieces fit tightly together and only in the lower level of the epidermis where the guard cells are do you find chloroplasts

Germination is when a seed, an embryonic plant that is resting, resumes its growth cycle. Flowering plants can have various germination cycles as short as a month to 150 years. When a plant completes its life cycle in a single growth season it is considered an annual. Perennials may take several seasons to many years to go from a germinated seed to a seed producing plant.

Flowers

Flowers come in all shapes, sizes, colors and arrangements, yet they all have certain characteristics that make them flowers. A flower starts as an embryonic primordium then develops into a bud that is found on the end of a specialized branch. The specialized branch at the end of a stalk is called the peduncle. The receptacle is a small pad-like swollen area on the very top of the peduncle. This serves as the platform for the flower parts. Whorls, which are three or more plant parts, are attached to the receptacle. The sepals are the outermost whorl and are usually green. Sometimes they are confused with leaves. They are usually three to five in number and are collectively referred to as the calyx. The second whorl of flower parts is the petals and is collectively referred to as the corolla. The corolla is usually extra-showy in order to attract pollinators. In wind-pollinated plants the corolla may be missing to maximize pollen exposure to the female flower parts. Just as the sepals in the calyx, the petals in the corolla may be fused together or separate individual units. Nestled inside the two outer whorls are the sexual organs of the flower. The stamen entail the male structure: a semi rigid filament with a sac called the anther dangling from the tip. Pollen grains develop in the anthers (a process which we will discuss in further detail later). Most anthers have slits or pores on the sides to accommodate pollen release. The female organs are collectively referred to as the pistil and include: a 'landing pad' at the top called the stigma, a slender stalk like style that leads to the swollen base called the ovary. The ovary will develop/ripen into a fruit.

There are names for the different ways that the flower parts are arranged with respect to the ovary. The ovary is said to be superior if the calyx and corolla are attached to the receptacle at the base of the ovary. If the receptacle grows up and around the ovary and the calyx and corolla are attached above it, then the ovary is said to be inferior. Inside the ovary is an egg-shaped ovule which is held in place within the ovary by means of a short stalk. The ovule is what develops into a seed. Fruits have seeds. Some flowers are produced all alone, while others are produced in clusters called inflorescences. An inflorescence is characterized by one peduncle with many little stalks serving individual flowers. The little stalks, in this case, are called pedicels and each stalk services one flower.

Fruit

A fruit is a mature or ripened ovary that usually contains seeds and can only come from flowering plants. A vegetable can consist of leaves, leaf petioles, specialized leaves, stems, roots, flowers and their peduncles, flower buds and or other parts of the plant. A fruit is by definition just the ovary part of a flower; therefore all fruits come exclusively from flowering plants.

Plant Defenses

Plants release hydrogen peroxide in response to the presence of a fungal invasion, which attacks by piercing the cell wall of a plant and breaking it down. This hydrogen peroxide (H^2O^2) is a double edged sword in its defense against the antigen. Hydrogen peroxide stops the breakdown of the cell wall because some pathogens will use pectinase, a digestive enzyme, to break down the cell wall barrier and invade the plant. The pectinase released by the fungus must be stopped. H^2O^2 is involved in stopping the action of this pectinase. Some of the hydrogen peroxide (H^2O^2) triggers the creation of phytoalexins.

Phytoalexins are similar to the antiviral proteins as a second line of defense. Phytoalexins are a group of hormones that inhibit protein synthesis and thus shut the cell down in the event of a pathogenic attack; much like in animal cells the shutting down of the protein production process.

- There are other barriers used by plants as a defense such as the following :
- Lignin is a strong type of molecule that provides plants with a defensive structure similar to that of fibrous proteins. It acts as a barrier and can be found in wood and is characteristically found in plants that have recently endured pathogen attack.
- Callose seals off sieve plates in the plant, effectively shutting off the transport of molecules around the organism. This is done to minimize the chance of the plant transporting infectious material inside itself, and halting the movement of materials that could be used by the pathogen in aid of replicating itself.
- Ethylene promotes leaf abscission. It is done to sever the plant of dead or dying plant matter. This is done to prevent the spread of infected material; therefore sacrificing infected sections of plant is more economical than taking the risk of the infection spreading.
- Galls and tannins are created by the plant to encapsulate foreign agents found within the plant. A gall is an instance where an infected cell that contains tannins becomes inflamed. These tannins play a protective role by segregating the foreign agent and its chemicals from the rest of the plant.

Plant Cell Functions and Processes

Oxidation-reduction reactions

OIL RIG, is a way to remember that oxidation is loss and reduction is gain. Oxidation results in the net loss of an electron or electrons, while reduction results in a net gain of an electron or electrons. The electrons come from compounds within the process or donated from previous processes. These chemical reactions are found throughout the processes within the cell to include photosynthesis and respiration.

Respiration

Respiration is the group of processes that utilizes the energy is stored through the photosynthetic processes. The steps in respiration are small enzyme-mediated steps that release tiny amounts of immediately available energy, the energy released is usually stored in ATP molecules which allow for even more efficient use of an organism's energy. Respiration occurs in the mitochondria and cytoplasm of cells.

- There are several forms of respiration:
  - aerobic
    - requires the presence of oxygen
  - anaerobic
    - occurs in the absence of oxygen
  - fermentation
    - occurs in the absence of oxygen
  - Certain types of bacteria and other organisms can carry on respiration without oxygen, so they will use either anaerobic respiration or fermentation. These two types of respiration compared to aerobic respiration releases quite a small amount of energy. Anaerobic respiration and fermentation is differentiated mainly in the way hydrogen is released and combined with other substances.

Photosynthesis

Photosynthesis is the process by which light energy is captured, converted and stored in simple sugar molecule. This process occurs in chloroplasts and other parts of green organisms. Photosynthesis transforms carbon dioxide into oxygen; therefore it is a backbone process: meaning that all life on earth depends on its function. Photosynthesis is the process that plants undertake to create organic materials from carbon dioxide and water, with the help of sunlight. Photosynthesis is the means that plants can obtain energy via light energy. The energy gained from light can be used in various processes mentioned below for the creation of energy that the plant will need to survive and grow. Photosynthesis is a reduction process, where hydrogen is reduced by a coenzyme, in respiration glucose is oxidized in an oxidation process.

The Chemical equation for Photosynthesis

$$6CO_2 + 12\,H_2O + \text{light energy} \rightarrow C_6H_{12}O_6 + 6O_2 + 6H_2O$$

Carbon + Water   Glucose + Oxygen + Water

Photosynthesis has two processes:

- Photolysis
    - the photochemical stage
- The Calvin Cycle
    - the thermo chemical stage
    - Photolysis
        - Photolysis occurs in the grana of a chloroplast where light is absorbed by the chlorophyll
            - Chlorophyll is a photosynthetic pigment that converts the light to chemical energy
        - Chlorophyll reacts with water (H^2O) and splits the oxygen and hydrogen molecules apart
        - The oxygen is released as a by-product and the hydrogen is then transported to be used by the Calvin cycle in the second stage of photosynthesis
        - The water is oxidized, hydrogen is removed and energy is gained in photolysis that will be required in the Calvin cycle

    - The Calvin Cycle
        - This process occurs in the stroma of chloroplasts
        - The carbon made available from breathing in animals, the carbon dioxide that is expelled enters this cycle
        - Like the Krebs's Cycle in respiration, a substrate is changed into carbon compounds to produce energy
        - In this phase of photosynthesis glucose is created for respiration from the carbon dioxide introduced into the cycle
        - The energy that is used up in the Calvin cycle is the energy that is made available during photolysis. The glucose that is made via the Calvin cycle can be used in respiration or a building block in forming starch and cellulose, materials that are commonly needed in plants

Limiting Factors in Photosynthesis

- Some factors affect the rate of photosynthesis in plants, are:
- Temperature plays a role in affecting the rate of photosynthesis. Enzymes involved in the photosynthetic process are directly affected by the temperature of the organism and its environment
- Light Intensity is also a limiting factor. If there is no sunlight, then the photolysis of water cannot occur without the light energy required.
- Carbon Dioxide concentration also plays a factor. It is due to the supplies of carbon dioxide required in the Calvin cycle stage

Comparison summary of photosynthesis and respiration:

Photosynthesis	Respiration
Energy stored in sugar molecules	Energy released from sugar molecules
Carbon dioxide and water used	Carbon dioxide and water released
Increases weight	Decreases weight
Requires light	Can occur in light or darkness
Occurs in chlorophyll	Occurs in all living cells
In green organisms, produces oxygen	Uses oxygen (aerobic respiration)
With light energy, produces ATP	With energy released from sugar, produces ATP

Plant Growth and Development

Plant growth can be determinate or indeterminate. Determinate plant growth means some plants will have a cycle of growth then a ceasing of growth, breakdown of tissues, and then death. They are fairly predictable. Other plants will be indeterminate. They will grow and remain active for hundreds of years. Their growth potential and cycle is indeterminate and there are many factors that can't really be predicated only hypothesized. Development refers to the growth and differentiation of cells into tissues, organs and systems of the plant from its beginning to its death or its life span.

Mitosis: Cell Cycle

Mitosis is a process by which a cell can reproduce itself including the number of chromosomes and the nature of the DNA will be identical to the original parent cell. Nothing we know of will grow or live indefinitely, so there must be some way to ensure the survival of the species. Reproduction is the only known way that a species survives and therefore is perpetuated or the species becomes extinct.

The cell cycle contains the process in which cells are either dividing or in between divisions. Cells that are not actively dividing are said to be in interphase, which has three different periods prior to mitosis, the division of the nucleous. The division of the rest of the cell occurs as an end result of mitosis and this process occurs in regions of active cell division, called meristems.

Mitosis is a process within the cell cycle that is divided into four phases
- Prophase
    - The chromosomes and their usual two-stranded nature becomes apparent
    - The nuclear envelope and membrane breaks down
- Metaphase
    - The chromosomes become aligned at the center of the cell
    - A spindle of fibers is develops
    - Some of the fibers attach to the chromosomes at their centromeres
- Anaphase
    - The sister chromatids of each chromosome, that is now called the daughter chromosomes, separate lengthwise and each group of daughter chromosomes migrates to the opposite ends of the cell
- Telophase
    - Is when the daughter chromosomes are grouped within a newly forming nuclear membrane which makes them separate nuclei
    - A wall forms between the two sets of daughter chromosomes thus creating two daughter cells

- In plants, as the cell wall is developing, vesicles of pectin merge forming a cell plate that eventually will become the middle lamella of the new cell wall.

- The key component of mitosis, to know, is that the daughter cells have the same chromosome number and are otherwise identical to the parent cell.

- In plants mitosis produces spores for the plants survival and its offspring. These offspring have identical cells and identical chromosomes to the parent cells and thus the processes are called asexual reproduction, without sexual reproduction.

Meiosis

Reproduction, the way for a species to perpetuate itself, is creating offspring. This can happen in several ways such as propagation, or by special cells called spores which are the products of mitosis. Most plants will undergo sexual reproduction which involves the production and recombining of sex cells called gametes, much like the reproduction of humans with sperm cells and egg cells that combine to form a single cell that is the offspring of the two cells. In flowering and cone-bearing plants this involves the production of seeds. The gametes produced are male and female, and when they combine together, the cells fuse and form a single cell called a zygote. The zygote is what will go on to become the plant embryo and eventually a mature, adult plant.

Meiosis is the process by which gametes, sex cells, are formed. It is unique because gametes have exactly half of the total number of chromosomes as the rest of the cells in the parent organism. When two gametes, each with half the number of chromosomes, get together they are able to restore the chromosome number to the same as the rest of the cells in the parent organism. When the zygote develops into a plant embryo and eventually a mature plant, it will have the exact number of chromosome specific to the species. The processes and steps in meiosis are very similar to mitosis yet are different.

All living cells have two sets of chromosomes, one from a male and one set from a female parent. The genes in the chromosomes control the characteristics of the offspring but the code from the male and female may not always be the same and therefore has to do with the genetics laws of how the offspring has which characteristics from which parent. For now, know that when the chromosomes code for the same characteristics from each parent they are called homologous chromosomes.

§ Phases of Meiosis:
- ○8 Meiosis forms from one cycle four cells with half the number of chromosomes as the parent cell. The daughter cells are usually never identical to each other or to the parent cell depending on the organism involved. Meiosis has two successive divisions which in plants occur without a pause. Mitosis takes roughly 24 hours, while meiosis takes up to two weeks and for some organisms can take longer from several weeks to even years.
- ○8 Division I (Reduction division)
  - ♑ the chromosome number is reduced to half the parent cell chromosome number. End result of division one is two cells.
  - ♑ Prophase I
    - א Chromosomes coil, becoming shorter and thicker, the two-stranded nature becomes apparent, two strands are called a chromatids and chromosomes are aligned in pairs. Each pair of chromosomes has four chromatids and they have a centromere attached in the center holding the four strands together.
    - א Nucleolus disassociates and nuclear envelope dissolves.
    - א Segments of the closely associated pairs of chromatids may be exchanged with each other between the pair members. This is called crossing-over. Each chromatid contains the original amount of DNA but now may have "traded" genetic material.
    - א The chromosomes separate. Some spindle fibers are forming and some are attaching to the centromeres of the chromosomes. The fibers extend from each pole of the cell.
  - ♑ Metaphase I
    - א The chromosomes align at the center of the cell, with the centromeres and spindle fibers apparent.
    - א The two chromatids, from each chromosome, function as a single unit.
  - ♑ Anaphase I
    - א The chromosomes move to the ends of the cell.
    - א The chromosomes do not separate from each other and at each end of the cell there is half of the cells total chromosome number.
    - א If crossing over occurred in prophase then the chromosomes will consist of original DNA and DNA from a homologous chromosome.
    - א The centromere remains intact in each pair of chromatids.
  - ♑ Telophase I
    - א What occurs in this step, depends on the species involved, as they may revert to interphase or proceed directly to division II.
    - א If they revert to interphase, they will only do so partially and the chromosomes will become longer and thinner.
    - א Nuclear envelopes will not form, but the nucleoli will generally recluster.
    - א Telophase is over when the original cell becomes two cells or two nuclei.
- ○8 Division II (Equational division)
  - ♑ The chromosome number stays the same, the cells replicate and result in four cells. The events closely resemble the events in mitosis, except that there is no duplication of DNA during the interphase that may or may not occur between the two divisions.

- Prophase II
  - Chromosomes of both nuclei become shorter and thicker. The two-stranded nature becomes apparent once again.
- Metaphase II
  - Chromosomes align their centromeres along the center.
  - Spindle fibers form and attach to each centromere, extending from one pole to the other.
- Anaphase II
  - The centromeres and chromatids of each chromosome separate and begin their migration to the opposite poles.
- Telophase II
  - The coils of chromatids—now called chromosomes again—relax and the chromosomes become longer and thinner.
  - Nuclear envelopes and nucleoli reform for each group of chromosomes.
  - New cell walls form between the four groups of chromosomes.
  - Each set of chromosomes in the four new cells, has exactly half of the chromosome number of the original number.

Plant Reproduction

Plants have a unique reproduction system that is referred to as Alternation of Generations. In plants, one member of every original pair of chromosomes end up in each resulting cell, which means each cell has one set of plants chromosomes. None of the daughter cells is identical to the parent cell. A cell with one set of chromosomes is called haploid and a cell with two sets is called diploid. It is the diploid cell that undergoes meiosis and results in four haploid cells.

Sex cells, or gametes, of an organism are haploid and when a zygote is formed, the zygote is diploid. This is always true, no matter how many chromosomes an organism might have. Alternation of generations refers to a plant's life cycle including sexual reproduction that is characterized by alternating between a diploid sporophyte phase and a haploid gametophyte phase. The structure, type and functions of a cell are all determined by chromosomes that are found in the nucleus of a cell. These chromosomes are composed of DNA, the acronym for deoxyribonucleic acid. This DNA determines all the characteristics of an organism, and contains all the genetic material that makes us who we are. This information is passed on from generation to generation in a species, so the information within them can be passed on for the offspring to harness in their lifetime.

Plant Cells and Animal Cells Differences

Cells are cells. The basis of each (cell animal, plant, specialized, or general) are similar but have differences because they are part of a different organism, are designed to be a part of a system and become specialized with a specific function. Due to this evolution of the simplest cell there are differences in animal cells and plant cells.

- The primary differences are as follows:
    Animal cells don't have a cell wall. They have a cell plasma membrane for the outer boundary. Without this cell wall animal cells require support from some type of skeleton externally or internally. During telophase of mitosis in animals, the cell pinches in the center to form two cells. Animal cells have Centrioles. The vacuoles in animal cells can be present but if they are present they are usually very tiny, whereas in plant cells, they are present and quite large.
    - Plant cells have a cell wall and this cell wall is what gives support and thicken to strengthen plants.
    - Plant cells have plasmodesmata to connect protoplasts but this is absent in animal cells as well as plastids also known as chloroplast. During the telophase in plant cells of mitosis a cell plate is formed at the beginning of the division for the structure. Animal cells don't create a cell plate because there is no cell wall.

The Implications and Importance of Plants to Humans

- Plants first and foremost provide a constant replenishment of oxygen and use the carbon dioxide that is expelled with each breath that every living animal takes.
- Stems from plants are important since they are vital for humans' survival.
    - Humans, from the beginning of time, have used stems in various forms for heat, shelter, paper, food, and so much more.
    - In today's society stems provide building material, paper products, paper fiber, food, or a derivative product from the stem.
- Leaves have their importance as well, some are good and some addictive but are part of our human existence.
    - Leaves provide us food, medicine, textile fibers, as well as hemp products and even tobacco products.
    - Leaves give us insecticides. Cocaine, Aspirin, Aloe Vera are all from leaves and all have benefits to us as humans.
    - Leaves also provide us with visual and other aesthetic values.

Blank

Protists

Microorganisms

Phylum Mastigophora

Flagellates

Sporozoa

Blank

Microorganisms

Microorganisms also known as Protists are much diversified. They are found in a variety of different types of habitats on the Earth. They vary in size and shape. Microorganisms have fundamentally the same body structure. Many have specialized body parts for carrying out specific body functions. Some microorganisms can actually create their own food materials. They reproduce rapidly and in large numbers. The protists are both harmful and yet some are helpful to the human race.

Bacteria

- is microscopic in size
- it's length is measured in microns
  - 1 micron (μ) is approximately 1/25,400 inch
- Shapes
  - Coccus
    - Spherical or round
  - Bacillus
    - Cylindrical or rod shaped
  - Spirillum
    - Spiral-shaped or curved
- Types
  - Autotrophic organisms
    - get nutrients and from the nutrients they obtain energy
    - They can manufacture their own food
      - phototrophic
        - Uses sunlight as energy
        - Through series of reactions sunlight changed into chemical energy
      - chemotropic
        - Uses inorganic compounds as a source of energy such as Nitrogen, Iron, and Sulfur compounds
        - Through series of reactions these compounds are changed into their own nutrients
  - Heterotrophic organisms
    - Must obtain their nutrients from living hosts or dead and decaying organisms
    - They cannot manufacture their own food and nutrients
      - Sarasitic
        - Use living plants, animals and humans as a source for nutrients
      - Saprophytic
        - Obtain their nutrients from dead and decaying organisms

- Reproduction of Bacteria
  - Mostly all bacteria reproduce asexually
    - This without a sperm and an egg
    - Also referred to as binary fission
  - Bacteria reproduce rapidly and reach maturity as soon as a few minutes
  - The offspring as soon as they are mature in minutes are capable of reproducing
  - Some do reproduce by sexual reproduction
    - Particle species have two mating types one y and one x
    - y does not have genetic particles present and x does
    - In reproduction, injects their chromosomes and sex determining particles into the y bacteria through small tubes that connect them
    - The x bacteria dies after this process and then fission takes place

- Bacteria's Importance
  - Bacteria can be a double-sided sword because it can be both beneficial and harmful to humans, animals and plants
  - Whether a specific species is beneficial, harmful or both depends on various factors:
    - The type of species it is
    - The nutrients used as a source of energy
    - Substances produced by the bacteria's metabolic activity
    - The specific situation or condition the bacteria is in
    - How it affects other organisms

- Beneficial Bacteria
  - Groups responsible for decay
    - They decompose complex organic compounds and convert them to simple chemical substances
    - The simple chemicals are available for plants and animals to live and grow
    - Nitrogen needed by all organisms due to decaying bacteria allow it to complete a cycle of going from the atmosphere (air) to water, soil and living things
    - Nitrogen, through various reactions and processes due to bacteria, goes from combined into complex molecules to being separated into simple nitrogen then all over again
  - Bacteria is used in various processes for man's benefit:
    - Tanning of leather
    - Processing flax into linen
    - Curing tobacco
  - Making food, such as
    - Cheese
    - Butter
    - Buttermilk
    - Vinegar
    - Sauerkraut

- Harmful Bacteria
  - Are parasites – an organism that lives on or inside a living organism (the host)
  - Presence of parasitic bacteria can result in disease
  - Ways it is harmful:
  - Destroys the tissue of the host
  - Bacteria produce poisonous substances called toxins
  - Toxins' strength depends on species
  - One of the strongest toxins produced by bacteria is botulism – botulism is food poisoning
  - Diseases in man are caused by bacteria, examples are:
    - Cholera
    - Tetanus
    - Dipextery
    - Pneumonia
    - Tuberculosis
    - Bubonic Plague
    - Syphilis

Phylum Mastigophora

- both animal like and yet plant like as well
  - Flagellates
    - Euglena is an example of a flagellate
      - contain in their body chlorophyll, why it is plant like
      - can't make own food must obtain it externally, why animal like
      - can be found almost anywhere as their habitat
      - they are the most adaptable of all living things
    - 0.01mm in length generally
      - has a tapered body
      - move by whipping an organelle called the flagella that is located at the end of the body

Phylum Protozoa

- Protozoa means literally "first animal"
- Animal like protists
  - Sarcaodina (Sarcodines)
    - Amoeba is an example of a sarcoadine
    - 0.25mm in length generally
    - No definite shape, constantly changing it shape
    - Move by pseudopodia, "false feet", they are temporary finger like extensions of the body used to extend in the direction it wants to move
    - Don't have mouths to obtain nutrients, use pseudopodia and then food vacuoles surround the food to digest it
  - Ciliophora (Ciliates)
    - Paramecium is an example of a ciliate
    - 0.12mm to 0.3mm in length generally
    - It shape is somewhat rigid and resembles the shape of the sole of a slipper
    - Often referred to as the "slipper animal"
    - Use cilia to move from one place to another, the cilia are small hair like extension from the body beat in a coordinated fashion in the direction it wants to move by moving the cilia in a forward motion and the pulling the water back very similar to the use of a boat oar
    - They have mouths to ingest food

Sporozoa (Sporozoans)

- Plasmodium is an example of a sporozoan
- Have a variety of different shapes
- They are parasites
- They infect a particular part of the host and never really need to move because they are either on or in their source of food
- These parasites cause diseases in living things that they infect
- They rely on other organisms to carry them from place to place like flies, leeches, and mosquitoes
- Malaria is an example of a disease caused by this protozoa

Animals

Lower Intervertebrates

Higher Intervertebrates

The Human Being

Blank

Lower Intervertebrates

- ∞ Sponges
  - ⌀ Aquatic and mostly marine
  - ⌀ Multicellular, however they act more or less independently
  - ⌀ Cells are not coordinated in functioning
  - ⌀ Respond to stimuli very slightly and only in the immediate area affected by the stimulus
  - ⌀ Most primitive of all multicellular animals
  - ⌀ They are the only animal that can rebuild itself out of their own individual original cells.
- ∞ Coelenterates
  - ⌀ Tissue level of organization among animals
  - ⌀ Jelly fish, hydra, sea anemones corals
  - ⌀ The flowers of the sea
  - ⌀ Highly colored
  - ⌀ Aquatic, mostly marine
  - ⌀ Carnivorous
  - ⌀ Basic structure is sack like body with tentacles, circular plan, no front or back
    - ℘ Two structures
    - ℘ Radial symmetry
      - ℽ Can be cut in half midway
    - ℘ Polyps
      - ℽ Round base, cylindrical stalk and central cavity
- ∞ Flatworms
  - ⌀ Organ-system level of organization among animals
  - ⌀ Have a flat body
  - ⌀ Aquatic
  - ⌀ First recognizable head which is facing forward and moves so this is anterior end
  - ⌀ Posterior end is the opposite end
  - ⌀ Dorsal is the upper or back
  - ⌀ Ventral is the under or lower
  - ⌀ They have a bilateral symmetry
    - ℘ Three groups:
      - ℽ Planarians
      - ℽ Flukes
      - ℽ Tapeworms
    - ℘ Body compose of three layers:
      - ℽ Ectoderm
      - ℽ Mesoderm
      - ℽ Endoderm
- ∞ Roundworms
  - ⌀ Can be soil or free being parasitic
  - ⌀ Slender, elongated bodies with tapered ends
  - ⌀ More developed structures than flatworms
  - ⌀ Has a digestive system
  - ⌀ Two openings to the central cavity
  - ⌀ Well developed muscular system, nervous system and reproductive system
  - ⌀ Sexual reproduction

- Mollusks
    - They are marine, freshwater or land
    - Important source of food for man
    - Snails, oysters, clams
    - Characteristics:
        - Soft-bodies some have shells
        - Mantle – protective fold
        - Radula – having ribbon of curved teeth that may extend from the mouth to tear food to pieces
        - Gills
        - Circulatory system with a pumping organ (heart)
        - Eggs fertilized either internally or externally, and the fertilized egg turns into a larva and eventually develop into an adult mullosk
    - Three groups:
        - Gastropods:
            - Spiral-shaped shells; if has one shell, has one opening
            - Move on ventral foot
            - Head with sensory tentacles
        - Bivalves
            - Clams, oysters, scallops and mussels
            - Bilaterally symmetrical and are flattened from side to side
            - they are bivalves due to two shells valves, hinged at the back
            - they have no head
            - the feed by filtering microorganisms
        - Cephalopods
            - Squid, octopus, cuttlefish, nautilus
            - Much more complex in structure
            - Have an active existance
            - They have tentacles around their mouth and
            - They are carnivourous

The Human Being

Basic Terms for Reference Points

- Positions are used throughout biology especially in regards to the human body. The anatomical position to which all other positions are in reference to is standing erect with the arms at the sides and palms turned forward with the head and feet pointed forward. The following are other positions used in reference to the body and in relation to all other directional terms used to describe organs, parts, regions etc.
  - Supine; the body laying face up
  - Prone; the body laying face down
  - Superior; upper above towards head
  - Inferior; downward lower towards feet
  - Anterior; front part or in front of or ventral
  - Posterior; back part or in back of or dorsal
  - Medial; or towards the midline of the item
  - Lateral; or away from the middle or towards the sides
  - Proximal; towards or nearest to the point of origin of the structure
  - Distal; away from or farthest from the point of origin
  - Superficial; nearest to the surface
  - Deep; farther away from the surface
- Then there are the terms sectioned of the body are based on planes.
  - Sagittal – lengthwise running front to back to be the right to left side.
    - Midsagittal plane is two equal halves running lengthwise
  - Frontal – lengthwise from side to side with anterior and posterior
  - Transverse – horizontal or crosswise to divide into an upper and lower portion.

Cells are the smallest structural units of the body. The organ systems are its largest structural units. The body functions as a unit as a group of integrated systems and function as a whole.

A living organism has organization. The body is a complex structure composed of smaller structures. This begins with atoms and molecules at the chemical level. The pure existence of life depends on a balance of the correct levels and proportions of chemical substances in the body. The body's organization of the atoms and molecules to cells that form tissues that make up organs that in turn makes up systems until finally you have a body that functions as a whole.

If broken down, the body cannot function and ceases to exist as a unified complex organism that interacts structurally and functionally with all its components to ensure survival. This relative consistency of the body's internal environment is referred to as homeostasis or the body's internal stability. There are external factors that constantly affect this balance. The body has built-in self-regulatory systems called a feedback loop which is an integrated communication control system. This feedback loop involves sensors that detect a change which notifies the control center which responds to an effector which has an effect on the condition and the sensor continually feed information back and forth to the control center. An example is when cold causes a disturbance in body temperature which is detected by the body's receptors which notify the brain which signal the muscles to shiver causing the body temperature to rise, bringing back the body's internal stability. This entire process involves the brain, nerve endings, and muscles. Everything is related to everything else. Homeostasis is part of the survival of the individual and of the genes and is the body's most important focus, "Survival of the fittest". This depends on the maintenance and restoration of the relative consistency of internal environment. The organs function together to maintain this stability. All functions of the body are related to age directly where peak efficiency is at a young age and decreases with time. Since age is directly related to the efficiency of the body functions lets briefly review the development and growth of the human body.

Development and Growth of the Body

The general growth of the human body begins at conception. The categories of the life span of a human are: Prenatal, Neonatal, Infancy, Childhood, Preadolescence, Adolescence, Adult, and an Older Adult.

Human Being's Life Span

- Prenatal
  - Prenatal is the period from conception to the birth of the fetus. This process is usually considered thirty-seven to forty weeks to be classified as a full term pregnancy. There are three phases within the prenatal period;
    - Embryonic Phase This is from fertilization to conception to the end of the eighth week of gestation.
      - Fetal phase is from the first day of the ninth week to the fortieth week of gestation.
    - Birth process is also called parturition. This is the period when changes take place for both the mother and the fetus as the stages of labor proceed. Labor is the process that results in the birth of a baby. The three stages of labor are:
      - Stage one which is the period from the onset of uterine contractions that cause the effacement (thinning) of the cervix to the complete dilation of the cervix
      - Stage two is the period from the time of maximum effacement and dilation of the cervix until the fetus, now considered a baby, exits from the uterus through the vagina (birth canal) to the exterior of the mother's body
      - Stage three is the process of the release and expulsion of the placenta through the vagina
- Neonatal Period
  - The neonatal period is considered the first four weeks of the newborns life after birth.
    - The baby has numerous changes that take place within seconds. The baby goes from total dependency on the mother to total self support: cardiovascular, circulatory, and respiratory systems
- Infancy
  - During the infancy period there are many developmental changes from the forth week after birth to eighteen months of age
  - These changes include doubling birth weight by four months and tripling birth weight by twelve months of age
  - The infant's length by twelve months is increased by fifty percent from birth. The infant's spine has a definite apparent lumbar curvature
  - The infant has rapid development of both nervous and muscular systems and a decrease of baby fat
- Childhood
  - Childhood is the period from the end of infancy or eighteen months to about six years of age.
  - The growth and development still continues at a rapid rate but monthly changes become less apparent by age six
  - They become less chubby, and lose the babyish look. The child begins to lose the baby teeth.
- Preadolescence
  - Preadolescent period is from the end of six years of life to the beginning of puberty, about the age of twelve to fourteen years old
  - The nervous and muscular systems continue to develop rapidly and they have developed numerous coordination skills

- During this time all of the baby teeth are lost and the permanent teeth have all erupted. Sometimes maybe even third year molars and wisdom teeth have erupted
- Adolescence
  - Adolescence is usually the period between thirteen and nineteen years of age
  - There is a rapid physical growth and reproductive sexual characteristic changes begin and continue steadily until the body's organs are sexually mature
  - At this point they are able to become sexually active and can reproduce
  - For females; changes include voice and facial changes. Hormones released cause changes in the breasts and the beginning of the menstrual cycle and they are now fertile and able to become pregnant
  - For males; hormones released cause changes in their voice, growth spurts, body and facial hair growth, and they become taller and have an increase in muscularity. At the end of this period puberty ceases and maturity is reached
- Adult
  - Adulthood is the period of maturity and no more true growth and development occurs
  - New cells are still being produced but simply for regeneration purposes
  - Adulthood is characterized by maintenance of the body, its organs, and its tissues
  - Maturity in adulthood includes maturation of bones, full closure of growth plates, and other structures take their adult placement
  - Also degeneration of the body and its functions begins
- Older Adult
  - Older Adult is when many changes take place due to aging
  - In general all of the body's systems begin to decrease optimal functioning and fail to work as efficiently
  - Bones change in texture, shape, and calcification and are more fragile. Bone spurs develop around joints
  - The skin begins to sag, skin wrinkles, and develop pigmentation spots
  - Hair thinning or even hair loss occurs
  - Bladder problems appear
  - For women they cease to be fertile and go through menopause

Tissues in the Body

As noted before cells make up tissues which make up organs which make up systems.

- There are four main types of tissues which make up organs
  - Epithelial
  - Connective
  - Muscle
  - Nervous
  - Epithelial Tissue covers the body, many of its parts and lines the body cavities.
    - The cells are packed close together from continuous sheets that have no blood vessels. It functions for protection, secretion, and absorption
  - Connective Tissue has the most varied forms. Is the most absorbent tissue and is the most widely distributed
    - Connective tissue is like delicate, paper thin webs, as well as strong, tough and even as a fluid
    - Its functions are as varied as its structure. It is for connection, protection, support, insulation, flexibility, to withstand pressure, transportation, a nutrient reservoir, and blood cell formation

- Muscle Tissue is considered the movement specialist of the body. Due to the high degree contractibility, muscle cells if injured are slow to heal and are replaced by scar tissue. There are three types of muscle tissue:
    - <u>Skeletal</u> attaches to bones and can be voluntarily controlled
    - <u>Cardiac</u> forms the walls of the heart and the heart beat is due to the involuntary regular contractions of the cardiac muscle tissue
    - <u>Smooth</u> is involuntary muscle tissue because it cannot be consciously controlled by the body. This tissue helps form the walls of blood vessels and hollow organs like the intestines and other tube like shaped body parts
- Nervous tissue is specifically for rapid communication through the body in relation to control of body functions and the body's structures
    - Nervous or nerve cells are made up of a cell body; one axon (carries nerve impulse away from the cell body) and one or more dendrites that carry nerve impulses towards the body cells

The Organs and the Systems of the Body

An organ is made up of tissues that are made up of cells. Two or more tissues work together and are organized in a specific way to perform a complex function that can't be done by any tissue alone and form a structure called an organ. These organs are grouped together and arranged so they can perform a complex function no single organ could accomplish and are called a system. The body has eleven major systems made up different groups of organs.

These systems are;

1. Integumentary
2. Skeletal
3. Muscular
4. Nervous
5. Circulatory
6. Endocrine
7. Lymphatic
8. Respiratory
9. Digestive
10. Urinary
11. Reproductive

System	Function	Structure/Organs
Integumentary	Protection Body temperature regulation Synthesizes chemicals Sophisticated sense organ	Skin Appendages: hair, nails, sweat glands oil glands Sense Receptors
Skeletal	Support Movement Mineral Storage Formation of Blood cells	Bones Joints

Muscular	Movement
	Body posture maintenance
	Heat production
	Support
		Muscles
		  Voluntary
		  Smooth
		  Cardiac

Nervous	Communication Integration Control Sensory stimulus recognition Production of nerve impulses	Brain Spinal Cord Nerves Sense Organs
Endocrine	Secretes Hormones directly into the blood Communication & integration control Control is slow & of long duration Hormone regulation of: growth, metabolism, reproduction, fluid &electrolyte balance	Pancreas Ovaries Testes
Circulatory	Transportation Regulation of body temperature Immunity (body defense)	Heart Blood vessels
Lymphatic	Transportation Immunity (body defense)	Spleen Thymus Lymph nodes Lymphatic Vessels

System	Function	Structure/Organs
Respiratory	Exchange of waste gas (co2) for oxygen in the lungs Controls area of gas exchange in the lungs alveoli Filtration of irritants from intake air Regulation of bodies acid base balance	Lungs Nose Bronchi Trachea Larynx
Digestive	Mechanical & Chemical breakdown (digestion) of food Absorption of nutrients Undigested waste product that is eliminated is called feces Appendix is a structural but not a functional part of the digestive system; however an inflammation of it is appendicitis.	**Primary:** Mouth Pharynx Esophagus Stomach Small Intestine Large Intestine Rectum Anal Canal **Accessory:** Teeth Salivary Glands Tongue Liver Gall Bladder Pancreas Appendix
Urinary	Cleaning or the cleaning of the blood of the waste products called urine Electrolyte balance Water balance Acid-base balance Urinary & reproductive functions in males Urethra	Kidneys Urinary Bladder Ureters Urethra
Reproductive	Survival of species Production of sex reproductive cells Growth development and birth of offspring Nourishment of offspring Production of sex hormones	**Male:** Gonads/Testes Prostate Penis Scrotum Vas Deferens Urethra **Female:** Ovaries Uterus Fallopian Tubes Vagina Vulva Breasts

Practice Test for Biology

1. What is it called for the body's internal environment to be kept stable and consistent for the survival of the individual and its genes?
   - A. Histogenesis
   - B. Hemopoiesis
   - C. Homeostasis
   - D. Hyperopia

2. What is the term used for instability due to a lack of the normal glucose concentration needed and the body does not function properly?
   - A. Glycogenolipis
   - B. Hypoglycemia
   - C. Hyperglycemia
   - D. Glucagon

3. What is the only one kind of cell that has a flagellum in the human body?
   - A. Ova cell
   - B. Sperm cell
   - C. Ovum cell
   - D. Daughter cell

4. A cube of sugar is placed at the bottom of a cup of coffee, sits for a few minutes, and the sugar then has disbursed through the coffee. This is an example of?
   - A. Diffusion
   - B. Osmosis
   - C. Dialysis
   - D. Filtration

5. During a process of diffusion, one side of a membrane has a 15% salt solution and the other side has a 5% salt solution. What type of movement on each side is this?
   - A. Up a concentration gradient, up a concentration gradient
   - B. Up a concentration gradient, down a concentration gradient
   - C. Down a concentration gradient, up a concentration gradient
   - D. Down a concentration gradient, own a concentration gradient

6. When you put a red blood cell into an isotonic solution, the red blood cell will:
   - A. Swell.
   - B. Shrink.
   - C. Not change.

7. Each cell has three principle parts, they are:
   - A. Cell wall, nucleus, plasma membrane
   - B. Cell membrane, mitochondria, nucleus
   - C. Plasma membrane, nucleus, cytoplasm
   - D. Cell membrane, nucleus, ribosome

8. What is it called when a cell "drinks" or acquires liquids or dissolved substances into the cell across the plasma membrane?
    A. Osmosis
    B. Pinocytosis
    C. Dialysis
    D. Phagocytosis

9. Which one is considered the least complex of all the structural parts of the body?
    A. Cell
    B. System
    C. Tissue
    D. Organ

10. What is the dominant function of any living thing or the body?
    A. Nourishment
    B. Reproduction
    C. Survival
    D. Protection

11. What are the names of the two different planes that are used in science that divide the body into sections of the upper and lower and the two equal halves of the right and left, respectively?
    A. Sagital plane, traverse plane
    B. Traverse plane, coronal plane
    C. Sagital plane, coronal plane
    D. Traverse plane, midsagital plane

12. The body's internal environment, such as temperature, remaining relatively constant is considered ?
    A. Histogenesis
    B. Homeostasis
    C. Hydrostatic
    D. Hypotonic

13. What part of the body is considered to be the most distal?
    A. None
    B. Ear
    C. Finger
    D. Toe

14. What is the term given to the study of the parts and the functions of an organism or of living things?
    A. Anatomy
    B. Biology
    C. Physiology
    D. Chemistry

15. Which type of muscle is considered voluntary?
    A. Skeletal
    B. Smooth
    C. Cardiac
    D. Visceral

16. Which muscular tissue type is an involuntary tissue?
    A. Skeletal
    B. Cardiac
    C. Smooth
    D. Visceral

17. Which stage of mitosis is the chromosomes aligning themselves across the center of the cell?
    A. Prophase
    B. Anaphase
    C. Telophase
    D. Metaphase

18. Which stage of mitosis is when the cytoplasm is divided, also called cytokineses?
    A. Prophase
    B. Anaphase
    C. Telophase
    D. Metaphase

19. Which stage of mitosis is when the nuclear envelope, the nuclear plasm and genetic code, is freed into the cytoplasm?
    A. Prophase
    B. Anaphase
    C. Telophase
    D. Metaphase

20. Which is a form of active transport?
    A. Osmosis
    B. Diffusion
    C. Ion pump
    D. Dialysis

21. What transport process is required for substances to "move" up a concentration gradient?
    A. Passive
    B. Engaging
    C. Active
    D. Synthesis

22. Which is considered the "protein factories"?
    A. Mitochondria
    B. Ribosomes
    C. Rough endoplasmic reticulum
    D. Smooth endoplasmic reticulum

23. What collects and transports proteins made in the cell?
    A. Mitochondria
    B. Ribosomes
    C. Rough endoplasmic reticulum
    D. Smooth endoplasmic reticulum

24. In the cell, which organelle is called the chemical processing and packaging center?
    A. Smooth ER
    B. Golgi Apparatus
    C. Mitochondria
    D. Lyposomes

25. The cell structure that is a molecule made up of sugar, phosphate, adenine, thymine, guanine and cytosine is often abbreviated as?
    A. ER
    B. RNA
    C. DNA
    D. ATP

26. What tissue is considered the most abundant, widely distributed tissue in the body, has relatively few cells in its cellular matrix and has multiple types, appearances and functions?
    A. Epithelial
    B. Connective
    C. Nervous
    D. Muscle

27. In a double helix, there are base pairs that are always composed of adenine-thymine or quinine-cytosine which compose the steps in a sequence which differs in different molecules. What is the name of this specific sequence?
    A. Genes
    B. DNA
    C. Chromosomes
    D. RNA

28. When a DNA molecule's strands are pulled apart, the unpaired bases will be paired up again, and each base always attracts its complimentary base. Which is the proper pairing of the four bases to form the two base pairs?
    A. Adenine-cytosine & thymine-quinine
    B. Quinine-thymine & adenine-cytosine
    C. Cytosine-thymine & adenine-quinine
    D. Thymine-adenine & cytosine-quinine

29. What vegetable is considered a monocot plant?
    A. Peas
    B. Corn
    C. Carrot
    D. Radish

30. Which plant would be classified as a dicot?
    A. Bradford pear tree
    B. Palm tree
    C. Centipede grass
    D. Kentucky red fescue grass

31. Avid gardeners use compost piles they tend to on their property and use in their flowerbeds, gardens and potting. What kind of proteist is responsible for the richness of this garden additive and rich soil?
    A. Flagellates
    B. Viruses
    C. Bacteria
    D. Amoebas

32. What type of bacteria is a decomposer of organisms by breaking down dead plants and animals into simple elements to be returned to the environment?
    A. Phototrophic
    B. Parasitic
    C. Saprophytic
    D. Demotrophic

33. Bacteria that enter a human body to obtain its nutrients are considered what type of bacteria?
    A. Phototropic
    B. Parasitic
    C. Saprophytic
    D. Demotrophic

34. If a bacteria can reproduce and reach maturity in 21 minutes and all offspring can reproduce, how many cycles of reproduction to maturity would take place in approximately 14 hours?
    A. 4
    B. 8
    C. 32
    D. 40

35. Bacteria reproduce asexually to produce new offspring, and the cell splits approximately two equal halves. What is the process by which this asexual reproduction takes place?
    A. Meiosis
    B. Mitosis
    C. Binary fission
    D. Binary division

36. What provides both the bacillus type and spirillum type bacteria with a means of movement?
    A. Cilia
    B. Flagella
    C. Tentacles
    D. Pseudopodia

37. What unit is used to measure length of bacteria?
    A. Micron
    B. Millimeter
    C. Centimeter
    D. Inch

38. What type of bacteria is considered an autotrophic bacterium that obtains its nutrients from inorganic compounds such as iron, sulfur and nitrogen?
    A. Chemotropic
    B. Phototropic
    C. Parasitic
    D. Saprophytic

39. Dead and decaying organisms are used by what type of bacteria to obtain its nutrients?
    A. Chemotropic
    B. Phototropic
    C. Parasitic
    D. Saprophytic

40. Paramecium use which of the following, that are short, hair-like projections, to move?
    A. Flagella
    B. Cilia
    C. Tentacles
    D. Pseudopodia

41. When an amoeba moves away from a stimulus, such as an intense light, this response is called a(n):
    A. Positive response
    B. Direct response
    C. Negative response
    D. Indirect response

42. What species is responsible for the replenishment of the nitrogen supply in the soil by its processes?
    A. Protists
    B. Protozoan
    C. Flagellates
    D. Bacteria

43. What microorganism has some characteristics that are animal-like and some that are plant-like?
    A. Euglena
    B. Paramecium
    C. Amoeba
    D. Plasmodium

44. Based on the levels of organization on the cellular level, living things that function independently and are single cells are called what?
    A. Colonial
    B. Unicellular
    C. Organism
    D. Multicellular

45. What are the two chemicals that are formed by plants and photosynthesis?
    A. Sugar and oxygen
    B. Sugar and water
    C. Sugar and chlorophyll
    D. Sugar and carbon dioxide

46. What is a gaseous byproduct given off by animals?
    A. Oxygen
    B. Carbon dioxide
    C. Hydrogen
    D. Nitrogen

47. What does an organism need to contain to be able to carry on photosynthesis?
    A. Chlorophyll
    B. Carbon dioxide
    C. Sugar
    D. Oxygen

48. Why do trees kill the grass around them?
    A. Use all the water in the soil
    B. Prevent sunlight from reaching the grass
    C. Poison the grass
    D. Take all the nutrients from the grass

49. What are the two raw materials needed for photosynthesis?
    A. Sunlight and oxygen
    B. Chlorophyll and water
    C. Carbon dioxide and water
    D. Carbon dioxide and Oxygen

50. What would earth not have if there were no green plants?
    A. Nitrogen
    B. Fungi
    C. Oxygen
    D. Sunlight

Practice Test for Biology Answers

1. C	26. B
2. B	27. C
3. B	28. D
4. A	29. B
5. D	30. A
6. C	31. C
7. C	32. C
8. B	33. B
9. A	34. D
10. C	35. C
11. D	36. B
12. B	37. A
13. D	38. A
14. C	39. D
15. A	40. B
16. B	41. C
17. D	42. D
18. C	43. A
19. A	44. B
20. C	45. A
21. C	46. B
22. B	47. A
23. C	48. B
24. B	49. C
25. C	50. C

Comprehensive Review Section for Chemistry

Introduction

Chemistry Fundamentals

Chemical Reactions and Equations

Calculations in Chemistry

Blank

Introduction

Chemistry is an experimental science in which a consistent system of measurements is used.

International System of Units

Scientists throughout the world use the International System of Units (Système International or SI)
- SI is based on the metric system.
  - In the United States the metric system in not used on an everyday basis.
    - It is necessary to perform conversions between the English system and the SI system.
    - The United States English system of measurement is considered the no common or standard system
  - A disadvantage of the SI system is that the size of the units sometimes end up being extremely large or small
    - Due to this disadvantage another set of conversions needed to be made within the SI system.
    - SI units are modified through the use of prefixes and the movement of the decimal placement based on these prefix equalities.

Dimensional Analysis

Dimensional analysis is a useful tool for solving problems that involve unit conversions.
- By knowing what you are given and what you need, ie the units, you can avoid many common errors encountered in chemistry problems.
- The common errors often simply are due to incorrect conversions or incorrect units for the answer.
- Dimensional analysis can also help when you are not sure where to begin with a problem.

Scientific Law

- Scientific Law is also called natural law
- Scientific Law or Natural law is a statement based on observed behavior of matter to which there are no known exceptions.
- The laws, before they became labeled, have undergone experiments to prove or disprove them and therefore have been validated to be laws.

These topics are reviewed and explained with problems in the "*Comprehensive Review Section of General Science*"

Chemistry Fundamentals

Matter

- Matter
  - Matter is anything that takes up space and has mass
  - Mass
    - Mass is a measure of the quantity of matter of an item.
    - It's unit of measurement is kg, g, mg, lb, oz, metric tonne, short ton

Energy

- Energy is the capacity to do work or transfer heat
- All chemical process are accomplished by energy changes
  - There are 2 principal types of energy:
    - Kinetic energy
      - Kinetic energy is a body in motion possesses energy because of its motion
      - Matter possesses energy by virtue of its motion
      - This energy is easily transferred between objects
    - Potential energy
      - Potential energy is the energy matter possesses because of its makeup, composition or its position
- Forms of energy
  - Light
  - Heat
  - Electrical
  - Mechanical
  - Chemical
- Energy Processes
  - There are two types of processes that involve some form of a energy change
    - Exothermic processes
      - Processes that release energy into its surroundings in either chemical reactions or physical changes
        - In exothermic processes that are chemical reactions, chemical energy usually is released as heat energy
        - Burning is an example of an exothermic processes
          - Burning is also referred to as a combustion reaction
      - Types of energy changes in exothermic processes
        - Heat energy
        - Light energy w/out heat
        - Electrical energy w/out heat or light
    - Endothermic Processes
      - Processes that absorb heat energy in either chemical reactions or physical changes
      - Types of energy changes

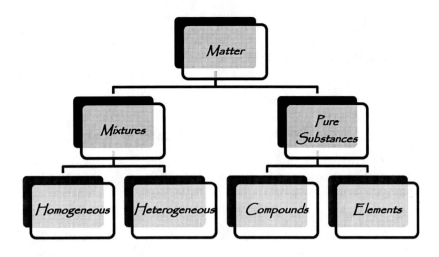

Substances

- All substances are either pure chemical substances or mixtures.
  - Pure Substances, Pure Chemical Substances,
    - Pure substances to be separated or broken down into individual components require some form of a chemical or nuclear reaction in order to separate them
    - Pure chemical substances can be further divided into elements or compounds
      - Elements
      - Compounds

Mixtures

- Mixtures can be separated or broken down into their separate individual components by using some form of a physical process
- Mixtures can be either heterogeneous or homogeneous.
- Heterogeneous
- Homogeneous
  - Homogeneous mixtures are also called solutions
- Substances have both chemical properties and physical properties
  - Chemical properties
    - Chemical properties of a substance are the characteristics that can be observed and are exhibited as matter undergoes chemical changes
    - Chemical properties of substances are always related to the kind of chemical changes that the substance undergoes
    - All chemical properties are intensive properties
  - Physical properties
    - Physical properties of a substance are characteristics that can be observed and describe the substance
    - Physical properties are the characteristics exhibited with no changes to its chemical composition, components, chemical identity or make up
    - Categories of Physical Properties
      - Color
      - Hardness
      - Density
      - Volume
      - Length
      - Mass
      - Rigidness
      - Expansioness
      - Compressability
      - Melting point
      - Freezing point
      - State/phase
      - Thermal conductivity
      - Electrical conductivity
      - Time
      - Electric current
      - Temperature
      - Luminous intensity
      - Amount of, quantity

- ℘ An example of a physical change is as follows
  - ♈ Water
    - ♌ The formation of gas water (steam) from liquid water, by boiling (heating it till it is at or above is boiling point)
    - ♌ The formation of solid water (ice) from liquid water, by freezing (taking it below its freezing point)
    - ♌ The formation of liquid water (water) from solid water(ice),by melting (heating it till it is above is freezing point
    - ♌ In all of the examples the liquid water (it's natural physical state) looks very different physically however, its chemical identity, makeup, and components is the same for all
- ℘ Physical properties can be classified as either intensive properties or extensive properties
  - ♈ Intensive property
    - ♌ An intensive property is independent of the amount of the sample
    - ♌ It does not vary based on the amount of the sample of the substance
  - ♈ Extensive property
    - ♌ An extensive property is dependent on the amount of the sample
    - ♌ It does vary based on the amount of the sample of the substance

Density

- ℠ Density is an intensive physical property
  - ⚶ Density is the inverse relationship of the mass of an object and it's volume
  - ⚶ Density is easily stated as the objects mass divided by its volume.

$$d = \frac{m}{v}$$

  - ⚶ Density's unit of measurement is g/ml for a liquid and g/cm^3 for a solid Note: $1ml=1cm^3$
  - ⚶ Note that most substances expand or contract when heated or cooled, therefore the density of a substance is dependent are temperature dependent

Laws of Matter and / or Energy

- ℠ There are three laws that are about Matter, and/or energy:
  - ⚶ Law of Conservation of Matter:
    - ℘ There is no observable or detectable change in the gravity of matter during a chemical reaction or during a physical change
  - ⚶ Law of Conservation of Energy:
    - ℘ Energy cannot be created nor destroyed in a chemical reaction or physical change. It can only be converted from one from to another
  - ⚶ Law of Conservation of Matter and Energy:
    - ℘ The combined amount of matter and energy in the universe is fixed
  - ⚶ The relationship between matter and energy was summarized by Albert Einstein's equation $E=mc^2$ or the energy released is equal to the product of the mass of matter transformed and the speed of light squared

States of Matter

- Matter of a substance may be changed by adding or removing heat energy from it.
- This physical property and physical change is referred to as "The Three States of Matter"
- Water being a substance of matter is a common and good example of how a substance can be changed or converted by adding or removing heat energy from a substance.
- The general process of how the substance, water, can be changed from one state of matter to another was explained previously under the "*physical properties/physical changes*" area.
  - "The Three States of Matter"
    - The states of matter are also referred to as the phase of matter or of the substance. Therefore the word state and phase are interchangeable.
  - The Three States of Matter is another way that all matter is classified.
    - Solid
    - Liquid
    - Gas
    - Solids
      - A solid has a definite shape and volume.
      - Ice
        - water as a solid
      - Silver, Aluminum, Iron and Copper are examples of substances that are solids in its natural state elementally.
    - Liquids
      - A liquid has a definite volume, but takes the shape of its container.
        - Water
          - water as a liquid
          - water is an example of a substance that is a compound and is liquid in its nature state
        - Mercury, Lithium, Sodium, Potassium, Calcium, and Bromine are examples of substances that are liquids in its natural state elementally
    - Gases
      - A gas has neither a definite volume nor a definite shape
        - Steam
          - water as a gas
        - hydrogen, oxygen, fluorine, chlorine, iodine and helium are examples of substances that are gases in their natural state elementally

Chemical Changes (reactions) & Physical Changes

- Matter goes through chemical changes and /or physical changes
- Energy is required for a chemical or a physical change to take place
- In both types of changes energy is either absorbed or released
  - Chemical Changes
    - Chemical changes take place on a molecular level
    - A chemical change always produces one or more new substances
    - In chemical changes one or more substances are used up or at least partially
    - In chemical changes energy is absorbed or released
    - During a chemical change the substances exhibit their chemical properties

- A chemical reaction (or chemical change) produces substances that are chemically different from the starting materials
  - Chemical Change examples are
    - Formation of water from hydrogen and oxygen in the atmosphere
    - Rusting of an iron pan
    - Mixing hydrochloric acid and sodium hydroxide to make salt and water
- Physical Changes
  - Physical changes are concerned with energy and states of matter
  - A physical change does not produce a molecular substance
  - A substances physical properties are usually chaged significantly as matter under goes a physical change
  - A physical change may clue you that a chemical change has also taken place
    - Changes in color
    - A change in temperature such as warming
    - A formation of a solid from two liquids
  - Changes in state or phase (melting, freezing, vaporization, condensation, sublimation) are physical changes
    - Physical Change examples are
    - Crushing a can
    - Melting an ice cube
    - Breaking a bottle

Phase Transitions

- Substances that go from one state (phase) to another go through a transition that is either endothermic or exothermic
  - Condensation - gas to liquid
  - Fusion (or freezing) - liquid to solid
  - Melting - solid to liquid
  - Sublimation - solid to gas
  - Vaporization - liquid or solid to gas

Solutions

- A solution is a homogeneous mixture of two or more components
- A solution is the final product when a substance is dissolved completely in a liquid
  - The dissolving agent is the solvent.
  - The substance which is dissolved is the solute.
  - The components of a solution are atoms, ions, or molecules, which makes them 10^{-9} m or smaller in diameter.
    - Example: sugar and water

Suspensions

- The particles in suspensions are larger than those found in solutions. Components of a suspension can be evenly distributed by a mechanical means, like by shaking the contents, but the components will settle out.
  - Example: oil and water

Colloids

- A mixture where particles of various sizes that are in between the particle sizes found in solutions and suspensions
- They can be mixed in such a way that they remain evenly distributed throughout the medium without settling out
- A colloidal dispersion consists of colloids in a dispersing medium
  - Milk

Other Dispersions

- Liquids, solids, and gases all may be mixed to form colloidal dispersions
  - Aerosols: solid or liquid particles in a gas
    - Smoke is a solid in a gas
    - Fog is a liquid in a gas
  - Sols: solid particles in a liquid
    - Milk of Magnesia is a sol with solid magnesium hydroxide in water
  - Emulsions: liquid particles in liquid
    - Mayonnaise is oil in water
  - Gels: liquids in solid
    - Gelatin is protein in water
    - Quicksand is sand in water
- Telling the differences
  - Suspensions will eventually separate
  - Solutions with a beam of light passing through it is not visible
  - Colloids with a beam of light passing through it will be reflected by the larger particles in the colloid and the light beam will be visible.

The Following are Changes that Affect the Composition of our Atmosphere.

- Oxygen gas changes to ozone during thunderstorms
- Freezing rain develops when a warm air mass overrides a cold air mass
- Carbon dioxide is a byproduct of the combustion of gasoline in an automobile engine and is produced
- Fog forms from water vapor when the temperature drops below the dew point
- Solid waste decomposes in landfills and produces methane gas

Types of Solutions

- Solutes
  - Substances dissolved in a liquid are called a solute
- Solvents
  - The liquid the solute is dissolved in is called the solvent
  - Water is the most abundant and common solvent
  - Water is the most abundant and common molecule found in the human body
    - A majority of the chemical reactions in the human body involve molecules dissolved in water
  - Water is also relatively the most abundant compound found on Earth

- Hydrophilic Molecules
    - Are molecules that easily dissolve in water
    - Are water loving molecules
    - They have polar groups or ionized functional groups
        - Polar groups
            - OH^-
        - ionized functional groups
            - COO^- or NH_2^+
- Hydrophobic Molecules
    - Are water-fearing molecules
    - Molecules that are not attracted to water
    - Molecules with electrically neutral covalent bonds
    - Molecules with carbon chains
        - When non-polar molecules are mixed with water two phases are formed.
            - Two layers are formed and they are usually distinct.
            - Oil and water when mixed and allowed to sit will be two distinct layers visible
- Amphipathic Molecules
    - This molecule has both hydrophilic and hydrophobic characteristics
    When mixed with water they form clusters with the hydrophilic molecules as polar bonds at the surface with contact with the water and the hydrophobic molecules as non polar bonds in the center of the clusters away from contact with water.

Concentration

- With regards to solutions, concentration is the amount of solute present in a unit volume of solution
- Concentration values do not reflect the number of molecules present

Acidity

- An acid is a molecule that releases protons in a solution
    - An acid releases Hydrogen ions
- A base is a molecule that can accept a proton
    - Acids and bases can be further divided into strengths
    - See the section on Acids and Bases

Bonding of Atoms

- Atoms are the basic building blocks of all types of matter
- Atoms form molecules when two or more are bonded together
    - A_1—bond—A_2 = Molecule: A_1A_2
- Atoms link to other atoms through chemicals bonds resulting from the strong attractive forces that exist between the atoms
    - Chemical bonds
        - In chemical bonds it is the valence electrons or the electrons found in an atom's outermost shell
        - The outer electrons interact when two atoms come towards each other due to the attraction from the + charges of the protons in the nucleus
        - Electrons repel each other but are attracted to the protons within atoms
        - This interaction of forces is how some atoms form bonds with each other and stick together

- The two main types of bonds between atoms are ionic bonds and covalent bonds
  - Ionic Bonds
    - Ionic bonds are formed when one atom accepts or donates one or more of its electrons to another atom
  - Covalent Bonds
    - A covalent bond is formed when electrons are shared between two atoms
    - Polar covalent bond is formed when the atoms do not always share the electrons equally
  - Metallic Bonds
    - Metallic Bond is when two metallic atoms share electrons
    - Electrons in metallic bonds may be shared between any of the metal atoms in is vicinity
- Electronegativity Values
  - If the values of two atoms are similar
    - Metallic bonds form between two metal atoms
    - Covalent bonds form between two non-metal atoms
    - Nonpolar covalent bonds form when the electronegativity values are very similar
  - If the values of two atoms are different
    - Polar bonds are bonds in which the electrons are shared unequally.
    - Ionic bonds are formed
    - Polar covalent bonds form when the electronegativity values are a little further apart
    - Unequal sharing of the electrons gives the atom with the higher share a slightly higher - charge where the other atom with the lesser share has a slightly higher + charge
- Hydrogen Bonds
  - Hydrogen bonds are weak bonds between the hydrogen atom in one polar bond and an oxygen or nitrogen atom in another polar bond
- Free Radical
  - An atom with a single electron in its outermost orbital is known as a free radical
  - Free radicals are highly reactive and short-lived
    - In an organism they are responsible for cellular breakdown
    - Free radicals acting on skin cells is sun damage to the skin

Atoms

- An atom is the smallest unit of matter with unique chemical properties
- Atoms are the chemical units of cell structure
- The particles within an atom are bound together by powerful forces
- Atoms cannot be divided using chemicals
- Atoms are composed of three fundamental particles
  - Protons
    - Protons carry a +1 positive charge
    - The number of protons is equal to the atomic number and determines the element
  - Neutrons
    - Neutrons have no charge
  - Electrons
    - Electrons carry a −1 negative charge
    - Electrons are attracted to the positive charge of the protons in the atoms nucleus
    - The number of protons usually equals the number of electrons
    - Elecrons are easier to add or remove from an atom than a proton or neutron

Atomic Number

- Is the number of protons in an atom
- Atoms that have the same atomic number but different mass numbers are called isotopes
- All atoms with atomic number 6 are carbon atoms
- Carbon atoms with mass numbers of 12 and 13 are isotopes of one another

Atomic Weight

- Is the number of protons and neutrons in an atom
- Is the average mass of atoms of an element

Isotopes

- Elements to exist in multiple forms
- Elements differ from one another by how many protons they contain
  - Protons and electrons always stay the same as the original element
- Varying the number of neutrons results in isotopes
- Varying the number of electrons results in ions
- Isotopes and ions of an atom with a constant number of protons are all variations of a single element
  - The human body depends upon four major elements for form and function: Hydrogen (H), Oxygen (O), Carbon (C), and Nitrogen (N)

Atomic Mass Number

- The mass number is the sum of the number of protons and neutrons of an element.
- Is not equal to the Atomic weight necessarily

Chemical Symbol

- Each element is assigned a unique chemical symbol
- The symbol for Hydrogen is H
- The symbol for Oxygen is O
- Some elements have symbols based on their names in languages other than English
- The symbol for iron is Fe, which is based on the Latin ferrum
- The atomic number, mass number, and chemical symbol are often combined to describe a given atom
- Atom of lithium (Li) with atomic number 3 and a mass number of 7 could be written $_3^7Li$.
- The atomic number and the symbol are both unique to a given element

Atomic Quantum Numbers

The properties of an atom's electron configuration are described by four quantum numbers: n, l, m, and s.

First Quantum Number

The first is the energy level quantum number, n. In an orbit, lower energy orbits are close to the source of attraction. The more energy you give a body in orbit, the further 'out' it goes. If you give the body enough energy, it will leave the system entirely. The same is true for an electron orbital. Higher values of n mean more energy for the electron and the corresponding radius of the electron cloud or orbital is further away from the nucleus. Values of n start at 1 and go up by integer amounts. The higher the value of n, the closer the corresponding energy levels are to each other. If enough energy is added to the electron, it will leave the atom and leave a positive ion behind.

Second Quantum Number

The second quantum number is the angular quantum number, l. Each value of n has multiple values of l ranging in values from 0 to (n-1).This quantum number determines the 'shape' of the electron cloud. In chemistry, there are names for each values of l. The first value, l = 0 called an s orbital; s orbitals are spherical, centered on the nucleus. The second, l = 1 is called a p orbital; p orbitals are usually polar and form a teardrop petal shape with the point towards the nucleus. l = 2 orbital is called a d orbital. These orbitals are similar to the p orbital shape, but with more 'petals' like a clover leaf. They can also have ring shapes around the base of the petals. The next orbital, l=3 is called an f orbital. These orbitals tend to look similar to d orbitals, but with even more 'petals'. Higher values of l have names that follow in alphabetical order.

Third Quantum Number

The third quantum number is the magnetic quantum number, m. These numbers were first discovered in spectroscopy when the gaseous elements were exposed to a magnetic field. The spectral line corresponding to a particular orbit would split into multiple lines when a magnetic field would be introduced across the gas. The number of split lines would be related to the angular quantum number. This relationship shows for every value of l, a corresponding set of values of m ranging from -l to l is found. This number determines the orbital's orientation in space. For example, p orbitals correspond to l=1, can have m values of -1, 0, 1. This would represent three different orientations in space for the twin petals of the p orbital shape. They are usually defined to be p_x, p_y, p_z to represent the axes they align with.

Fourth Quantum Number

The fourth quantum number is the spin quantum number, s. There are only two values for s, +½ and -½. These are also referred to as 'spin up' and 'spin down'. This number is used to explain behavior of individual electrons as if they were spinning in a clockwise or counterclockwise. The important part to orbitals is the fact that each value of m has two electrons and needed a way to distinguish them from one another.

These four numbers, n, l, m and s can be used to describe any electron in a stable atom. Each electron's quantum numbers are unique and cannot be shared by another electron in that atom. This property is called the Pauli Exclusion Principle. A stable atom has as many electrons as it does protons. The rules the electrons follow to orient themselves around their atom are simple once the rules governing the quantum numbers are understood.

The orbital names s, p, d, and f stand for names given to groups of lines in the spectra of the alkali metals. These line groups are called sharp, principal, diffuse, and fundamental.

The orbital letters are associated with the angular momentum quantum number, which is assigned an integer value from 0 to 3. s correlates to 0, p = 1, d = 2, and f = 3.The angular momentum quantum number can be used to give the shapes of the electronic orbital; s orbitals are spherical; p orbitals are polar. It may be simpler to think of these two letters in terms of orbital shapes.

The electron configuration of an atom denotes the distribution of electrons among available shells. The standard notation lists the subshell symbols, one after another. The number of electrons contained in each subshell is stated explicitly. The electron configuration of beryllium, with an atomic number of 4, is $1s^2 2s^2$.

Periodic Table

- The periodic table is the most important organizing principle in chemistry
- The periodic table lists two main numbers for each element
  - The atomic number is an integer that equals the number of protons
    - The atomic number for each element is written above its symbol
    - The periodic table is a list of elements arranged by atomic number
  - The atomic mass or a weighted average of all the isotope masses
- The number of neutrons is not given in the periodic table because it will vary with different isotopes
- The mass number of an element is the sum of the protons and neutrons
  - This also is not given in the periodic table because it varies with each isotope

Periods and Groups

- Elements in the periodic table are arranged in periods (rows) and groups (columns)
- Atomic number increases as you move across a row or period
  - Each square on the periodic table gives information about an element
  - element's symbol
  - atomic number
  - atomic weight.

Periods

- Rows of elements are called periods
  - Periods are labeled 1 to 7
  - The period number of an element signifies the highest energy level for an electron of the element
- The number of elements in a period increases as you go down the periodic table because there are an increase in the sublevels in each level as the energy level increases of the atom

Groups

- Columns in the table are called groups
- Columns of elements are to help define element groups
  - Groups are elements that have the same outer electron arrangement
    - The outer electrons are called valence electrons
    - Roman numerals listed above each group are the usual number of valence electrons

- Elements in a group share similar chemical properties or common properties
- Groups are labeled 1 to 18
  - Groups 1, 2, and 13 to 18 are called the main group elements
  - Groups 3 to 12 are the transition elements
  - The bottom two rows are called the lanthanides and actinides, respectively

Representative vs. Transition Elements

- There are two sets of groups
- Group A elements are called the representative elements
- Which have s or p sublevels as their outer orbitals
- Group B elements are the nonrepresentative elements
- Which have partly filled d sublevels (the transition elements) or partly filled f sublevels (the lanthanide series and the actinide series)
- An example of how the atomic electron configuration would be written as the valence electron configuration of a group VA element will be s^2p^3 with 5 valence electrons

Metals vs. Nonmetals

- Metals tend to lose electrons to form positive ions, whereas nonmetals tend to gain electrons to form negative ions

Elemental Symbol

- When writing the symbol for an element, a superscript indicates the mass number and a subscript indicates the atomic number
  - $^{14}_{6}C$ has a mass number of 14 and an atomic number of 6
- Most elements occur naturally as a mix of different isotopes.
  - An element's atomic mass is the weighted average of the isotope masses

Location on the Periodic Table

- Metals are located on the left side and the middle of the periodic table
  - Group IA and Group IIA (the alkali metals) are the most active metals
    - The transition elements, groups IB to VIIIB, are also considered metals

Molecular Geometry

- Molecular geometry or molecular structure is the three-dimensional arrangement of atoms within a molecule. It is important to be able to predict and understand the molecular structure of a molecule because many of the properties of a substance are determined by its geometry.
- Valence Electrons
    - The outermost electrons of an atom
    - The electrons that are most often involved in forming bonds and making molecules.

- Bonding Pairs are the pairs of electrons shared between atoms in a molecule and hold the atoms together.
- Count how many electron pairs are present, including both bonding pairs and lone pairs
    - A is used to represent the central atom
    - B indicates atoms surrounding A
    - E indicates the number of lone electron pairs
    - Bond angles are predicted in the following order:
- lone pair versus lone pair repulsion > lone pair versus bonding pair repulsion > bonding pair versus bonding pair repulsion

Geometry	Type	# of Electron Pairs	Examples
Linear	AB_2	2	$BeCl_2$
trigonal planar	AB_3	3	BF_3
tetrahedral	AB_4	4	CH_4
trigonal bipyramidal	AB_5	5	PCl_5
octohedral	AB_6	6	SF_6
Bent	AB_2E	3	SO_2
trigonal pyramidal	AB_3E	4	NH_3
Bent	AB_2E_2	4	H_2O
Seesaw	AB_4E	5	SF_4
T-shape	AB_3E_2	5	ClF_3
Linear	AB_2E_3	5	XeF_2
square pyramidal	AB_5E	6	BrF_5
square planar	AB_4E_2	6	XeF_4

Nomenclature

Atoms

- An atom is made up of a positively-charged nucleus surrounded by negatively-charged electrons
- The atom is neutral when there are equal numbers of protons and electrons. Ions are formed when there are unequal numbers of protons and electrons in an atom
  - A positive ion is called a cation
  - A negative ion is called an anion
- Ionic bonds form when one atom completely transfers one or more electrons to another atom, resulting in the formation of ions
- Positively charged ions (cations) are strongly attracted to negatively charged ions (anions)

Naming Chemical Compounds

- All chemical compounds can be named systematically by following a series of rules
  - Binary ionic compounds
    - Binary ionic compounds are named by identifying first the positive ion and then the negative ion
    - Polyatomic ions
      - Polyatomic ions involves memorizing the names and formulas of the most common ones
  - Anions
    - The chemical formula of covalent compounds can be easily determined from the systematic name of the compound
    - Greek prefixes are used to indicate the number of atoms of each element present in the compound
  - Chemical compounds
    - Common and systematic names
      - Common names are historical and tend not to identify the elements that make up the compound fs
      - Systematic name allows for correct identification of the cations and anions that together make up the ionic compound
  - Molecular compounds
    - Are composed solely of nonmetals
    - Binary molecular compound
      - Is a compound that contains only two elements
      - Prefixes are used to specify the number of atoms of each element
        - sulfur hexafluoride, SF_6

Roman Numerals

- Elements that can form more than one element a Roman numeral in parentheses follow the name of the element
- The Roman numeral naming convention has wider appeal because many ions have more than two valences than using the -ous or -ic
- Usually this is in metals
  - Fe^{3+} Iron (III)
  - Cu^+ Copper (I)
  - Cu^{2+} Copper (II)

-ous and -ic

- the endings -ous or -ic are used to denote the ionic charge of cations
- the endings are added to the Latin name of the element to represent the ions with lesser or greater charge
  - Iron
    - Fe^{2+} Ferrous
    - Fe^{3+} Ferric
  - Tin
    - Sn^{2+} Stannous
    - Sn^{4+} Stannic
  - Copper
    - Cu^+ Cuprous
    - Cu^{2+} Cupric

-ide

- The -ide ending is added to the name of a monoatomic ion of an element
  - Hydrogen
    - H^- Hydride
  - Flourine
    - F^- Fluoride
  - Oxygen
    - O^{2-} Oxide
  - Sulfur
    - S^{2-} Sulfide
  - Nitrogen
    - N^{3-} Nitride
  - Phosoporous
    - P^{3-} Phosphide

-ite and -ate

- Oxyanions are polyotomic ions that are anions that conatin oxygen
- When two oxyanions are formed from an element the rules are
  - The one with less oxygen is given a name ending in -ite
  - The one with more oxgyen is given a name that ends in -ate
    - Nitrogen and Oxygen
      - NO_2^- Nitrite
      - NO_3^- Nitrate
    - Sulfur and Oxygen
      - SO_3^{2-} Sulfite
      - SO_4^{2-} Sulfate

hypo- and per-

- When there are four oxyanions the prefixes hypo- and per- prefixes are used with the -ite and -ate suffixes
  - The hypo-prefix indicate less oxygen
  - The per - prefix indicates and more oxygen
    - ClO^- Hypochlorite
    - ClO_2^- Chlorite
    - ClO_3^- Chlorate
    - ClO_4^- Perchlorate

bi- and di- hydrogen

- Polyatomic anions sometimes gain one or more H^+ ions to form anions of a lower charge. These ions are named by adding the word hydrogen or dihydrogen in front of the name of the anion. It is still common to see and use the older naming convention in which the prefix bi- is used to indicate the addition of a single hydrogen ion.
  - HCO_3^- Hydrogen carbonate or bicarbonate
  - HSO_4^- Hydrogen sulfate or bisulfate
  - $H_2PO_4^-$ Dihydrogen phosphate

Acids & Bases

There are several methods of defining acids and bases.

Properties of Acids

- taste sour
- the word 'acid' comes from the Latin acere, which means 'sour'
- acids change litmus (a blue vegetable dye) from blue to red
- their aqueous solutions conduct electric current
  - an electrolyte
- react with bases to form salts and water
- evolve hydrogen gas (H_2) upon reaction with an active metal (such as alkali metals, alkaline earth metals, zinc, aluminum)

Properties of Bases

- taste bitter
- feel slippery or soapy
- bases don't change the color of litmus; they can turn red litmus back to blue
- their aqueous solutions conduct electric current
  - electrolytes
- react with acids to form salts and water

Examples of Common Acids

- citric acid (from certain fruits and veggies, notably citrus fruits)
- ascorbic acid (vitamin C, as from certain fruits)
- vinegar (5% acetic acid)
- carbonic acid (for carbonation of soft drinks)
- lactic acid (in buttermilk)

Examples of Common Bases

- detergents
- soap
- lye (NaOH)
- household ammonia (aqueous)

Electrolytes

- Strong electrolytes are completely dissociated into ions in water
- The acid or base molecule does not exist in aqueous solution, only ions
- Weak electrolytes are incompletely dissociated

Strong Acids

Strong acids completely dissociate in water, forming H^+ and an anion. There are six strong acids. The others are considered to be weak acids. You should commit the strong acids to memory:

- HCl - hydrochloric acid
- HNO_3 - nitric acid
- H_2SO_4 - sulfuric acid
- HBr - hydrobromic acid
- HI - hydroiodic acid
- $HClO_4$ - perchloric acid
- $H_2SO_4 \rightarrow H^+ + HSO_4^-$

Weak Acids

- Molecules that contain an ionizable proton
- A molecule with a formula starting with H usually is an acid
- A weak acid only partially dissociates in water to give H^+ and the anion
    - hydrofluoric acid, HF, and acetic acid, CH_3COOH
- Anions with an ionizable proton
    - $HSO^{4-} \rightarrow H^+ + SO_4^{2-}$
- Cations
    - transition metal cations
    - heavy metal cations with high charge
        - NH_4^+ dissociates into $NH_3 + H^+$

Strong Bases

- The hydroxides of the Group I and Group II metals usually are considered to be strong bases
- Strong bases dissociate 100% into the cation and OH^- (hydroxide ion)
    - LiOH - lithium hydroxide
    - NaOH - sodium hydroxide
    - KOH - potassium hydroxide
    - RbOH - rubidium hydroxide
    - CsOH - cesium hydroxide
    - $Ca(OH)_2$ - calcium hydroxide
    - $Sr(OH)_2$ - strontium hydroxide
    - $Ba(OH)_2$ - barium hydroxide

Weak Bases

- do not furnish OH^- ions by dissociation
- Weak bases are anions of weak acids
- Weak Bases react with water to generate OH^- ions
    - ammonia, NH_3,
    - diethylamine, $(CH_3CH_2)_2NH$.

Binary Acids

- Binary acids like Binary Compounds consist of two elements
- The prefix hydro- in front of the full name of the nonmetallic element
- The ending -ic is added for it being ab=n acid
    - Hydrofluoric Acid - HF
    - Hydrochloric Acid - HCl
    - Hydrobromic Acid - HBr
    - Hydroiodic Acid - HI
    - Hydrosulfuric Acid - H_2

Ternary Acids

- Ternary acids usually contain hydrogen, a nonmetal, and oxygen
- The -ic ending is added to the root name of the most common form of the acid
- The -ous ending is added to the most common form of the acid with one less oxygen atom
- The hypo- prefix is added to the -ous acid with one less oxygen atom and keeps the -ous ending
- The per- prefix and the -ic ending is added to the most common form of the acid with one more oxygen
    - Nitric Acid - HNO_3
    - Nitrous Acid - HNO_2
    - Hypochlorous Acid - HClO
    - Chlorous Acid - $HClO_2$
    - Chloric Acid - $HClO_3$
    - Perchloric Acid - $HClO_4$
    - Sulfuric Acid - H_2SO_4
    - Sulfurous Acid - H_2SO_3
    - Phosphoric Acid - H_3PO_4
    - Phosphorous Acid - H_3PO_3
    - Carbonic Acid - H_2CO_3
    - Acetic Acid - $HC_2H_3O_2$
    - Oxalic Acid - $H_2C_2O_4$
    - Boric Acid - H_3BO_3
    - Silicic Acid - H_2SiO_3

Bases

- Sodium Hydroxide - NaOH
- Potassium Hydroxide - KOH
- Ammonium Hydroxide - NH_4OH
- Calcium Hydroxide - $Ca(OH)_2$
- Magnesium Hydroxide $Mg(OH)_2$
- Barium Hydroxide - $Ba(OH)_2$
- Aluminum Hydroxide - $Al(OH)_3$
- Ferrous Hydroxide - $Fe(OH)_2$
- Iron (II) Hydroxide - $Fe(OH)_2$
- Ferric Hydroxide- $Fe(OH)_3$
- Iron (III) Hydroxide - $Fe(OH)_3$
- Zinc Hydroxide - $Zn(OH)_2$
- Lithium Hydroxide - LiOH

Gases

Gases

- All pure substances display similar behavior in the gas phase
- At 0° C and 1 atmosphere of pressure, one mole of every gas occupies about 22.4 liters of volume
- In a gas at 1 atmosphere, the molecules are approximately 10 diameters apart
- Gases occupy their containers uniformly and completely, liquids and solids due not
- Molar volumes of solids and liquids vary greatly due to states of matter properties from one substance to another
- Gases are easier to compress since their molecules are farther apart where in a liquid they are not.
- A gases volume can be reduced by an increase of pressure
  - If you double the pressure of a gas you then decrease its volume to a half its previous volume.
  - If you double the mass of a gas then you double its pressure
  - If you increase the temperature of a gas you then increase its pressure.
- Regardless the gas they have the same properties
  - Therefore you can derive a mathematical quantitative equation that relates volume, pressure, temperature, and the quantity of gas
- The Laws of Gases in formulas are key to understanding the more complex behavior of real gases

Ideal Gas Law:	Boyle's Law:	Law of Charles and	Dalton's Law:
$PV = nRT$	$PV = k_1$	Gay-Lussac:	$P_{tot} = P_a + P_b$
		$V = k_2T$	

where:
P is pressure, P_{tot} is total pressure, P_a and P_b are component pressures
V is volume
n is number of moles
T is temperature
k_1 and k_2 are constants
R is the ideal gas constant

Ideal Gas or Perfect Gas

An ideal gas is a gas whose pressure P, volume V, and temperature T are related by the ideal gas law
$PV = nRT$
Ideal gases are gas molecules with negligible size with an average molar kinetic energy dependent only on temperature. At low temperature, most gases behave enough like ideal gases that the ideal gas law can be applied to them.

Chemical Reactions & Chemical Equations

A chemical reaction is a process that is usually characterized by a chemical change in which the starting materials (reactants) are different from the products. Chemical reactions tend to involve the motion of electrons, leading to the formation and breaking of chemical bonds. There are several different types of chemical reactions and more than one way of classifying them.

- A chemical reaction is the process that occurs when two or more substances combine to produce a chemical change.
  - The important terms to remember are:
    - chemical equation
      - name given to the shorthand used to describe the steps of a chemical reaction
    - reactants
      - the starting materials for a chemical reaction; the substances that combine in the reaction
    - products
      - the substances that are formed as a result of a chemical reaction
    - chemical reaction rate
      - the speed at which a chemical reaction occurs
    - activation energy
      - the external energy that has to be added in order for a chemical reaction to occur
    - catalyst
      - a substance that helps a chemical reaction to occur (lowers the activation energy), but does not participate in the reaction itself

Inorganic Chemical Reactions

- Elements and compounds react with each other in various ways.
- There are four major categories
  - Combination Reactions
  - Decomposition Reactions
  - Single Displacement Reactions
  - Double Displacement Reactions
    - Combination Reactions
      - Two or more reactants form one product in a combination reaction
        - sulfur dioxide when sulfur is burned in air
          - $S\ (s) + O^2\ (g) \rightarrow SO^2\ (g)$
    - Decomposition Reactions
      - A compound breaks down into two or more substances and usually results from heating or electrolysis
        - Mercury (II) oxide broken down into its component elements
          - $2HgO\ (s) + heat \rightarrow 2Hg\ (l) + O^2\ (g)$
    - Single Displacement Reactions
      - An atom or ion of a single compound is replacing an atom of another element
      - Can be subdivided into more reactions such as redox
        - Copper ions in a copper sulfate solution is displaced by zinc metal forming zinc sulfate
          - $Zn\ (s) + CuSO^4\ (aq) \rightarrow Cu\ (s) + ZnSO^4\ (aq)$

- Double Displacement Reactions
    - Elements from two compounds displace each other to form new compounds
    - Also called metathesis reactions
    - Can occur when one product is removed from the solution as a gas or precipitate
    - Can occur when two species combine to form a weak electrolyte that remains un-dissociated in a solution.
        - Solutions of calcium chloride and silver nitrate are reacted to form insoluble silver chloride in a solution of calcium nitrate
            - $CaCl^2 (aq) + 2\ AgNO3 (aq) \rightarrow Ca(NO^3)^2(aq) + 2\ AgCl (s)$
    - A neutralization reaction is a specific type of double displacement reaction that occurs when an acid reacts with a base, producing a solution of salt and water
        - Hydrochloric acid and sodium hydroxide react to form sodium chloride and water
            - $HCl (aq) + NaOH (aq) --\!-\!> NaCl (aq) + H2O (l)$

Oxidation-Reduction or Redox Reaction

In a redox reaction the oxidation numbers of atoms are changed. Redox reactions may involve the transfer of electrons between chemical species.

The reaction that occurs when In which I_2 is reduced to I^- and $S_2O_3^{2-}$ (thiosulfate anion) is oxidized to $S_4O_6^{2-}$ provides an example of a redox reaction:

$2\ S_2O_3^{2-}(aq) + I_2(aq) \rightarrow S_4O_6^{2-}(aq) + 2\ I^-(aq)$

Balancing Chemical equations

- A chemical equation describes what happens in a chemical reaction.
- The equation identifies the reactants and products, the formulas of the substances, the phases of the substances, and the amount of each substance
    - Balancing a chemical equation is the mathematical relationship between the quantity of reactants and products
        - The quantities are expressed as grams or moles

Steps to Balance an Equation

- There are essentially three steps to the process:
    - Write the unbalanced equation
        - Chemical formulas of reactants are listed on the left hand side of the equation
        - Products are listed on the right hand side of the equation
        - Reactants and products are separated by putting an arrow between them to show the direction of the reaction. Reactions at equilibrium will have arrows facing both directions
    - Balance the equation.
        - Apply the Law of Conservation of Mass to get the same number of atoms of every element on each side of the equation
            - Start by balancing an element that appears in only one reactant and product
        - Once one element is balanced, proceed to the next one and balance it and continue till all until all elements are balanced
        - Balance chemical formulas by placing coefficients in front of them
        - Do not add subscripts, because this will change the formulas
    - Indicate the states of matter of the reactants and products
        - Use (g) for gaseous substances
        - Use (s) for solids
        - Use (l) for liquids
        - Use (aq) for species in solution in water
        - Write the state of matter immediately following the formula of the substance it describes

Nuclear Decay

Nuclear Equations

- Unstable atomic nuclei will spontaneously decompose to form nuclei with a higher stability.
  - The decomposition process is called radioactivity
    - The energy and particles which are released during the decomposition process are called radiation
    - Natural radioactivity is when an unstable nuclei decomposes in nature
      - There are three major types of natural radioactivity:
        - Alpha
        - Beta
        - Gamma
    - The decomposition in a Lab is induced radioactivity

Alpha Radiation Decay

- Alpha radiation consists of a stream of positively charged particles, called alpha particles
- $^{238}_{92}U -> {}^{4}_{2}He + {}^{234}_{90}Th$
- The helium nucleus is the alpha particle
- Alpha (α) radiation consists of helium nuclei
- The helium nucleus is a small particle containing two protons and two neutrons ($^{4}_{2}He$)

Beta Radiation Decay

- Beta radiation is a stream of electrons, called beta particles
- $^{234}_{90}U -> {}^{0}_{-1}e + {}^{234}_{91}Pa$
- The electron is the beta particle
- Beta (β) radiation consists of electrons ($^{0}_{-1}e$)

Gamma Radiation

- Gamma rays are high-energy photons with a very short wavelength
  - The emission of gamma radiation results from an energy change within the atomic nucleus
  - Gamma emission changes neither the atomic number nor the atomic mass
- Electron capture is the capture of an inner shell electron by a proton in the nucleus
  - The process emits gamma (γ) radiation and results in a proton converting to a neutron
  - Gamma radiation consists of high-energy electromagnetic radiation

Positron

- Positron (particle with the same mass as an electron, but a charge of +1 instead of -1) emission isn't observed in natural radioactivity, but it is a common mode of decay in induced radioactivity
- Positron emission results from the conversion of a proton in the nucleus to a neutron
- The ejected positron ($^{0}_{1}e$) is a particle that has the same mass as an electron but an opposite charge
- Balancing nuclear equations is different than balancing chemical equations
  - In nuclear reactions you have to account for the protons, neutrons, and electrons, and write the symbols for various chemical elements

🎵 In a nuclear equation, the products and reactants are symbolized as

$$^A_Z X$$

X is the chemical symbol for the element

A is the mass number

Z is the atomic number

🔊 When balancing nuclear equations:
- ℘ The total of the superscripts (mass numbers, A) in the reactants and products must be the same
- ℘ The total of the subscripts (atomic numbers, Z) in the reactants and products must be the same

Fisson

🔊 In a nuclear fission reaction a heavy nucleus divides to form smaller nuclei and one or more neutrons

🔊 The fission reactions of uranium-235 and plutonium-239 are the principal ones that generate energy in nuclear power plants
- ℘ Example of fission process:
  - 🎵 uranium-235

$$^{235}_{92}U + ^1_0 n \longrightarrow ^A_Z Ba + ^{94}_{36}Kr + 3^1_0 n$$

  - 🎵 plutonium-239

$$^{235}_{92}U + ^1_0 n \longrightarrow ^A_Z Sr + ^{143}_{54}Xe + 3^1_0 n$$

Decay Series

🔊 Unstable nuclei undergo a spontaneous emission of particles, electromagnetic radiation, or both

🔊 A radioactive nucleus breaks apart, the products may be unstable

🔊 They go through another radioactive decay process

🔊 This decay process continues until a stable element is formed

The decay series for uranium-238 is as follows

$$^{238}_{92}U \longrightarrow ^A_{29}Th + \alpha$$

$$^A_{90}Th \longrightarrow ^{234}_{Z}Pa + \beta$$

$$^{234}_{Z}Pa \longrightarrow ^A_{92}U + \beta$$

$$^A_{92}U \longrightarrow ^{230}_{Z}Th + \alpha$$

$$^{230}_{Z}Th \longrightarrow ^A_{88}Ra + \alpha$$

Calculations in Chemistry

Molecules

- ✇ A molecule is a combination of two or more atoms that are held together by covalent bonds
  - ℘ A molecule is the smallest unit of a compound that still displays the properties associated with that compound.
    - ℐ Molecules may contain two atoms of the same element
      - ℒ O_2
      - ℒ H_2
    - ℐ Molecules may consist of two or more different atoms
      - ℒ CCl_4
      - ℒ H_2O.
  - ℘ Molecules are usually discussed in terms of their molecular weights and moles
  - ℘ Ionic compounds, such as NaCl and KBr, do not form true molecules.

Molecular Weight and Formula Weight

- ✇ The molecular weight of a molecule is calculated by adding the atomic weights of the atoms in the molecule
- ✇ The formula weight of an ionic compound is calculated by adding its atomic weights according to its empirical formula

The Mole

- ✇ A mole is a unit of measurement.
  - ℘ Moles is a consistent way to convert between atoms/molecules and grams
    - ℐ A mole is the quantity of anything that has the same number of particles found in 12.000 grams of carbon-12
    - ℐ A mole of carbon atoms is 6.022×10^{23} carbon atoms
      - ℒ This is equal to Avogadro's number is 6.022×10^{23}
- ✇ The mass in grams of one mole of a compound is equal to the molecular weight of the compound in atomic mass units
  - ℘ One mole of a compound contains 6.022×10^{23} molecules of the compound
- ✇ Formula for determining the number of moles of a sample
$$mol = weight\ of\ sample\ (g)\ /\ molar\ weight\ (g/mol)$$

Molar Mass

- ✇ The mass of 1 mole of a compound is called its molar weight or molar mass
- ✇ The units for molar weight or molar mass are grams per mole
- ✇ The molar mass is the mass of one mole of a sample
  - ℘ Add the atomic masses (atomic weights) of all of the atoms in the molecule
    - ℐ Find the atomic mass for each element by using the mass given in the Periodic Table
    - ℐ Multiply the subscript (number of atoms) times the atomic mass of that element
      - ℒ Then add the masses of all of the elements in the molecule to get the molecular mass
  - ℘ Molar mass usually is expressed in grams (g) or kilograms (kg)

Molar Mass of an Element

- The atomic weights given in the periodic table are an average of the weights of the isotopes of an element
  - The number of protons and neutrons in an element are not always the same
    - The molar mass of sodium metal is the mass of one mole of Na
      - The molar mass of sodium 22.99 g
        - The sum of the protons and neutrons in the atom would be 22
    - The molar mass of oxygen is the mass of one mole of oxygen
      - Oxygen forms a divalent molecule
        - The atomic weight of oxygen is $16.00\ g$
          - O_2 is two atoms of oxygen; therefore the atomic weight is times two
            - The molar mass of oxygen is $2\ x\ 16.00\ g\ =\ 32.00\ g$
              - The mass of one mole of O_2 is $32.00\ g$

Molar Mass of a Molecule

- The molar mass of water is the mass of one mole of H_2O.
  - Add together the atomic masses of all of the atoms of hydrogen and water in a molecule of water:
    - 2 x 1.008 g (hydrogen) + 1 x 16.00 g (oxygen) = 18.02 g
    - Avogadro's number is the number of particles found in one mole of a substance
      - It is the number of atoms in exactly 12 grams of carbon-12
      - This value is approximately 6.022 x 10^{23} particles per mole

Conversion for Mole to Gram or Gram to Mole Conversions.

- Determine the number of moles of CO_2 in 454 grams
  - Look up the atomic masses for carbon and oxygen from the Periodic Table
  - The atomic mass of C is 12.01 and the atomic mass of O is 16.00
    - The formula mass of CO_2 is $12.01\ +\ 2(16.00)\ =\ 44.01$
    - One mole of CO_2 weighs $44.01\ grams$
      - Conversion factor to go from grams to moles is $1\ mol/44.01\ g$
        - Moles of CO_2 = $454\ g\ x\ 1\ mol/44.01\ g\ =\ 10.3\ moles$

Practice Test for Chemistry

1. The three basic components of an atom are:
   A. Protons, neutrons, and ions
   B. Protons, neutrons, and electrons
   C. Protons, neutrinos, and ions
   D. Protium, deuterium, and tritium

2. An element is determined by the number of:
   A. Atoms
   B. Electrons
   C. Neutrons
   D. Protons

3. The nucleus of an atom consists of:
   A. Electrons
   B. Neutrons
   C. Protons and neutrons
   D. Protons, neutrons, and electrons

4. A single proton has what electrical charge?
   A. No charge
   B. Positive charge
   C. Negative charge
   D. Either a positive or negative charge

5. Which particles have approximately the same size and mass as each other?
   A. Neutrons and electrons
   B. Electrons and protons
   C. Protons and neutrons

6. Which two particles would be attracted to each other?
   A. Electrons and neutrons
   B. Electrons and protons
   C. Protons and neutrons
   D. All particles are attracted to each other
   E. None - they are all very different in size and mass

7. The atomic number of an atom is:
   A. The number of electrons
   B. The number of neutrons
   C. The number of protons
   D. The number of protons plus the number of neutrons

8. Changing the number of neutrons of an atom changes its:
    A. Isotope
    B. Element
    C. Ion
    D. Charge

9. When you change the number of electrons on an atom, you produce a different:
    A. Isotope
    B. Ion
    C. Element
    D. Atomic mass

10. According to atomic theory, electrons are usually found:
    A. In the atomic nucleus
    B. Outside the nucleus, yet very near it because they are attracted to the protons
    C. Outside the nucleus and often far from it - most of an atom's volume is its electron cloud
    D. Either in the nucleus or around it - electrons are readily found anywhere in an atom

11. How many moles of NF_3 are in 12 g?
    A. 0.042
    B. 0.083
    C. 0.17
    D. 0.36

12. What is the correct formula for calcium nitrate?
    A. $CaNO_3$
    B. $Ca(NO_3)_2$
    C. $CaNO_2$
    D. $Ca(NO_2)_2$

13. Which of the following is the strongest acid in aqueous solution?
    A. HNO_3
    B. NH_4Cl
    C. HNO_2
    D. HF

14. Which molecule has a linear geometry?
    A. O_3
    B. CH_4
    C. SO_2
    D. CO_2

15. Which species has the smallest number of electrons?
    A. Ca^{2+}
    B. Ar
    C. K^+
    D. Cl

16. Evaluate this expression:

$$\frac{(8.1 \times 10^{-2})(6.8 \times 10^{-1})}{(2.56 \times 10^{-6})}$$

    A. 4×10^{-7}

    B. 6×10^{-5}

    C. 2×10^{4}

    D. 0×10^{5}

17. Consider this balanced chemical equation. $4Al(s) + 3O_2(g) \rightarrow 2Al_2O_3(s)$

    How many moles of Al will remain if 0.60 moles of O_2 react with 0.90 moles of Al?

    A. 0.10

    B. 0.30

    C. 0.45

    D. 0.80

18. How many moles of H_2SO_4 are in 25mL of a 2.0 M H_2SO_4 solution?

    A. 0.025

    B. 0.050

    C. 2.0

    D. 50.0

19. Which of these has the lowest percent by mass oxygen?

    A. CO

    B. CO_2

    C. SO_2

    D. SO_3

20. A sample of gas at 273 K has a pressure of P_1 and a volume of V_1. When the pressure is changed to P_2, what is the volume V_2? (Assume the temperature remains constant.)

    A. $\frac{P_1 P_2}{V_1}$

    B. $\frac{P_1 V_1}{P_2}$

    C. $\frac{P_2 V_1}{P_1}$

    D. $\frac{P_2}{P_1 V_1}$

21. Which element is a liquid at 25°C and 1 atm?

    A. Fluorine

    B. Chlorine

    C. Bromine

    D. Iodine

22. Which technique can be used to determine the number of components in a plant pigment?

    A. Calorimetry

    B. Chromatography

    C. Colorimetry

    D. Gravimetry

23. A reaction has $\Delta H° > 0$ and $\Delta G° > 0$ at 25°C. This reaction
    A. Is at equilibrium at 25°C.
    B. Could not be spontaneous under standard conditions at any temperature.
    C. Could be spontaneous under standard conditions at temperatures above 25°C.
    D. Could be spontaneous under standard conditions at temperatures below 25°C.

24. The effect of temperature on the rates of chemical reactions is primarily a result of the
    A. Size of the colliding molecules
    B. Orientation of the colliding molecules
    C. Enthalpies of the reactants and products
    D. Kinetic energies of the colliding molecules

25. The value of the rate constant for a gas phase reaction can be changed by increasing the:
    A. Amount of product
    B. Pressure of the reactant
    C. Temperature of the reaction vessel
    D. Volume of the reaction vessel

26. Which properties of electromagnetic radiation are inversely related?
    A. Amplitude and frequency
    B. Energy and wavelength
    C. Energy and frequency
    D. Wavelength and amplitude

27. Which must represent an atom in an excited state?
    A. $1s^2 2s^2 2p^1$
    B. $1s^2 2s^2 2p^2$
    C. $1s^2 2s^2 2p^2 3s^1$
    D. $1s^2 2s^2 2p^5$

28. Which quantum numbers represent the orbitals being filled in the ground state for the elements Sc (21) to Zn(30)?
    A. $n = 3, l = 1$
    B. $n = 3, l = 2$
    C. $n = 4, l = 1$
    D. $n = 4, l = 2$

29. In which series are the species listed in order of increasing size?
    A. N, O, F
    B. Na, Mg, K
    C. Cr, Cr^{2+}, Cr^{3+}
    D. Cl, Cl^-, S^{2-}

30. In which molecule does the chlorine have the most positive partial charge?
    A. HCl
    B. BrCl
    C. OCl_2
    D. SCl_2

31. Which molecule contains the shortest carbon-carbon bonds?
    A. C_2H_2
    B. C_2H_4
    C. C_3H_8
    D. C_6H1_2

32. How many valence electrons are in one ion of thiosulfate, $S_2O_3^{2-}$?
    A. 26
    B. 28
    C. 30
    D. 32

33. Which suffix is used to designate a carbohydrate?
    A. –ase
    B. –ate
    C. –one
    D. –ose

34. Which functional group is not commonly found in proteins?
    A. Alcohol
    B. Aldehyde
    C. Amide
    D. Amine

35. The gentle oxidation of ethanol, CH_3CH_2OH, produces
    A. Ethanal, CH_3CHO
    B. Ethanoic acid, CH_3CO_2H
    C. Carbon Monoxide, CO
    D. Carbon Dioxide, CO_2

36. When the concentration of a particular reactant is tripled and the initial rate of the reaction increases by a factor of nine, what is the order of the reaction with respect to this reactant?
    A. Zero
    B. One
    C. Two
    D. Three

37. A substance, X, undergoes a first order reaction X → Y with a half life of 20 minutes. If the initial concentration of X is 2.0 M, what will its concentration be after 40 minutes?
    A. 0.25 M
    B. 0.50 M
    C. 1.0 M
    D. 1.4 M

38. The chemicals in a lightstick give off light as they react. When the lightstick is placed in warm water the glow increases. This is because the
    A. Activation energy for the process is lowered.
    B. Average kinetic energy of the reactants increases.
    C. Higher temperature catalyzes the reaction.
    D. Higher temperature changes the wavelength of light emitted.

39. Which statement is correct about a system at Equilibrium?
    A. The forward and reverse reactions occur at identical rates.
    B. The concentrations of reactants must equal the concentrations of the products.
    C. The concentrations of reactants and products can be changed by adding a catalyst.
    D. The concentrations of reactants and products are not affected by a change in temperature.

40. Which range includes the average oxidation state of S in $Na_2S_4O_6$?
    A. less than 0
    B. 0 to +2
    C. +2 to +4
    D. greater than +4

41. What is the coefficient for O_2 when the equation $NH_3 + O_2 \rightarrow NO + H_2O$ is balanced with the smallest whole number coefficients?
    A. 2
    B. 3
    C. 4
    D. 5

42. Which type of radiation has the highest frequency?
    A. Infrared
    B. Microwave
    C. Ultraviolet
    D. X-ray

43. How many orbitals have the quantum numbers: $n = 4, l = 3, m_l = 0$
    A. 7
    B. 3
    C. 1
    D. 0

44. What is the ground state electron configuration of a $_{27}Co$ atom in the gas phase?
    A. $1s^2 2s^2 2p^6 3s^2 3p^6 3d^7$
    B. $1s^2 2s^2 2p^6 3s^2 3p^6 3d^9$
    C. $1s^2 2s^2 2p^6 3s^2 3p^6 3d^8 4s^1$
    D. $1s^2 2s^2 2p^6 3s^2 3p^6 3d^7 4s^2$

45. Which molecule is least stable?
    A. OF_2
    B. OF_4
    C. SF_2
    D. SF_4

46. Which term describes the formation of acetic acid from ethyl alcohol?
    A. Addition
    B. Esterification
    C. Neutralization
    D. Oxidation

47. Which class of compounds does not include C=O double bonds in its molecules?
    A. Esters
    B. Aamides
    C. Alcohols
    D. Acids

48. Which set of quantum numbers (n, l, m_l) is forbidden?
    A. 3, 2, 0
    B. 3, 1, −1
    C. 2, 0, 0
    D. 1, 1, 0

49. Which characteristic of an atomic orbital is most closely associated with the magnetic quantum number, m_l?
    A. Size
    B. Shape
    C. Occupancy
    D. Orientation

50. The most notable difference between a saturated and an unsaturated fat containing the same number of carbon atoms is that the saturated fat:
    A. Melts at a higher temperature
    B. Melts at a lower temperature
    C. Releases much more energy when metabolized
    D. Releases much less energy when metabolized

51. Which statement is always true for a spontaneous reaction?
    A. The entropy change for the system is negative
    B. The enthalpy change for the system is negative
    C. The entropy change for the universe is positive
    D. The free energy change for the system is positive

52. The heat of a reaction is measured in a bomb calorimeter. This heat is equal to which thermodynamic quantity?
    A. ΔE
    B. ΔG
    C. ΔH
    D. ΔS

53. Which set of quantum numbers corresponds to an electron in a 4d orbital?
    A. $n = 4, l = 1, m_l = -1, m_s = \frac{1}{2}$
    B. $n = 4, l = 2, m_l = -2, m_s = -1/2$
    C. $n = 4, l = 3, m_l = 3, m_s = \frac{1}{2}$
    D. $n = 4, l = 3, m_l = -1, m_s = -1/2$

54. What is the energy of a photon from a laser that emits light at 632.8 nm?
    A. 3.14×10^{-19} J
    B. 1.26×10^{-31} J
    C. 2.52×10^{-33} J
    D. 4.19×10^{-40} J

55. Which process releases the most energy?
    A. $Mg^{2+}(g) + e \rightarrow Mg+(g)$
    B. $Mg+(g) + e \rightarrow Mg(g)$
    C. $Na^{2+}(g) + e \rightarrow Na+(g)$
    D. $Na+(g) + e \rightarrow Na(g)$

56. In which list are the ions arranged in order of increasing size?
    A. $F- < S^{2-} < Al^{3+} < Mg^{2+}$
    B. $F- < S^{2-} < Mg^{2+} < Al^{3+}$
    C. $Mg^2+ < F- < Al^3+ < S^{2-}$
    D. $Al^3+ < Mg^{2+} < F- < S^{2-}$

57. Which species is diamagnetic?
    A. NO
    B. N_2^+
    C. O_2
    D. O_2^{2-}

58. Which formula represents an alkyne? (Assume all are noncyclical.
    A. C_2H_2
    B. C2H4
    C. C5H10
    D. C8H18

59. Cellulose and starch are biological polymers. Humans are able to digest starch but not cellulose. This difference is due primarily to a difference in the
    A. Identity of the monomers in the two polymers.
    B. Number of monomer units in the two polymers.
    C. Orientation of the bonds joining the monomers.
    D. Percentage

Practice Test for Chemistry Answers

1. B	21. C	41. D
2. D	22. B	42. D
3. C	23. B	43. C
4. B	24. D	44. D
5. C	25. C	45. D
6. B	26. B	46. D
7. C	27. C	47. C
8. A	28. B	48. D
9. B	29. C	49. D
10. C	30. A	50. A
11. C	31. A	51. C
12. A	32. D	52. A
13. A	33. D	53. B
14. D	34. B	54. A
15. D	35. A	55. C
16. C	36. C	56. D
17. A	37. B	57. D
18. B	38. B	58. A
19. C	39. A	59. C
20. B	40. C	

Blank

Comprehensive Review for Physical Science

Introduction

General terms and Relationships

Laws in Physics

Kinematics

Force

Work/Energy

Waves

Sound

Light

Relativity

Thermodynamics

Electricity

Magnetism

Heat

The Earth's Atmosphere

Blank

Introduction

Physics is a systematic study of the natural world that attempts to quantify reality through the application of observation with logic and reason. To study this science you have to have certain foundational information to build upon it. Physics is the scientific study of matter and energy and how they interact with each other. Energy in physics can take the form of motion, light, electricity, radiation, gravity, etc. Physics will deal with matter that is as small as the particles that make up the atom and the particles that make up those particles to stars and even entire galaxies. This is all to be explained in greater detail later in this section.

Physics is an experimental science and uses the scientific method to formulate and test hypotheses that are based on observation of the natural world. Physic's goal is to use the results of experiments to formulate scientific laws, that are quantified or in mathematical language to which can then be used to predict other phenomena. There are a number of physical constants used throughout physics, as part of the equations used to calculate certain values. This listing is found at the end of this section for your reference.

Without matter and energy there can be no life. Living verses non living things, what are the differences? A living thing has properties that make it living. Living things reproduce; convert food into what it needs and responds to environmental stimuli or to its surroundings. A living thing or organism is never at rest even when it appears to be. Organs and systems are always in motion, cells are digesting food and excreting waste; glands, muscles, nerves and tissues are responding to stimuli.

General Terms and Relationships

Matter is anything that takes up space and has mass. It can be living or non living. An atom is made up of fundamental particles that are bits of matter they are electron, proton and neutron. Matter and energy are closely linked and have a close association with life.

Energy is the ability or a capacity to do work; it is not a visible or tangible object. It neither takes up space nor has weight. Work is almost any form of gainful activity. In Physics' work means to move an object. To move an object you must apply force. Force is the pushing or pulling of an object. Force is any quantity that is capable of producing a change in motion. To be considered a force the only requirement is that it has the capacity to change but doesn't necessarily change. Work is measured as the foot-pound. One foot-pound is the amount of work done in the American system when you exert a force of one pound through a distance of one foot. W=F x D. In the metric system there are two forms of measurement: gram-centimeter or kilogram-meter. Energy comes in various forms such as light, heat, sound, electricity and then there is also chemical energy, atomic energy, and mechanical energy. Mechanical energy actually generates other forms of energy by the movement of machines producing mechanical energy. Energy is released when matter changes form or spins into motion. Matter and energy are different forms of the same thing since matter can be changed into energy and vice versa. All living things obtain their energy from some form of matter and then convert it into the energy form that they need. Matter has certain properties; it has volume, weight, mass and inertia. Matter exists in one of three states at all times; these three states are a solid, liquid, or gas. Water is a common example of a form of matter that easily can change from one form of matter into another. Volume is a measurement of the amount of space that matter occupies. The volume of a solid or liquid never changes where a gas's volume changes according to the shape of its container. A solid has a specific shape and volume and to change it something must be done to it. A liquid only has a constant volume but its shape is based on its container. A gas has no definite shape and takes on the shape of what it is in, however with a gas its volume changes with the size of the container since it is condensed into a small container and expands when in a larger container, therefore it takes on the volume of its container.

Weight is the measurement of the pull of gravity on the item. An example of this is be the weight of an object on earth is 18 lbs, in space it is weightless and on the moon it weighs 3lbs; since the moon's gravitational pull is one sixth that of the earth and in space there is no gravitational pull. The items mass however has not changed it is constant. Mass and weight are measured in the same basic unit of grams. On earth the greater the mass the greater the weight of an object, it is directly proportional to each other. In different conditions this is not true, for example the mass of an 18 lb object on earth is the same on earth and the moon but the objects weight is not the same on the moon but is 3lbs because of the change in the gravitational pull on the object.

Laws in Physics

Sir Isaac Newton developed the Three Laws of Motion, which describe basic rules about how the motion of physical objects changes. Newton was able to define the fundamental relationship between the acceleration of an object and the total forces acting upon it. Three Laws of Motion

- Newton's First Law of Motion states that in order for the motion of an object to change, a force must act upon it, a concept generally called inertia.
    - Newton's First Law of Motion
        - Everybody continues in its state of rest, or of uniform motion in a straight line, unless it is compelled to change that state by forces impressed upon it.
          This is sometimes also called the Law of Inertia, or just inertia. Inertia is the resistance an object has to a change in its state of motion
        - The law basically makes two points:
            - An object that is not moving will not move until a force acts upon it.
            - An object that is in motion will not change velocity (or stop) until a force acts upon it.
- Newton's Second Law of Motion defines the relationship between acceleration, force, and mass.
    - Newton's Second Law of Motion
        - The acceleration produced by particular force acting on a body is directly proportional to the magnitude of the force and inversely proportional to the mass of the body.
- Newton's Third Law of Motion states that any time a force acts from one object to another, there is an equal force acting back on the original object. If you pull on a rope, therefore, the rope is pulling back on you as well.
    - Newton's Third Law of Motion
        - To every action there is always opposed an equal reaction; or, the mutual actions of two bodies upon each other are always equal, and directed to contrary parts.

Newton's Law of Gravity

Newton's law of gravity defines the attractive force between all objects that possess mass.
The force of gravity is stated as: Every particle of matter in the universe attracts every other particle with a force that is directly proportional to the product of the masses of the particles and inversely proportional to the square of the distance between them.

The force of gravity is also known as weight. An attractive force of one particle therefore is always directed toward the other particle regardless their different mass and sizes. The particles pull on each other with equivalent force however it is noted that the particle with less mass (which may or may not be the smaller particle, depending upon their densities) will accelerate more than the other particle.

"Law" of Gravity

Newton developed his "Law of Gravity" to explain the attractive force between a pair of masses. Yet it later became apparent that Einstein had developed The Theory of general relativity which has provided a more comprehensive explanation for the phenomenon of gravity. Newton's law of gravity is an accurate low-energy approximation that works for most of the cases.

Fundamental Forces

The fundamental forces (or fundamental interactions) are the ways that individual particles interact with each other which are Gravity, Electromagnetism, Weak Interaction and Strong Interaction.
Gravity
- It is a purely attractive force which reaches through even the "empty" void of space to draw two masses toward each other. It keeps the planets in orbit around the sun and the moon in orbit around the Earth.
- Gravitation is described under the theory of general relativity, which defines it as the curvature of space-time around an object of mass. This curvature, in turn, creates a situation where the path of least energy is toward the other object of mass.
- Electromagnetism
  - Electromagnetism is the interaction of particles with an electrical charge. Charged particles at rest interact through electrostatic forces, while in motion they interact through both electrical and magnetic forces.
- Weak Interaction
  - The weak interaction is a very powerful force that acts on the scale of the atomic nucleus, also known as a phenomena such as beta decay.
- Strong Interaction
  - The strongest of the forces is the aptly-named strong interaction, which is the force that keeps protons & neutrons bound together. As in the helium atom it is strong enough to bind two protons together despite the fact that their positive electrical charges cause them to repulse each other, also known as a phenomena of the alpha decay

The current quantum mechanical interpretation of these forces is that the particles do not interact directly, but rather manifest virtual particles that mediate the actual interactions. All of the forces except for gravity have been consolidated into this "Standard Model" of interaction.

Center of Gravity

Every particle of an object interacts with every particle of the other object. Since it is understood that forces (including gravity) are vector quantities, these forces are viewed as having components in the parallel and perpendicular directions of the two objects. The center of gravity of an object is generally identical to its center of mass but this is not always the case of irregular shaped items, therefore the idea of a gravitational field was developed. The gravitational field is defined as the force of gravity at a given point divided by the mass of an object at that point. The units of the gravitational field are m/s^2. When an object moves in a gravitational field, work must be done to get it from one place to another (starting point 1 to end point 2).

Mass-Energy Relationship

Einstein was able to show that mass and energy were related, formula $E = mc^2$.

The Law of Conservation of Mass-Energy:

The total energy in a closed or isolated system is constant, no matter what happens. Another law stated that the mass in an isolated system is constant. When Einstein discovered the relationship $E = mc^2$, it was said to refer to the conservation of mass-energy. The total of both mass and energy is retained, yet some may change forms. The ultimate example of this is a nuclear explosion, where mass transforms into energy. The most relative example to society worldwide would be the relationship was proven of the released the energy of mass when the nuclear bombs dropped in WWII on Hiroshima and Nagasaki.

Speed of Light

It needs to be noted that actually no object with mass can accelerate to precisely the speed of light. A photon, a mass less object, has the ability to move at the speed of light, but there is no acceleration since it is always moving exactly at the speed of light and never has a starting point.

In theory a physical object could move at a speed greater that the speed of light, but this would never be able to be achieved if the object was to reach such a speed through acceleration. A physical object's speed has a limit, the speed of light. The speed of light has a kinetic energy that goes to infinity, and due to this it can never be reached by acceleration. It needs to be noted that no physical object or entity has ever yet displayed this property.

Kinematics

Kinematics is the study of motion where one ignores the forces producing the motion. Position, motion, speed, velocity, and acceleration are terms used to interpret the endless motion of all objects in kinematics. Position refers to the location of an object. Ironically to give a position of an object, another object or reference point must be used or implied also. Motion is when an object is undergoing a "continuous" change and we state an object is moving. Since position is relative on something else to state the position, motion is therefore also relative to something else.

Scalar or Vector Quantity

For future reference, terms used by the general public can be intermixed or misused and can be clarified for science by using the reference words, vector quantities or scalar quantities especially in physical science. Vector quantities are expressed by use of a magnitude (a unit) and a direction, so it depends on the initial and final state of the object regardless of its path. Scalar quantities are those only expressed by use of magnitude (a unit) not by a direction. Speed is scalar where velocity is always a vector quantity with a direction given. Distance is another example of scalar and displacement is vector.

The fundamental forces (or fundamental interactions) of physics are the ways that individual particles interact with each other which are gravity, Electromagnetism, Weak Interaction (or Weak Nuclear Force), Strong Interaction (or Strong Nuclear Force).

Distance

Distance is referred to as the amount of ground an object has covered during its motion. Distance is a scalar quantity where displacement is a vector quantity, referred to as the amount an object is been overall changed in its position or being out of place.

Speed

Speed is referred to as how fast an object is moving or the rate at which an object covers distance. Speed is a scalar quantity. In general a fast moving object covers a large distance in a relatively short amount of time and vice versa; for a slow moving object covers a short or small distance in a relatively short amount of time. If there is no movement it has a zero speed. Average speed is the distance traveled per time traveled.

Velocity

Velocity however is a vector quantity and is the rate at which an object changes its position. To have a zero velocity, there can be motion, and speed however, if the start position is the same as the end position then there has been zero velocity. If an object in motion is to maximize its velocity then it must maximize the amount it is displaced from its original position moving further from the starting point without changing directions or returning to its starting position. Velocity keeps track of direction. Average velocity is the position change or displacement per the amount of time the position change took place.

Acceleration

Acceleration is the rate at which an object changes its velocity. So as long as an object is changing its velocity or its position it is then considered accelerating. A constant acceleration is where an objects velocity changes the same constant amount each consecutive amount of time ratio. However an object with a constant velocity is not accelerating but an accelerating object is one that has a constant change in its velocity. Due to this the distance traveled/time is not a constant value.

A falling object usually accelerates as it falls. A free falling object that is accelerating at a constant rate will cover different distances each consecutive second so it is stated that objects with a constant acceleration, the distance traveled is directly proportional to the square of the time of travel. The following are typical acceleration values in units of velocity/time; $m/s/s$, $mi/h/s$, $km/hr/s$, m/s^2. Free falling objects are in a state of acceleration at $9.8m/s/s$ or (g) or the velocity of the object is changing by $9.8\ m/s$ every second. Due to this constant, the velocity of an object can be found for any object which has been dropped from a position of rest at any given amount of time and $v^f=g \times t$ and the distance an object has fallen from a position of rest can be found by $d = 0.5 \times g \times t^2$

The direction of the acceleration vector depends on two things, if the object is speeding up or slowing down and if the object is moving in the positive or negative direction. If the object is slowing down its acceleration is in the opposite direction of its motion.

Positive acceleration is when the acceleration of the object is in the positive direction. If an object is speeding up and has a positive velocity, moving in a positive direction, then the acceleration is in the same direction as the velocity. If an object is slowing down and has a negative velocity, or moving in a negative direction, it is still a positive acceleration since the object is in the opposite direction as the velocity.

Negative acceleration is the acceleration of the object in a negative direction. If an object is slowing down and is moving in a positive direction or has a positive velocity, it is negative acceleration. When an object is slowing down, the acceleration is in the opposite direction of the velocity. If an object is speeding up and has a negative velocity or is moving in a negative direction and an object with the acceleration in the same direction as the velocity. The direction of the velocity vector is the same as the direction which an object is moving.

The use of positive and negative always has a physical meaning. It is used here to describe the velocity and the acceleration of a moving object; positive and negative describe a direction. Because both velocity and acceleration are vector quantities, a full description of the quantity demands the use of a directional adjective. North, south, east, west, right, left, up and down are all directional adjectives. Positive often means to the right or up and negative often means to the left or down. So an object that has a negative acceleration is the same as its acceleration to the left or down or whatever has been designated as negative. Negative accelerations do not refer to acceleration values which are less than 0. An acceleration of $-2\ m/s/s$ is an acceleration with a magnitude of $2\ m/s/s$ which is directed in the negative direction.

The four kinematic equations which describe an object's motion are:

Solving for displacement (d)

$$d = v_i \times t + \frac{1}{2} \times a \times t^2$$

$$d = \frac{v_i + v_f}{2} \times t$$

Solving for final velocity (v_f)

$$v_f = v_i + a \times t$$

$$v_f^2 = v_i^2 + 2 \times a \times d$$

There are a variety of symbols used in the above equations. Each symbol has its own specific meaning. The symbol d stands for the displacement of the object. The symbol t stands for the time for which the object moved or the given interval of time. The symbol a stands for the acceleration or average acceleration of the object. And the symbol v stands for the velocity of the object; a subscript of i after the v (v_i) indicates that the velocity value is the initial velocity value and a subscript of f (as in v_f) indicates that the velocity value is the final velocity value.

Force

Forces

A force is a push or pull upon an object resulting from the object's *interaction* with another object. Whenever there is an *interaction* between two objects, there is a force upon each of the objects. When the *interaction* ceases, the two objects no longer experience the force. Forces only exist as a result of an interaction.

The net force is the vector sum, resultant vector, of all the forces acting upon an object. The resultant vector (whether a displacement vector, force vector, velocity vector, etc.) is the result of adding the two or more individual vectors together.

A force is not needed to keep an object in motion. An object in motion does not come to a rest position because of the *absence* of a force; rather it is the *presence* of a force that brings it to a rest position. That force being the force of friction.

Circular Motion

Uniform circular motion is the motion of an object in a circle with a constant or uniform speed. An object transverses a distance around the perimeter of the circle. One complete cycle around a circle's perimeter is its circumference. The circumference of a circle, the time to complete one cycle and the objects speed is simply an application of average speed. The circumference can be found from the radius of the circle and therefore two times pi times the radius over the period (T), the time, to make one cycle around the circle is the average speed of the circle. When objects are moving around different radii of circles in the same period the object of the larger radius is traveling a greater speed than that of the smaller radius, so average speed and radius of the circle are directly proportional. An object moving in a circle has its direction constantly changing however, the velocity vector is directed in the same direction the object is moving. The acceleration of the object is in the same direction as the velocity change vector and is towards the center of the circle. Force in relation to circular motion is that every object that is in motion in a circle involves a force which is directed inward. This is considered centripetally and to be a centripetal force there must be the motion of an object in a circle with an inward net force to sustain the inward acceleration.

Mass

The tendency of an object to resist changes in its state of motion varies with mass. Mass is that quantity which is solely dependent upon the inertia of an object. The more inertia an object has, the more mass it has; therefore, the more massive an object the greater tendency it has to resist changes in its state of motion. The state of motion of an object is defined by its velocity or the speed with a direction. Inertia is the tendency of an object to resist changes in its state of motion, its velocity, or accelerations.

An object at rest has zero velocity and will remain with a zero velocity if there is an absence of an unbalanced force and such object will not change its *state of motion* unless acted upon by an unbalanced force. Which is the same for an object with a velocity greater than zero will remain at that velocity if there is an absence of an unbalanced force and therefore such object will not change its *state of motion* unless acted upon by an unbalanced force. Unbalanced forces actually cause acceleration.

Forces Balanced/Unbalanced

Forces acting upon an object have to be determined and then each forces direction has to be determined before an object can be said to have balanced or unbalanced forces acting upon it. If two individual forces are of equal magnitude and opposite direction, then the forces are said to be balanced. An object is said to be *acted upon by an unbalanced force* only when there is an individual force which is not being balanced by another individual force of equal magnitude and in the opposite direction of the first individual force.

Equilibrium

If an object is at equilibrium, then the forces are balanced. This is the key to describe if a particular situation is considered to be at equilibrium. If it is at equilibrium then the net force is zero and the acceleration is $0\ m/s/s$. Objects at equilibrium must have an acceleration of $0\ m/s/s$ but that does not mean the object is at rest. It means one of two things: it is either at rest and staying at rest, or in motion and continuing in motion with the same speed and direction. If an object is at rest and is in a state of equilibrium, then the object is at static equilibrium. Static means stationary or at rest. The forces acting upon an object in equilibrium are commonly used to analyze situations involving objects at static equilibrium.

Free-falling object

A free-falling object is an object which is falling under the sole influence of gravity. Therefore, any object that is only being acted upon by the force of gravity is said to be in a state of free fall. All true free-falling objects have two distinct motion characteristics. They do not encounter air resistance and, on Earth, accelerate downwards at a rate of $9.8\ m/s/s$. This $9.8 m/s/s$ is a constant for all free falling objects of acceleration on Earth called acceleration of gravity (g).

Momentum

Momentum is the quantity of motion that an object has. An object that is in motion has momentum. Momentum is a mass in motion. All objects that are moving have momentum and the amount of momentum an object has is dependent upon two variables mass and velocity directly. The units for momentum would be mass unit's time's velocity units. The standard metric unit of momentum is the $kg \bullet m/s$. In reference to momentum the more momentum an object has the greater amount of force or a longer amount of time or both would be required to bring an object to a halt. As the force acts upon the object for a given amount of time, the object's velocity is changed; and therefore, the momentum is changed. An unbalanced force always accelerates an object to either speed it up or slow it down. For an object to slow down a force acts upon the object opposite to the object's motion and if the force acts in the same direction as the object's motion it speeds the object up. A force will change the velocity of an object and therefore the momentum of the object is changed.

An impulse is the quantity of force times the time and equals the mass times the change in velocity or the change in momentum. It's formula is written as such: $F \times t = m \times \Delta v$. Therefore it is in a collision. Objects experience an impulse and this impulse causes and is equal to the change in momentum. A special kind of collision is called a rebound which involves both a direction change as well as a speed change. An elastic collision is when an object rebounds with the same speed, therefore, it has the same momentum and kinetic energy as it had prior to the collision. Elastic collisions are characterized by a large velocity change, a large momentum change, a large impulse, and a large force.

Work / Energy

When a force acts upon an object to cause a displacement of the object, work has been done upon the object. There are three parts to be considered to be work: there must be a force, a displacement, and a cause. Therefore, for a force to be considered as having done *work* on an object there must be a displacement and a reason that object is to be displaced. Work is any unit of force times any unit of displacement and is equivalent to a unit of work. Work (and energy) use the standard metric unit of the Joule (J) and one Joule is equivalent to one Newton of force causing a displacement of one meter. In order to calculate the work done on an object the three quantities that have to be known are force, displacement and the angle between the force and the displacement. The angle between the force and the displacement vector is theta and is $\cos\theta$ for calculation in the work formula.

- Energy types
  - Potential energy
    - Gravitational potential energy
    - Elastic potential energy.
  - Kinetic Energy
    - Vibrational Kinetic Energy
    - Rotational Kinetic Energy
    - Translational Kinetic Energy
  - Mechanical Energy
  - Power

Potential Energy

Potential Energy is the stored energy as a result of its position possessed by an object. When an objects position is altered from its usual equilibrium position, the object is able to store energy by virtue of its position which is the objects potential energy.

There are two types of potential energy, gravitational potential energy and elastic potential energy. Energy that is stored as a result of the Earth's gravitational attraction for the object is gravitational potential energy. The gravitational potential energy is relative to its vertical position or height. There are two dependent variables, mass of object and the height it is raised. These two variables have a direct relationship with gravitational potential energy. A zero height position must be arbitrarily assigned and the height is then this zero height position. Gravitational potential energy of an object is directly proportional to its height above the zero position.

Elastic Potential Energy

Elastic potential energy is the energy stored in elastic materials due to the result of their stretching or compressing. The amount of energy stored in the material is directly proportional to the amount of stretch of the material. Springs are a special device which can store elastic potential energy due to either compression or stretching. Compression of a spring requires a force, the greater the compression the greater the force to compress it further. The force amount is directly proportional to the stretch or compression, and this constant of proportionality is considered the spring constant (K). These types of springs follow Hooke's Law.

A spring is at an equilibrium position when it is neither being stretched nor compressed; it is the position the spring naturally assumes when no force is applied to it. In regard to potential energy, it would then be considered the zero-potential energy position. The potential energy of springs is half times the spring constant times the squared amount of compression relative to the equilibrium position.

Kinetic energy

Kinetic energy is the energy of motion. An object which has motion has kinetic energy regardless if the motion is vertical or horizontal. Kinetic energy is a scalar quantity and doesn't have a direction. Kinetic energy comes in many forms: vibrational, rotational, and translational.

- Vibrational Kinetic Energy is energy due to vibrational motion.
- Rotational Kinetic Energy is energy due to rotational motion.
- Translational Kinetic Energy is energy due to motion from one location to another.

Translational Kinetic Energy depends upon two variables: the mass of the object and the speed (v) of the object. The Kinetic Energy of an object is directly proportional or dependent to the square of its speed. The measurement for Kinetic Energy is the Joule (J) just like work and potential energy. During the process of doing work, mechanical energy is known as the object that is doing the work exchanging energy with the object upon which the work is done.

Mechanical Energy

Mechanical energy can be either kinetic or potential energy. Objects have mechanical energy if they are in motion and / or if they are at some position relative to a zero potential energy position. An object that possesses mechanical energy is able to do work. It is this mechanical energy that enables the object to apply a force on another object to cause it to be displaced. Mechanical energy is the ability to do work. Total Mechanical energy is the sum of potential energy and the kinetic energy of the object. There are conditions when the Total mechanical Energy will be a constant value and where it is a changing value. These conditions are dependent on the work-energy relationship.

Power

Power is the rate at which work is done; work/time ratio. Power uses the units of measurement of the watt and Joules/sec. When power is delivered by a machine it is referred to as horsepower. One horsepower is approximately equivalent to 750 watts. Machines are usually designed and built to do work on objects and are typically described by a power rating, the rate at which the machine can do work upon other objects. The amount of work, power and time are inversely proportional. A human being or an animal is also considered a machine capable of doing work on an object and actually can be given a power rating.

Power is work/time and work is equal to force times displacement and velocity is displacement/ time. Therefore, power can be considered force times velocity. So a machine which is strong enough to apply a large force to cause a displacement in a short amount of time is a powerful machine and is considered a strong, fast machine.

Waves

Waves are everywhere in nature. Waves have properties, a nature and behaviors completely unique to them. Two of the most common waves are light waves and sound waves. The properties of waves are amplitude and wavelength.

Waves

- Disturbances
  - A disturbance that is repeated or periodic is a wave.
  - A wave is a disturbance that travels through a medium from one location to another location
  - A pulse is a single disturbance moving throughout a medium from one location to another
- Periodic
  - A repeated event is considered periodic
  - A disturbance that is repeated is periodic
  - A periodic wave refers to a disturbance that moves through a medium from one location to another.
    - Medium is a substance or material which carries the wave
    - The medium is a collection of particles or parts that are capable of interacting with each that are adjacent to each other
- The particles are disturbed from their equilibrium position, or rest position, and then they begin a push pull process on their adjacent particles
  - This process continues consecutively and therefore the disturbance moves through the medium and due to the force acting on the particles they return to their rest or original position
  - In a disturbance there is always some force acting on the particles to restore them to their original position
- A wave involves movement of a disturbance without the movement of matter
  - The particles of the medium simply vibrate about a fixed position as the pattern of the disturbance moves from one location to another
  - Waves are an energy transport phenomenon
    - As a disturbance moves through the medium from one particle to the other energy is being transported from one end of the medium to the other
    - A wave transports its energy without transporting any matter
- Waves are categorized on the basis of :
  - The direction of movement of the particles relative to the direction which the waves travel
    - There are 3 types:
      - longitudinal
      - transverse
      - surface
  - The wave's ability or inability to transmit energy through a vacuum, empty space
    - There are 2 types:
      - Electromagnetic
      - Mechanical
      - Longitudinal Waves
        - The particles of the medium move in a direction parallel to the direction which the wave moves
        - As energy is transported left to right the medium particles move left and right
        - The particles move parallel to the direction of the pulse
        -

- Transverse
  - The particles of the medium move in a direction perpendicular to the direction which the wave moves
  - As energy is transported left to right the medium particles move up and down
  - The particles move perpendicular to the direction of the pulse
- Surface
  - The particles of the medium undergo a circular motion
  - Only has particles on the surface of the medium that undergo the circular motion
  - The motion of the particles tends to decrease as one proceeds further from the surfaces original point of disturbance
- Any wave moving through a medium has a source
  - The source of the vibration is the location where the wave is introduced into the medium
- Electromagnetic waves:
  - These waves are capable of transmitting it's energy through a vacuum(empty Space)
  - These waves are produced by the vibration of charged particles
  - These waves are light waves
- Mechanical waves:
  - These waves are incapable of transmitting it's energy through a vacuum(empty Space)
  - These waves require a medium to transport their energy from one location to another
  - These waves are sound waves

Wave Parts

- The parts of a wave are: equilibrium/rest position, crest and trough
  - Equilibrium/rest position
    - The center position between the crest and the trough
  - Crest
    - Is the point on the medium which exhibit's the maximum amount of positive or upwards displacement from the equilibrium/rest position
  - Trough
    - Is the point on the medium which exhibit's the maximum amount of the negative or downwards displacement from the equilibrium/rest position

Amplitude

- Is the vertical change of the wave from rest and is the vertical measurement of the wave
- Is the maximum displacement of a particle on the medium from its rest position
- Is measured as a distance from rest to crest or rest to trough
  - The amount of energy carried by a wave is directly related to the amplitude of the wave
    - The amplitude of a transverse pulse is related to the energy which the pulse transports through the medium
    - The energy put into a pulse only affects the amplitude but not the wavelength, frequency or the speed of the pulse
      - A low energy wave has low amplitude
        The energy amplitude relationship: $E \infty A^2$

Wavelength

- Is the length of one complete wave cycle, a repeated pattern that is periodic and regular over both time and space
- Is the length of one spatial repetition
- Is measured as a distance from crest to crest or from trough to trough
  - In longitudinal waves the vibrations cause the particles to be compressed or rarefraction
    - Compressed
      - Compression is a region where a point in the medium through which a longitudinal wave is traveling that has the maximum density
    - Rarefraction
      - The region where the medium particles are stretched apart maximizing the distance is rarefraction and in a longitudinal wave has the minimum density
- Measuring wavelengths
  - Transverse wavelength is measured crest to crest or trough to trough
  - Longitudinally wavelength is measured from compression to compression or from rarefraction to rarefraction

Frequency

- Frequency is how often the particles of the medium vibrate when a wave passes through the medium
- Frequency is the number of complete vibration cycles of a medium per a given amount of time
- Frequency is a rate quantity, cycles/second
  - The quantity frequency would be in units of cycles/second, waves/second or vibrations/second
    - Frequency's unique unit of measurement is Hertz (Hz) were 1 Hz is equal to 1 $cycle/second$
      - 8 cycles per 4 seconds is 2Hz or 8 cycles per 16 seconds is 1/2Hz

Period

- The time for the event to repeat itself is the period
  - Period is a time quantity, seconds/cycle
  - A repeated event is considered periodic

Wave Speed

- Wave speed is the distance traveled by a given point on a wave in a given period of time and is meters traveled per second

Wave Behaviors

- Boundary Behaviors are associated with the bending of the path of a wave
  - Reflection
    - A wave reaches the end of the medium and is bounced off or reflected from the next medium
    - The wave stays in the original medium and just reverses its direction of travel
    - Commonly found in sound waves
  - Refraction
    - A wave reaches the end of the medium and has a change in the wave's direction as it passes from one medium to another
    - The wave stays in the original medium and just reverses its direction of travel
    - Commonly found in sound waves

- Diffraction
  - Diffraction is a change in a wave's direction as they pass through an opening or around a barrier
  - The bending of waves when an opening or obstacle has a size smaller than or equal to the wavelength
    - A sound is heard around to corners
    - A cheerleader's megaphone is a diffraction of sound waves

Wave Interferance

- Wave Interference is the phenomenon when two waves meet while passing along the same medium
  - There are two types of wave interference, constructive interference and destructive interference
    - Constructive Interference
      - Is when the two interfering waves along the same medium at any location have a displacement in the same direction
    - Destructive Interference
      - Is when two interfering waves at any location along the medium have a displacement in the opposite direction

Sound

Sound waves have frequencies from a few cycles per second up to millions of cycles per second.

Audible Range

- The audible range is due to the frequency as well as the intensity of the sound
- The human ear can hear frequencies that are of an audible range from about 20 to about 20,000 cycles per second
- A sound of 3,000 cycles per second is what the human ear is most sensitive to
- The number of cycles per second the human ear receives is the consequence of the frequency resulting in the highness or loudness of the pitch

Loudness

- The loudness of a sound wave is related to the amount of energy being transferred.
  - Loudness is related to the wave's amplitudes and how the ear perceives sound which is measured by the quantity of intensity of a sound wave
  - Loudness is not related to the frequency or the wavelength of a sound

Intensity

- Intensity is the rate of energy transferred per unit of time
  - Intensity's unit of measure is in watts or J/s and the wave front area is m^2(meters squared)
  - The decibel scale is used to measure the intensity level of a sound
    - The intensity the human ear can detect is from the $10 - 12 \, w/m^2$ to $10 \, w/m^2$
    - $10 \, w/m^2$ is the maximum intensity of sound the human ear hears before it is painful.

Resonance

- When sound waves come in contact with objects vibrations tend to be produced in these objects
  - The reaction of a particular object to sound waves depends on its own frequency of vibration
  - Objects similar in physical properties to the vibrating sound tend to vibrate more noticeably
    - Resonance is a tuned condition that exists when an external frequency corresponds to the objects natural frequency of vibration

Light

Particle –Wave Duality of Light

- Everything that moves has a wave length associated with it
- Light is usually only defined or described as a wave
  - Einstein's description of light was as a photon being a particle of electromagnetic radiation
  - This conflicting and confusing dilemma caused the phrase "dual nature of light" to be created as a way to explain that light can act as both a wave and a particle
- Speed of light (c) in a vacuum is

$$c = 3 \times 10^8 \ m/s$$

  - Even though light travels at a prescribed speed, it can have different wavelengths and frequency
    Speed of wave = wavelength x frequency

$$c = \lambda f$$ c= velocity of electromagnetic radiation
λ = wavelength of electromagnetic radiation
f = frequency of electromagnetic radiation

  - Waves produced by moving particles are considered matter waves
  - Therefore matter as well as light has properties of both waves and matter
    - By this any moving particles wavelength can be found by

$$\lambda = h/mv$$ λ = lambda = wavelength of the moving particle
m = mass of the particle
v = velocity of the particle
h = Planck's constant

Plank's Constant

- Plank's Constant states that is energy is radiated or absorbed in discrete amounts
  - Plank's Constant is equal to $6.625 \times 10^{-34} \ J \cdot s$
  - A photon is a particle of electromagnetic radiation
  - A photon has a wavelength due to Einstein's description of light
    - All photons carry an amount of energy which is proportional to its frequency
      - Energy of a photon can be found by $E = hv$ or $E = hc/\lambda$ or $E = c/mv$

$$E = hv \ \text{or} \ E = hc/\lambda \ \text{or} \ E = c/mv$$

E= energy c = speed of light m = mass of the particle
h = Planck's constant λ = wavelength v = velocity of the particle
v= frequency

$$c = \lambda f$$ c= velocity of electromagnetic radiation
λ = wavelength of electromagnetic radiation
v= frequency of electromagnetic radiation

- Units of wavelength of light

meters, m or 1 x 10^{-2} m   Nanometer, nm or 1 x 10^{-9} m   Angstrom, Å or 1 x 10^{-10} m

ఴ Electromagnetic Spectrum
- ∾ Many types of light or radiation
- ∾ Radiation associated with heat given off by objects at room temperature

Radio waves	Microwaves		infrared				visible light	Ultra violet		x-rays		Gamma rays		

10^0 10^{-1} 10^{-2} 10^{-3} 10^{-4} 10^{-5} 10^{-6} 10^{-7} 10^{-8} 10^{-9} 10^{-10} 10^{-11} 10^{-12} 10^{-13}

Wavelength in meters

10^8 10^9 10^{12} 10^{13} 10^{14} 10^{17} 10^{19} 10^{20} 10^{21}

Wavelength in Hz

- ∾ Radio waves
  - ℘ Wavelength is > 1×10^{-1} m
  - ℘ Frequency is < 3×10^9 Hz
- ∾ Microwaves
  - ℘ Wavelength is 1×10^{-1} m to 1×10^{-2} m
  - ℘ Frequency is from 3×10^9 Hz to 3×10^{12} Hz
- ∾ Infrared
  - ℘ Wavelength is from 1×10^{-2} m to 1×10^{-7} m
  - ℘ Frequency is from 3×10^{12} Hz to 4.3×10^{14} Hz
- ∾ Visible light Spectrum
  - ℘ Visible spectrum is from 4×10^{-7} m to 7×10^{-7} m wavelength Infrared spectrum
    - ϒ Decrease wavelength and increase frequency the type of electromagnetic radiation become more dangerous
    - ϒ Visible light color spectrum is:
      - ℓ Red 4×10^{-7} m wavelength
      - ℓ Orange
      - ℓ Yellow
      - ℓ Green
      - ℓ Blue
      - ℓ Violet 7×10^{-7} m wavelength
  - ℘ Frequency is from 4.3×10^{14} Hz to 7.5×10^{14} Hz
- ∾ Ultraviolet
  - ℘ Wavelength is from 4×10^{-7} m to 1×10^{-9} m
  - ℘ Frequency is from 7.5×10^{14} Hz to 3×10^{17} Hz
- ∾ X-rays
  - ℘ Wavelength is from 1×10^{-9} m to 1×10^{-11} m
  - ℘ Frequency is from 3×10^{17} Hz to 3×10^{19} Hz
- ∾ Gamma Rays
  - ℘ Wavelength is > 1×10^{-11} m
  - ℘ Frequency is > 3×10^{19} Hz
- ∾ Higher wavelengths correspond to the red end up to 10^{-5} m outside visible spectrum is the infrared
  - ℘ Lower wavelengths are towards the violet end and down to 10^{-8} are ultraviolet rays

Relativity

Fundamentals of Relativity

- Classical relativity involves a simple transformation between a moving object and an observer in another inertial frame of reference
- Principle of Relativity (First Postulate): The laws of physics are the same for all inertial reference frames
- Principle of Constancy of the Speed of Light (Second Postulate): Light always propagates through a vacuum (i.e. empty space or "free space") at a definite velocity, c, which is independent of the state of motion of the emitting body
- Special Relativity The result of Einstein's findings was to introduce new coordinate transformations, called Lorentz transformations, between inertial frames of reference that are at slow speeds, these transformations were essentially identical to classical relativity model, yet at high speeds like near the speed of light they produce very different results
- Theory of General Relativity, Albert Einstein explained gravitation as the curvature of space-time around any mass. Objects with greater mass caused greater curvature, and thus exhibited greater gravitational pull. It has been shown that light actually curves around massive objects such as the sun, which supports this theory since space itself, curves at this point and light will follow the simplest path through space.

Theory of Relativity

- The "theory of relativity" to describe these concepts, originally only applied to special relativity because there was no general relativity yet
- Special relativity yields several consequences when applying Lorentz transformations at high velocities (near the speed of light)
  - They are as follows
    - Time dilation
    - Length contraction
    - Velocity transformation
    - Relativistic velocity addition
    - Relativistic Doppler effect
    - Simultaneity & clock synchronization
    - Relativistic momentum
    - Relativistic kinetic energy
    - Relativistic mass
    - Relativistic total energy

However Einstein's predictions of special relativity eventually have been shown to be true. An example is that clocks flown around the world slowed down by the duration predicted by the theory. The coordinate transformations didn't have to be created since the Lorentz transformations Einstein needed already existed. Einstein was a master in science and theory and by taking his and others previous work and adapting it to new situations, just as he did in this example with the Lorentz transformations; he was able to make new predictions. Another example, he took and used Planck's solution and applied it to the ultraviolet catastrophe in black body radiation to craft his solution to the photoelectric effect, and thus developed the photon theory of light.

The Lorentz Transformations

It was Hendrik Antoon Lorentz, a mathematician and physicist, who proposed the idea of a "local time" to explain relative simultaneity and worked on similar transformations to explain the null result other experiments and so coordinate transformations were published. It was Henri Poincare who with some modifications to the algebraic formulations he named the "Lorentz transformations," thus attributing them to Lorentz. The transformations that Einstein used were essentially identical to the transformations applied to a four-dimensional coordinate system using three spatial coordinates ($x, y, \& z$) and one time coordinate (t). Thus the transformed new coordinates are denoted as the ($x', y', \& z'$) to be referred to as the x-prime, y-prime and z-prime coordinates. For a special relativity velocity it would be described that the velocity is in the xx' direction, with velocity μ.

Einstein took basic concepts, applied them to theoretical frameworks and proved them to be not merely mathematical tricks but fundamental aspects of nature in their own right. The Theory of Special Relativity showed that among inertial frames of reference there was no "preferred" frame. The development of general relativity came about as an attempt to show that this was true among non-inertial frames of reference as well such as accelerating ones.

General Relativity

Einstein's "equivalence principle," was that observing an experiment on the Earth (with gravitational acceleration g) would be identical to observing an experiment in a rocket ship that moved at a speed of g. The equivalence principle is simply stated as assuming the complete physical equivalence of a gravitational field and a corresponding acceleration of the reference system on such an item.

Einstein's General theory of relativity was that the universe is a geometrical system with three spatial dimensions and one time dimension. By the presence of mass: energy: and momentum or collectively stated as mass-energy density or stress-energy, there is a bending of this space-time coordinate system. Gravity is therefore the movement along the "simplest" or least-energetic route along this curved space-time.

Gravity can be depicted as the relationship between the curvature of space-time and mass-energy density with a direct constant proportion from Newton's Law of Gravity with the gravitational constant, G and the dependence of the speed of light, c is from the theory of special relativity:

$$(\text{Curvature of space-time}) = (\text{mass-energy density}) \times 8\pi G / c^4$$

If there is a zero or near zero for mass-energy density, which would be considered empty space; space-time is flat. Classical gravitation is a special case of gravity's manifestation in a relatively weak gravitational field, where the c^4 is a very big denominator and G is a very small numerator so it makes the curvature correction small.

General relativity explains gravity in relation to the curvature of a light object and that it necessarily doesn't have much of an effect on a heavier object; however, the curvature created by the heavier object does have an effect on the lighter object. In application it is this relationship of the two objects that keeps us from floating off into space, gravity. The curvature that is created by the Earth keeps the moon in orbit, and at the same time the curvature created due to gravity by the moon is enough to affect the tides on earth from the pull of its gravitation.

Special relativity and all of its findings support that of general relativity including the fact the theories are consistent.

Thermodynamics

Laws of Thermodynamics:

The laws of thermodynamics are actually specific manifestations of the law of conservation of mass-energy as it relates to thermodynamic processes.

- The zeroeth law of thermodynamics makes the notion of temperature possible
- The first law of thermodynamics demonstrates the relationship between internal energy, added heat, and work within a system
- The second law of thermodynamics relates to the natural flow of heat within a closed system
- The third law of thermodynamics states that it is impossible to create a thermodynamic process which is perfectly efficient

Electrostatic Laws:

Coulomb's law and Gauss's law are formulations of the relationship between electrically charged particles to create electrostatic force and electrostatic fields. The formulas, it turns out, parallel the laws of universal gravitation in structure. There also exist similar laws relating to magnetism and electromagnetism as a whole.

Invariance of the Speed of Light:

Einstein's major insight, which led him to the Theory of Relativity, was the realization that the speed of light in a vacuum is constant and is not measured differently for observers in different inertial frames of reference, unlike all other forms of motion.

First Law of Thermodynamics

The change in a system's internal energy is equal to the difference between heat added to the system from its surroundings and work done by the system on its surroundings.
Though this may sound complex, it's really a very simple idea. If you add heat to a system, there are only two things that can be done -- change the internal energy of the system or cause the system to do work (or, of course, some combination of the two). All of the heat energy must go into doing these things. The energy that goes into a system cannot be lost along the way, but has to be used to do something, either change internal energy or perform work.

Second Law of Thermodynamics

It is impossible for a process to have as its sole result the transfer of heat from a cooler body to a hotter one.

Third Law of Thermodynamics

The third law of thermodynamics is essentially a statement about the ability to create an absolute temperature scale, for which absolute zero is the point at which the internal energy of a solid is precisely 0.

Quantum physics is the study of the behavior of matter and energy at the molecular, atomic, nuclear, and even smaller microscopic levels. It was discovered that the laws that govern macroscopic objects do not function the same in such small realms as some of the other general laws do.

Electricity

Electrical Force

- The electrical force between two charges is proportional to the product of the two charges.
  - There is a directly proportional relationship between the charge and the electrical force
    - Therefore, if one charge is double the electric force is doubled and if both charges are doubled then the electric force quadruples
- Coulomb determined that the electric force varies inversely as the squared charges distance
  - Therefore, if the original force is decreased to 25% between the two forces when the distance between two forces doubles
  - When 2 forces move closer together the force between them increases

Electric Field

- An electric field is a property of a charge that experiences a force due to the presence of the other changes.
$$F = \text{charge} \times \text{electric field}.$$
  - Electric fields vary from point to point both in magnitude and direction due to the force a charge is dependent on the magnitude of the charges involved and the distance separating the charges
  - The electric field is always in the same direction as the electric force
  - Charges in the vicinity of other charges will have a force act on the charges and they begin to move
  - When an electrical force moves a charge a certain distance, the force does work on the charge
  - The charge in the electrical potential over this distance is defined by work done by the force

$$\text{Work done} = \text{force} \times \text{distance} = \text{charge} \times \text{potential difference}$$

Potential Difference

- Potential difference is how much work the electric field does in moving a charge from one place to another
- Potential difference is the change in electric potential
  - Units are Joules/Coulomb which is = volts
  - Batteries are rated by the potential differences across their terminals. A 9 volt battery the potential difference between the + and − terminals precisely 9 volts
  - In an electrical outlet on your home the difference between the + and − sides is 110 volts

Current

- A potential difference is established between two points and some charges are released
- These charges are acted on by an electrical force and therefore, move
  - The measurement of the amount of charge flowing by a given point at a certain time interval is considered a current
  - A current is the charge flowing through that point per unit time
    Current = charge/time
  - Current is expressed in units of charge
    - Current has its own unit of measure
    - Coulombs/second or = Amperes (A)

Electrical Currents

- In electrical currents, physical currents consist of electrons moving in wire from lower to higher electrical potential, electrons are negatively charged so the net effect is equal to a positive current flow from higher to lower electrical potential
- 2 types of currents
    - Direct current (DC)
    - Alternating Current (AC)
  - Direct Current
  - DC is a current which always flows in one particular direction
  - An example is a flashlight battery
  - Alternating Current
  - AC is one which alternately flows in one direction the then the other
  - An example is a household outlet

Resistance

- Resistance makes the potential difference applied across two points and the current generated are proportional
  - Voltage and current are proportional and this consistency is the resistance in Ohms Law
    - Units for resistance are volts/amperes = Ohms (Ω)

$$v = current \times resistance$$

  - Materials with a high resistance will allow a small current relative to a material that has a low resistance will allow a larger current
    - therefore, in relation to heat resistance and conductivity,
  - Electrical conductivity is proportional to the inverse of the resistance
    - A relationship exist that good electrical conductors have low resistance and vice versa
  - A good electrical conductor is copper
  - A poor electrical conductor is concrete

Electrical Power

- The power rating of an appliance is the rate at which it uses electrical energy
- Power companies charge you the total amount of energy we use during a specific period. The consumption is in Kilowatt Hours (KWh). 1 Kilowatt hour is the energy used by 1Kilowatt appliance (that uses 1000 Joules per second) that is run for one hour.

$$1KWh = Joules/second \times 3600seconds = 3,600,00 \ Joules$$

  - The energy of An electrical appliance, the power output, the potential difference across it and the current running through it is equal to the charge times the potential difference
  - (charge per unit time) times (potential difference) is equal to energy per unit time therefore is equal to :

$$Power = current \times voltage$$

Electrical Units

  - watt = Joules / second
  - volt = Joules / coulomb
  - Amperes = coulombs / second
  - Ohms = volts / Ampere

Magnetism

- Magnetic Forces are explained in terms very similar to those used for electric forces
  - There are two magnetic poles;
    - North
    - South
  - Like poles repel and opposite poles attract

Magnetic Field

- A magnetic field is when moving charges experience a force
- is a magnetic field that a current carrying wire will also experience a force, since a current consists of moving charges
- The strength of a magnetic field is measured in units or Teslas (T). Compasses use magnetism with the Earth's magnetic field
- 1 Tesla is actually a relatively strong field the Earth's magnetic field is like 0.0001T

Magnetism

- Magnetism is the vicinity of a magnetic field in which a moving charge will experience a force
- Magnetism differs from electricity
  - In magnetic poles always occurs in North and South pairs
  - There are no monopoles

Magnetic Forces

- Magnetic forces cause charged particles to change their direction
  - The magnetic force that acts on a charged particle is always perpendicular to the direction it's moving
  - The charged particles direction of motion is changed but the speed of the particles is unchanged
  - If the force is perpendicular to the motion then no work is done
  - Magnetic forces do not do work on charged particles and cannot increase their kinetic energy
    - Electric Motor
  - An electric motor is a machine which converts electrical energy into mechanical energy, either being rotational or kinetic energy
  - In the motor a current is passed through a loop which is immersed in a magnetic field
    - Speaker
  - A speaker is a device that uses the magnetic forces existing on current carrying wires
  - A speaker is a device that takes an electrical signal and converts it back into a sound wave
    - Electrical signals in the form of an AC current are sent through a loop which is immersed in a magnetic field

Magnetism from Electricity

- Currents are induced on an object when the object is brought into the vicinity of their magnet fields
  - A compass
    - The compass needle is deflected when brought into the vicinity of a current carrying wire
- Electromagnet
  - An electromagnet is a coil of wires which when a current is passed through the oil of wires it will generate a magnetic field

Magnetic Material

- Three types of magnetic material;
  - Nonmagnetic
    - Most materials have no obvious magnetic properties. The atoms magnetic fields are randomly aligned and tend to cancel out
  - Permanent magnets
    - Magnetic fields of the individual atoms are aligned in one preferred direction, giving rise to a net magnetic field
  - Ferromagnets
    - There are domains in which the magnetic fields of the individual atoms align, but the orientation of the magnetic fields of the domains is random, so no net magnetic field
    - They are useful when an external magnetic field is applied to them. The magnetic fields of the atoms line up in the direction of this external field, due to the nature of the magnetic forces and the external magnetic field is enhanced

Currents from Magnetism

- A change in magnetic fields through loops of wire will cause currents to be induced
  - The rotation comes from the falling water or steam
    - falling water
      - hydroelectric plant
    - steam
      - coal or nuclear plant
- A changing magnetic field put through the plane of wires causes a current to be generated
- Examples of these kinds of items are:
  - Electric generator
    - It rotates the current in the magnetic field
    - The electric motor is similar to the electric generator
      - They differ because
        - The electric motor produces the current but rotation of its parts
        - The electric generator produces a current by rotation in the magnetic field
  - Microphone
  - Magnetic tape reader

Heat

Temperature

- Temperature is the measure of the average kinetic energy of matter in an object
  - Temperature is subject to other things to determine whether a substance is warm or cold in respect to the other object
  - Therefore temperature like position is relative to the reference point of
- Temperature is measured in units of Celsius, Fahrenheit and Kelvin scales
- The Kelvin Scale is considered the absolute temperature scale.
  - The lowest possible temperature known is 0°K or absolute zero.
    - On the Kelvin Scale at 273.16°K is the temperature at which water exists simultaneously as a gas, liquid and a solid.
      - This is simultaneous existence of water is referred to as the triple point.
  - Temperature also has a freezing point or the ice point.
    - The boiling point or steam point is when water boils to form steam and steam condenses to form water simultaneously.
      - The Fahrenheit temperature is 212°F and the Celsius temperature is 100°C.
      - The boiling point is the state of matter change from a liquid to a gas.
    - The ice point is the temperature at which water freezes and ice melts simultaneously.
      - The Fahrenheit temperature is 32°and the Celsius temperature is 0°.
      - The freezing point is the state of matter change from a liquid to a solid.
- Temperature when the substance comes in contact with another object determines if it will gain or lose heat.
  - Temperature increases and gets higher when a substance is heated or energy is applied to it.

Temperature conversions:

$$°K = °C + 273$$
$$°F = \left(\frac{9}{5}°C\right) + 32$$
$$\Delta°F = \left(\frac{9}{5}\right)\Delta°C$$

Heat

- Heat is a form of energy that causes matter's components to rapidly move and to move farther away from each other.
  - An object that is hot has a high temperature and contains heat or exerts heat.

The Earth's Atmosphere

Our Atmosphere

- The Atmosphere is the gaseous shell of air that surrounds the earth
- The Air humans breathe is air
- Earth's atmosphere that humans breathe is composed of nitrogen, oxygen, argon and carbon dioxide
- Percentage composition of Earth's atmosphere is as follows
    - Nitrogen 78%
    - Oxygen 21%
    - Carbon Dioxide 0.03%
    - Argon 0.9%

The Atmosphere and Life Cycle

- Nitrogen (N_2), Oxygen (O_2), and Carbon dioxide (CO_2)
    - These elements are all part of the life cycle of plants and animals
    - These elements are constantly being replenished and consumed from the atmosphere as byproducts of these various life cycles
        - Carbon monoxide is the product of incomplete combustion
    - Nature has a way so that it maintains the right balance of the required nutrients from the atmosphere

Atmospheric Divisions

- The atmosphere has various regions divided by vertical variations such as density and volume, temperature, homogeneity, and heterogeneity of gases and ozone and ion concentration
- The levels of the Atmosphere are;
    - Troposphere
    - Stratosphere
    - Mesosphere
    - Thermosphere

Troposhpere

- The lower Troposphere atmospheric conditions are referred to as weather
    - Weather is the changes of the atmosphere closest to the earth's surface and is reflective by the local variations in a specific region
        - The Troposphere varies from at the equator as high as 10 ½ miles to about 5 miles @ the poles At the top of the Troposphere the temperature falls as low as ⁻60° F to ⁻50° F

- The Atmosphere's properties measurements include
    - Temperature – the measurement of the heat energy. The kinetic theory of gases says energy directly proportional to temperature
    - Pressure – the face per unit area one atmosphere of pressure is equal to 14.7 lb/in^2.
    - Humidity – the measure of water vapor in the air
    - Wind speed is measured by an anemometer and direction by a wind vane or a wind sock

Atomospheric Relationsip to Density

- When the temperature of an air mass is increased it expands to a larger volume
  - Density is mass per volume or $\rho = {}^{m}/_{v}$
    - Therefore, the increase in volume causes a decrease in density
- As the atmosphere extends vertically its density continues to decrease
  - Air that is cold is heavier and moves downward displacing light warmer air
    - This is one means for vertical air movement
  - Warm air's volume is lighter or less dense
  - Cool air's volume is heavier or denser

Atmospheric Pressure

- Pressure is the force per unit area
  - Every human's body and every inch or the body sustains an average weight or 14.7 lbs at sea level
    - This weight of 14.7 lbs at sea level is equal to a pressure of 14.7 lb/in^2
    - Atmospheric pressure is closely related to density
      - Atmospheric pressure is force per area
        - 1 atmosphere of pressure is equal to 14.7 lb/in^2 or 1 atm
  - A region of rising air is one of low pressure
    - There are distinct changes when measuring temperature of the atmosphere versus altitude
    - There is an inverse relationship between temperature and altitudes
      - The atmospheric temperature decreases with an increase in altitude
- Lapse rate is the rate at which the temperature decreases with height
  - The average rate of $3\frac{1}{2}$°F per 1000 ft up to about 10 miles
    - This is also the average lapse rate of stationary air

Air Movement

- Air motion is due to the gases of the atmosphere subject to the forces arising from gravity and pressure differences due to temperature variations
  - The pressure of a gas is directly proportional to its temperature
    - Air movement in the atmosphere is caused by the difference in pressure due to a temperature change
      - Wind is the horizontal motion of air
      - Air currents are collectively the vertical air motions being either updrafts or downdrafts

Clouds

- Clouds have a major role in maintaining the earth's heat balance
  - Purposes
    - Reflect solar radiation
    - Insulate the earth from heat loss
    - Precipitation process is associated with clouds
      - All forms of precipitation originate in clouds
        - Precipitation in major forms is called rain and snow
          - Rain is measured by a rain gauge
          - Snow is reported by its depth in inches
    - The hydrologic cycle
      - The way moisture is distributed over the earth

- Clouds are visible droplets of water vapor or ice crystals that are buoyant masses
  - Clouds are classified according to shape, appearance, and altitude
    - There are four basic root names also referred to as families :
      - Cirrus (Ci)
        - curl or wispy fibrous forms fibrous forms
      - Cumulus(Cu)
        - heap or billowy round forms
      - Stratus(St)
        - layered forms or stratified
      - Nimbus(Nb)
        - a cloud from which precipitations is occurring from or threatens to occur
  - Clouds are also classified according to height:
    - High Clouds
      - From 20,000 ft and above
      - Visible water vapor in the form of ice crystals due to the temperature at that altitude
    - Middle Clouds
      - Between 6,000 ft and 20,000 ft
    - Low Clouds
      - Ground level up to 6,000 ft
      - Thin layers of water vapor and fogs
        - Fog consists of visible water vapor
          - Fog forms for two reasons
            - Moist air moves over a colder surface and the air is cooled below the dew point and condensation occurs
            - Stationary air overlying a surface area is cooled
    - Clouds with vertical development
      - Between 1,500 ft up to 60,000 ft
      - These clouds are formed by rising air currents
      - The winds and air currents cause many variations in cloud shapes
      - Cloud height also called "cloud ceiling" is important in aviation as well as meteorology
      - Meteorologists can determine the cloud height of the cloud coverage using the principle for light, reflection of the light from its emission to its detection, the time it takes for this and the constant of the speed of light

Blank

Practice Test for Physical Science

1. A sound wave is different than a light wave in that a sound wave is
   A. Produced by an oscillating object and a light wave is not.
   B. Is capable of traveling through a vacuum.
   C. Is capable of diffracting and a light wave is.
   D. Capable of existing with a variety of frequencies and a light wave has a single frequency.

2. Acceleration is a vector quantity and which limit of measure is typically used as its label?
   A. ms
   B. m/s
   C. m/s/s
   D. m/s/s^2

3. Which abbreviation is a constant value?
   A. g
   B. Hz
   C. J
   D. Watt

4. Which unit of measure is used by work and energy?
   A. g
   B. Hz
   C. J
   D. Watt

5. The centripetal force that acts on an object in a circular motion is a description of which force?
   A. Spring
   B. Applied force
   C. Net force
   D. Gravity

6. What is the name given to a force acting upon an object to cause a displacement?
   A. Work
   B. Power
   C. Potential energy
   D. Kinetic energy

7. Jack and Jill ran up the hill to fetch a pail of water. If Jack is twice as massive as Jill but Jill ran up the hill and reached the pail of water sooner than Jack, who did the most work?
   A. Jack
   B. Jill
   C. Jack and Jill
   D. Neither Jack nor Jill

8. Jack and Jill ran up the hill to fetch a pail of water. If Jack is twice as massive as Jill but Jill ran up the hill and reached the pail of water sooner than Jack, who is the most powerful?
   A. Jack
   B. Jill
   C. Jack & Jill
   D. Neither Jack nor Jill

9. John has a toy dart gun made from wood with a spring used to shoot the darts. What type of energy does the gun possess?
   A. Gravitation potential
   B. Elastic potential
   C. Potential
   D. Kinetic

10. John has a toy dart gun made from wood with a spring used to shoot the darts. Due to the energy the gun possesses, when the dart is released what is done to the dart?
   A. The dart has a force applied and is compressed
   B. The dart has an energy applied to it to have power
   C. The dart has a force applied to it to do work
   D. The dart has work done to it from the spring that applied a force

11. John has a toy dart gun made from wood with a spring used to shoot the darts. When John shoots his dart gun at the target board and it falls to the ground, what has been done to the dart and target board?
   A. Work, power
   B. Power, power
   C. Power, work
   D. Work, work

12. What type of energy is possessed by all of the following; a student, a baseball pitcher, a football, a quarterback, a tractor, and a bicycle?
   A. Gravitation potential
   B. Chemical potential
   C. Mechanical potential
   D. Elastic potential

13. When you disconnect a part of a circuit you:
   A. Spoil the dry cell
   B. Waste electricity
   C. Make an open circuit
   D. Make a closed circuit

14. A dry cell is related to electricity in that it:
   A. Uses electricity
   B. Stops electricity
   C. Supplies electricity
   D. Changes electricity

15. A bulb will glow when it is in a (an):
    A. Flashlight
    B. Short circuit
    C. Open circuit
    D. Closed circuit

16. When a switch is used in a circuit it is:
    A. Always closed
    B. Never closed
    C. Always open
    D. Sometimes open

17. Every time a switch is closed:
    A. Electricity can flow
    B. Electricity cannot flow
    C. Electricity is made
    D. Electricity is destroyed

18. Copper is usually used in electrical wires. What is the reasoning for the use of copper?
    A. Copper is an Insulator
    B. Copper is a Conductor
    C. Copper is a light substance
    D. Copper is a heavy substance

19. A wire become hot from electricity because:
    A. The wire is made of copper
    B. Electricity has a high voltage
    C. Electricity is moving and takes energy from the wire
    D. Electricity is moving and gives energy to the wire

20. What relationship is there due to electricity and its wires temperature and the light given off?
    A. The hotter the wire no light is given off
    B. The colder the wire no light is given off
    C. The hotter the wire the dimmer the light
    D. The hotter the wire the brighter the light

21. From what energy does a generator make electrical energy?
    A. Light
    B. Heat
    C. Steam
    D. Magnets

22. When does electricity stop flowing from a generator?
    A. When the coil is moving
    B. When the magnet is moving
    C. Neither the coil nor the magnet is moving
    D. Either the coil or the magnet is moving

23. Calculate how many kilowatt- hours of energy would be used if a 60 watt light bulb is kept on for 1 full day?
    A. 1.44
    B. 6.00
    C. 600
    D. 1440

24. The power company charges you 0.09 cents per kWh regularly and anything over 800 kWh's during the summer there is a 0.025 cents per kWh seasonal charge added. Your monthly usage for July was 4,000,000 watts per hour; calculate how much your bill would be?
    A. $ 288.00
    B. $ 360.00
    C. $ 440.00
    D. $ 460.00

25. If electricity costs $0.10 per kWh how much would it cost to run a 1000 watt heater for 10 hours?
    A. 0.10
    B. 1.00
    C. 10.00
    D. 100.00

26. A flashlight uses a 9 volt battery and has a current of 1 Ampere, how much energy is being used in watts?
    A. 1
    B. 9
    C. 81
    D. 11

27. Your lamp in your bedroom has a 60 watt light bulb plugged into a 110 volt wall outlet, what is the current running through the light in Amperes?
    A. .183
    B. .545
    C. 1.83
    D. 5.45

28. The Earth's atmosphere is primarily composed or what element?
    A. Oxygen
    B. Carbon
    C. Argon
    D. Nitrogen

29. What type of cloud is fluffy looking and you can imagine shapes and images from them?
    A. Cirrus
    B. Cumulus
    C. Stratus
    D. Nimbus

30. Which type of radiation has the highest frequency?
    A. Infrared
    B. Microwave
    C. Ultraviolet
    D. X-ray

31. In comparing an electric motor and an electric generator which is the correct statement about their relationship to each other?
    A. They are exactly the same.
    B. They are completely different.
    C. They are similar with no differences.
    D. They are similar but are different.

32. Magnetic forces can cause numerous things to happen to a particle or an object. What is not caused by a magnetic force?
    A. Change direction
    B. Do work
    C. Experience a force
    D. Induce a current

33. If five wave crests pass by a given point in one second, what would be the frequency in Hz?
    A. 0.20
    B. 0.50
    C. 2.00
    D. 5.00

34. At the beach, 10 wave's crests pass the same rock in one second, what is the period of the wave in seconds?
    A. 0.01
    B. 0.10
    C. 1.00
    D. 10.00

35. What is the wavelength in meters of a radio waves produced by a radio station which has a frequency of 900 Kilohertz?
    A. 30 m
    B. 300 m
    C. 90 m
    D. 900 m

Practice Test for Physical Science Answers

1. A	13. C	25. B
2. C	14. C	26. B
3. A	15. D	27. B
4. C	16. D	28. D
5. C	17. A	29. B
6. A	18. B	30. D
7. A	19. D	31. D
8. B	20. D	32. C
9. B	21. D	33. D
10. D	22. D	34. B
11. D	23. A	35. B
12. B	24. C	

Please Note:

Learning Styles is an Optional Test

Check with Your School to See If This Is Part of Your Entrance Test

Blank

Learning Styles

Learning is overall the process of committing (representations) information, data, etc. to memory where it may be processed. The learner processes information, data, etc. by the way he/she organizes, stores, and finds relationships by linking new to old knowledge. Learning is not just memorizing the answers and regurgitating someone else's meaning. Learning is the search for meaning, understanding wholes, as well as, the parts from what has been presented or derived from the senses. Learning is comprised of both acquisition and metacognition.

Metacognition is how the learner processes to memory the information, data, etc. that has been acquired or presented to the learner in order to learn for later use and knowledge. Metacognition is broken up into two categories, investigative and contemplative, as to how information, data, etc. is processed by the learner.

Contemplative Metacognition is when information, data, etc. is being processed in such a way that the learner is meditative, reflective, thinks internally and usually thinks before doing something. A contemplative metacognition person tends to think about the details of how to do something before he/she does it; he/she focuses on the details and often misses the big picture. This type learner is a cognitive learner and tends to come up with new ways of doing things. This learner tends to be more cautious or conservative. He/she views things from a different perspective and looks for meaning and make careful observations. A contemplative metacognition learner processes very differently from an investigative learner.

Investigative metacognition or contemplative metacognition is the way that information, data, etc. is thought of or about in order to learn (process to memory) for later use. Investigative metacognition is when information, data, etc. is being processed in such a way that the learner is externally active, analyzes it after the fact, probes it, experiments, and usually does something and then thinks about it. He/she is reactive rather than proactive. An Investigative metacognition person tends to jump into something before he/she has thought it through, similar to an impulsive behavior type. He/she tends to be "seeing is believing", needs variety, needs to try things out, and he/she looks at the big picture first then looks at the details later. This type of learner tends to be active, prefers simulations, likes to be involved in case studies and usually learns by doing something.

Acquisition is the method by which information, data, etc. is presented to the learner, to allow him/her to acquire (take in) the information, data etc. in order to then learn (process it to memory) for later use. In order to learn (process it to memory) the learner must think of or about the information, data, etc..

Acquisition is broken up into two categories related to how information, data, etc. is presented to the learner. Theoretical acquisition or factual acquisition are the ways that information, data, etc. can be presented to the learner in order to acquire (take in) the information, data, etc.

Theoretical acquisition is when information , data, etc. is being presented to the learner in such a way that the information , data, etc. would be categorized or described as being hypothetical, idealistic, abstract, theoretical, based on perception, relative, creative, unique, out of the ordinary, subjective, or non-concrete.

Factual acquisition is when information, data, etc. is being presented in such a way that the information, data, etc. would be categorized or described as being matter of fact, factual, corporeal, concrete, material, objective, physical, experiential, clearly stated as to meaning, or straightforward.

The three methods of acquiring information, data, etc. are auditorial, visual and acquired. Auditorial learning would include such presentation of information, data, etc. by lecture, tapes, compact discs, and/or discussions. Visual learning would include such presentation of information by reading, videotapes, overheads, charts, graphs, and/ or observations. Acquired learning would include such presentation of information by hands on teaching methods, labs, field work, or watching someone else do the act.

The three methods of processing information, data, etc. are audio, visual, and physical processing. Audio processing would include such things as discussions, recording notes, and replaying them, reading out loud, listening to others opinions and getting their feedback and "you get more out of what you hear than anything else" idea. Visual processing would include such things as watching or looking at something to learn or process it, writing down notes or reorganizing the notes at a later time or drawing things to see them. Physical processing would include such things as doing something, trying it or physically taking part in it.

Just like any classification there are two extremes and a fuzzy area in between where one becomes the other. Often people are not completely characterized by one or the other. People often have some characteristics of each one but will tend to be more one than the other. There are always those that fit directly into one of the classifications and are only that way. This person would be considered the absolute if he/she has no characteristics of the other classification. In the real world and in every situation there is probably no one that is an absolute except in theory.

How to Understand Learning Styles and its Relationships

Analysis of the following areas: Metacognition and Acquisition. Metacognition includes contemplative and investigative and Acquisition includes factual and theoretical. The modes of acquiring data, etc. (auditorial, visual and acquired) are included. The methods of processing information, data, etc. (audio, visual, and physical) are also included. Metacognition cannot be compared to Acquisition.

Just as in any classification system there are two extremes and a fuzzy area between where one becomes the other. Often people are not completely characterized by one extreme or the other. Learners have been forced to learn in teacher preferred styles over the years and many have learned to learn in a variety of ways. This accounts for those who do not seem to be one way or another. People often have some characteristics of each part of the category but will tend to be more one than the other. There are always those that fit directly into one of the classifications and are only that way. This person would be considered the absolute if he/she has no characteristics of the other classification. In the real world and in every situation there is probably no one that is an absolute except in theory.

Metacognition

- Metacognition is how the learner processes to memory the information, data, etc. that has been acquired or presented to the learner in order to learn for later use and knowledge. Metacognition is broken up into two categories, investigative and contemplative, as to how information, data, etc. is processed by the learner.
  - *Contemplative metacognition*: is when information, data, etc. is being processed in such a way that the learner is meditative, reflective, thinks internally and usually thinks before doing something.
    - A contemplative metacognition person tends to think about the details of how to do something before he/she does it; he/she focuses on the details and often misses the big picture.
    - This type learner is a cognitive learner and tends to come up with new ways of doing things. This learner tends to be more cautious or conservative.
    - He/she views things from a different perspective and looks for meaning and make careful observations.
    - A contemplative metacognition learner processes very differently from an investigative learner.
  - *Investigative metacognition*: or contemplative metacognition is the way that information, data, etc. is thought of or about in order to learn (process to memory) for later use.
    - Investigative metacognition is when information, data, etc. is being processed in such a way that the learner is externally active, analyzes it after the fact, probes it, experiments, and usually does something and then thinks about it.
    - He/she is reactive rather than proactive.
    - An Investigative metacognition person tends to jump into something before he/she has thought it through, similar to an impulsive behavior type.
    - He/she tends to be "seeing is believing", needs variety, needs to try things out, and he/she looks at the big picture first then looks at the details later. This type of learner tends to be active, prefers simulations, likes to be involved in case studies and usually learns by doing something.

Interpretation
- Contemplative and investigative must be looked at together.
  - This tends to be an inverse relationship.
  - If a person is high in one then that person usually is lower in the other.
  - A person who is about equal in both is able to use both to process information.

Acquisition

- Acquisition is the method by which information, data, etc. is presented to the learner, to allow him/her to acquire (take in) the information, data etc. in order to then learn (process it to memory) for later use.
  - In order to learn (process it to memory) the learner must think of or about the information, data, etc...
- Acquisition is broken up into two categories related to how information, data, etc. is presented to the learner.
  - Theoretical acquisition or factual acquisition are the ways that information, data, etc. can be presented to the learner in order to acquire (take in) the information, data, etc.
    - *Factual*:
      - Factual acquisition is when information, data, etc. is being presented in such a way that the information, data, etc. would be categorized or described as being matter of fact, factual, corporeal, concrete, material, objective, physical, experiential, clearly stated as to meaning, or straightforward.
    - *Theoretical*:
      - Theoretical acquisition is when information , data, etc. is being presented to the learner in such a way that the information , data, etc. would be categorized or described as being hypothetical, idealistic, abstract, theoretical, based on perception, relative, creative, unique, out of the ordinary, subjective, or non-concrete.

Interpretation

- Factual and theoretical must be looked at together.
  - This tends to be an inverse relationship.
  - If a person is high in one then that person usually is lower in the other.
  - A person who is about equal in both is able to use both to process information.

Learning Style/Acquisition

The three methods of acquiring information, data, etc. are acquired, auditorial, and visual.

- *Acquired Learning*:
  - Would include such presentation of information by hands on teaching methods, labs, field work, or watching someone else do the act.
- *Auditorial Learning*:
  - Would include such presentation of information, data, etc. by lecture, tapes, compact discs, and/or discussions
- *Visual Learning*:
  - Visual learning would include such presentation of information by reading, videotapes, overheads, charts, graphs, and/ or observations.

Interpretation

- To evaluate the type of method the person uses to acquire information these three methods are ranked from highest to lowest.
  - The highest is the preferred method.
  - The closer the scores are the more the person is able to adapt to the situation at hand and learn from any of the methods.

Just like any classification there are two extremes and a fuzzy area in between where one becomes the other. Often people are not completely characterized by one or the other. People often have some characteristics of each one but will tend to be more one than the other. There are always those that fit directly into one of the classifications and are only that way. This person would be considered the absolute if he/she has no characteristics of the other classification. In the real world and in every situation there is probably no one that is an absolute except in theory.

Inter/Intra Personal

This area determines if a person is a more social or solitary learner and is based on how high the person's percentage is for that category. The higher the percent, the higher the person's tendency towards that type of setting for learning would be. If the percent is about equal, the person can learn equally well in either setting.

- *Social learners*:
    - Social learners do better when one or more people interact with them. This learner would rather be in groups for activities, study groups, or bouncing information back and forth with another individual.
- *Solitary learners*:
    - Solitary learners do better when they have no other human interaction to learn. This learner would rather have an independent study, computer course, or do a project alone. This learner studies alone.

Blank

Please Note:

Cyberspace Aptitude Analysis
Is an Optional Test

Check with Your School to See If This Is
Part of Your Entrance Test

Blank

Cyberspace Aptitude Analysis

CAA is a tool that assesses the relationship between computer ease, internet ease, internet success, internet satisfaction and what kind of a user the person is overall. Cyberspace aptitude determines the level of computer/web interaction that a person already possesses. A person will be classified as Non-User, Novice, Intermediate, Master or Expert. An explanation of these classifications will be provided with the results.

The internet is not necessarily only using the web it is utilizing the operations of a network of information and connection between millions of computers. It is an enormous network. The different areas have been designated

User Type Classification	Categories of Knowledge and Use Content
None User	Acquire Web Components
Novice	Chat
Intermediate	E-Commerce
Master	E-mail
Expert	Entertainment
	General
	Internet Broadcast
	Search/Research
	Spec Interest Groups

Understanding Data that is given from the CAA

There are 2 ways to consider the data to have a better understanding of your people and their cyberspace abilities. The first way is based on the overall score and then secondly to look at each subcategory of Cyberspace Aptitude Analysis. Looking at the overall score will help to determine, based on his/her score on the CAA section, whether the person would be classified as a none user, novice, intermediate, master or an expert in general. Looking at the subcategories will help to determine what his/her strengths and weaknesses are and what type of cyberspace user he/she is. The chart below will help to determine the user level, either from the score (raw data of points acquired) or from the percentage. This data is based on administration to a large population of diversified people.

	Score Range	% Range
None User	0-50	0%-20%
Novice	51-75	21%-30%
Intermediate	76-125	31%-50%
Master	126-175	51%-70%
Expert	176-248	71%-100%

By looking at the types of components the person is stronger in, some inferences can be made regarding whether the person uses the web for fun, business, entertainment, school, work, etc. For example, someone who is high in Chat, Entertainment and Search/Research and extremely low in all other areas could be inferred as a person who uses the web purely for fun. A person who is high in Email and Spec Interest Groups and very low in all other areas could be inferred as a person who uses the web in a business setting where this information is important. These are not facts but inferences based on relationships between the categories.

User Types Explanation

There are five types of CAA users: a none user, novice, intermediate, master, expert. A user will be classified as an overall user type based on his/her overall score but he/she then can be evaluated by user types based on the score in the individual categories. Each user can be at different levels for each of the different categories. A comparison would be that a student could be better in one subject in school than another but still be a good student, just at different levels in different subjects.

The different categories that are tested are: Acquire Web Components, Chat, E-Commerce, E-mail, Entertainment, General, Internet Broadcast, Search/Research, Special Interest Groups. There are many different parts of the internet / web and skills that are included in each of these categories of use of cyberspace.

In order to have a better understanding of what type of a user a person is, we have described each user type so they can be understood more easily. These types are related to cyberspace not computer use. A person can be very computer literate and be proficient using a computer but be a non user of cyberspace. Cyberspace and computer use are somewhat related but there is no direct correlation that would suggest that just because a person can use a computer and various programs on the computer that person can use web components and be proficient at them.

Non-User

A non-user of cyberspace is a person who has no knowledge or very little of the web and any of its components. This person is one, who if they use any component of the internet it is in a very simple basic way and usually has to have help from others throughout the entire process. The components the person uses may be because of a requirement that has been school or job related and it is repetitive. This type user knows very little about very few if any of the internet's / web's components. This type user may recognize the names of the internet components but has no understanding of what they are, how they work, and any benefits they can provide to his/her life, job, or school. This type user often is one who is apprehensive and prefers the non-automated way of doing things. This user also may not be a person who has ever been exposed to the internet nor had the opportunity to be involved in the learning of what the internet is and what it can entail.

Novice

A novice of cyberspace is a person who has minimal knowledge of the web and any of its components. This person is one who when he/she uses a component of the internet it is in a basic way and he/she knows one way to do it and he/she doesn't deviate from it. The person often has to go to someone with a question if it is out of the scope of what was learned first. The components the person uses may have originally been learned due to a requirement that has been school or job related and now has begun to use it more but still in a relatively basic way. This type user knows a little about some of the internet's / web's components. This type user may recognize the benefits internet components can provide to his/her life, job, or school but have no clear understanding of what they are really are and how and why they work the way they do. This type user often is one who is apprehensive but is learning to try the automated way of doing things and venturing out of the conventional ways of doing things.

Intermediate

An intermediate user of cyberspace is a person who has a basic understanding and basic knowledge of the web and any of its components. This person is one who when he/she uses a component of the internet it is in an intermediate way and he/she has a more casual relationship with the web components. This person will often try new things and try to look into how to do something before going to someone for help but yet are still timid and apprehensive to try too complex of a task. This user has a firm grasp on how to do things and tries things just because of curiosity. This type user knows usually more than one way of doing something or getting to something. This person will know how to do things but will usually not know too much about the how, why and what makes it all work together to come out with the end result. This type user puts the benefits of the web to use in his/her life to make things easier and provide more satisfaction to his/her life, job, or school. This type user often is one who is not apprehensive but is learning all the time what else he/she can do with the web and its components.

Master

A master user of cyberspace is a person who has an extensive understanding and knowledge of the web and any of its components. This person is one who when they use a component of the internet it is on a higher level than most and prefer to use the web component and will deviate from any conventional use other than the web if at al possible. This user has a very extensive relationship with the internet and requires the least amount of assistance with things related to the web. Typically a Master will posses all of the previous groups of user's levels but go beyond this to programming and trying to do new things with the components that are already there. This user is familiar with the mechanics of the web and all of the components that it builds upon. This user is capable of trouble shooting problems but will still have to get help from others at times. This user is the troubleshooter and experimenter and will find alternate ways of doing things on a complex level throughout all levels of the web. This user goes behind the scene and gets data. This user is one who has decided to take his/her pursuit of knowledge beyond the standard entry level developer of web components. This user knows how and why things work the way they do. This is a person that can cause damage to your systems if he/she gets access to it because this user knows a lot about a lot. This user puts every aspect of the web to play in his/her life; he/she would be lost if not connected.

Expert

An expert user of cyberspace is a person who has the ultimate understanding and knowledge of the web and any of its components. This person is one who when he/she uses a component of the internet it is on a higher level than any others. This user has an ultimate relationship with the internet and requires no assistance with things related to the web. Typically, an expert makes existing things do new things with the components that are already there or creates new parts to those components. This user is often the creator of programs and data on the web. This user is familiar with the mechanics of the web and all of the components that it builds upon. This user is the trouble shooter and are "the know it all's" of the web. This user is the authority. This user is the person you go to for help from any of the other levels. This user goes behind the scene and gets data and makes it do what he/she wants it to do and how he/she wants it to do it. This user is on the leading edge and is on the forefront of what is to come and can be. This user doesn't question "what can the web do for me "but says "what can I make the web do." This user knows how and why things work the way they do. This user is the person that can cause ultimate damage to your systems if he/she gets access to it because he/she knows the most about it. This user puts every aspect of the web to play in his/her life, and would be lost if not able to be connected to it. The web is his/her world.

Categories of Knowledge and Use Content

Acquire Web Components

Acquire Web Components is a category that entails computer and internet operations to acquire information from the web in ways that are not "click here" type operations. Some of these operations include FTP sites (File Transfer Protocol), saving pictures or text on a web page, acquiring source code from a web page or a site, etc. This category is how you get data from the web and the internet without it simply being given to you word for word or being downloaded to you by clicking on a button. It is more advanced operations that require a higher level of knowledge on how to obtain things from the internet.

Chat

Internet chat encompasses the various methods used to conduct real time text based communication between individuals or groups. While there are many different programs used to conduct chat sessions most of them share the same features and operating procedures. Typically those who wish to communicate using online chat use one of two methods, they can enter a Chat room online or log into an Instant Messenger. A Chat room is a specifically designed telnet session that allows users to log into the website with their username and relay messages to anyone else associated with the open telnet session. In a Chat Room there is no order or rule as to when, how or what is discussed and it is not uncommon for several conversations to take place at one time. Instant Messenger usually enables users to have a more concise exchange of ideas. Both methods offer the advantage of being able to exchange information in real time over great distance.

E-Commerce

E-commerce is simply shopping online or the transaction of money for some goods or services using an electronic means instead of the conventional form of money exchange. This entails transactions made on line using various forms of money and payments and using conventional institutions in unconventional ways via the internet. Ecommerce can entail buying and selling stocks, applying for loans, buying insurance, making payments, paying bills, filing taxes, checking credit cards and banking balances, buying merchandise, selling merchandise, etc. There are very few limitations to what is entailed with Ecommerce, which is simply electronic commerce.

E-mail

  Email for short is electronic mail. It is the means by which you are able to send messages and receive messages quickly, almost instantaneously. This is the most commonly used feature of the internet. Email is not part of the web but a component of the internet (the network of computers). Email has protocols and requirements to make it function properly. Email components include: email program or a reader, mail server, post office, email address, email service, attachments, in/outbox, and a sent/deleted box. Without many of these components the mail will not go anywhere just like with the USPS; without proper postage your mail doesn't get delivered properly if at all. Email allows text, images, documents, and programs to be sent by using the features of email.

Entertainment

This category entails the use of the internet to enrich our lives with fun and entertainment. This could entail radio, TV, video's , music, games, video games, gambling, literature, or anything that would be considered extracurricular activities, greeting cards, pictures, scrap booking, or anything that would be usually done for entertainment.

General

This category is a basic understanding of the internet, the world wide web and how it works. It includes terms and jargon often used to describe processes, components and languages that are part of Cyberspace. History and the internet and the web's purpose and focus are also included in this category. This is more than simply understanding that the internet is a set of networked computers with connections and software that allows people to use the connections to access other computers. The web is the total collection of data or collection of information that is on those computers that are part of the internet that are hyperlinked data and/or documents. The web supplies the content to the user but any function of the internet can be done by using the web. The internet can exist without the web, however, the web cannot exist without the internet and a browser is the key to the web. The internet is a communication tool just like the telephone.

Internet Broadcasting

Internet Broadcasting is broadcasting via the internet verses cables, satellites, radio waves, tv waves, etc. It is transmitting via the internet and the computers that make up the internet. This includes listening to the radio, broadcasts of news, watching video clips, playing music, carrying on telephone conversations and video telephone. Distance learning is included in this since it is a broadcast over the web to various students in a group setting but learning on the internet versus an actual classroom. Internet Broadcasting consists of different ways that would be considered conventional to most people except uses the internet's technology instead of the conventional technology that has been used by most of years. It is an unconventional way of doing things that will eventually become conventional to the next generation just like cell phones are common place were 20 years ago they were an unconventional way of making a phone call were today it is just like picking up the phone at home on a "land line".

Search/Research

The internet is a huge space of information stored on huge numbers of computers just waiting for you to access it. It would seem easy, however, it is not that easy to access the right information without understanding how to find it. The user has to use search engines of one form or another and each one has its own limitations and its own search query indexes. There are some basic rules that all search engines use and various processes that can help but there is no one search engine that searches and indexes all of the web pages available. Search engines are computer programs not human so they do not read into what is typed into the program. In order to search the web effectively for anything, just like writing a research paper, the user first needs to develop a search strategy that will make it more effective and timely. Searches use rules and formulas and rely on keywords and symbols to select what matches an inquiry.

Spec Interest Groups

The internet allows the person to communicate with others on specific topics that he/she has an interest in. There are ongoing group discussions about specific topics that a person has interest in. There are ongoing group discussions about specific topics that use both Usenet and Listserv. Usenet allows users to read and post comments on an electronic bulletin board. There are also forums that are on specific topics of discussion and the user is normally required to login and branch out in many directions from the centralized topic. There are various newsgroups with specified subject matter and have specified designated codes to easily recognize which subject matter it is centralized to. Listserv are electronic mailing lists that are ongoing group discussions that deliver email messages to your email address that you signed up with in a mass distribution to all members. You can also receive emails from other members of these mail lists in reference to topics. Usenet and Listserv are not exclusive to each other they can be used together for some newsgroups and newsgroups can be available in both forms. These newsgroups can be created by virtually anyone. Both types of newsgroups can be managed and maintained with very little human involvement once it is created and functioning.

We would like to thank you for your purchase of this Study Guide for DET. We appreciate your business and look forward to a continued relationship throughout your education.

We would like to wish you the best of luck on your upcoming test and all of your future endeavors.

We would like to offer you to check back with us on our website, www.arnettce.com for other products, services and novelty items.

Sincerely,

The Staff

Arnett CE, Inc.